Orpheus with His Lute

Poetry and the Renewal of Life

———— ◇ ————

Elisabeth Henry

Southern Illinois University Press
Carbondale and Edwardsville

Published in the United States, its dependencies,
and Canada by Southern Illinois University Press,
P.O. Box 3697, Carbondale, IL 62902-3697

First published in 1992 by
Bristol Classical Press
an imprint of
Gerald Duckworth & Co. Ltd.
The Old Piano Factory
48 Hoxton Square, London N1 6PB

Printed and bound in Great Britain by
Billing and Sons Ltd., Worcester

Library of Congress Cataloging-in-Publication Data

Henry, Elisabeth.
    Orpheus with his lute: poetry and the renewal of life / Elisabeth Henry.
       p. cm.
    Includes bibliographical references.
    1. Orpheus (Greek mythology) – Art. 2. Arts, European. 3. Orpheus
(Greek mythology) I. Title.
NX 652.O7H46 1992
700 – dc200   91-34929
                                                     CIP

ISBN 0–8093–1769–9

Contents

Preface

THE impetus to write this book came from a Workers Educational Association class which pursued the figure of 'The Hero' with me for twenty weeks during the winter of 1986-7. Orpheus never found a place in this course, authentic Greek hero though he undoubtedly was; we had to ask why. Two years later, he had twenty weeks to himself, with the same group, and led us in quite different directions.

At this point I found myself returning to work I had done as much as thirty years earlier, with postgraduates at Sheffield University, in a series of seminars on education and the arts. As I remember them, the name of Orpheus was never mentioned in those discussions. But some of the questions we had asked then returned to my mind: What did the ancient poets mean when they talked of the Muses? Why was the Romantic artist stereotyped as dying lovelorn in a garret? Why should music and poetry be thought valuable for the community, and for the young? These and other widely-ranging ideas of artistic experience might, I now felt, have been more coherently defined and related if we had recognised the almost Protean presence of Orpheus in everything we were talking about.

So, after all these years, there was a demand for acknowledgement, and it seemed that all these questions must be addressed afresh, by attending to the Orpheus myth and to those who have sung it for us, painted it, recounted it, lived it. The purpose of this study was to discover what these extremely various interpretations could say to us about the experience of the artist and of those who respond to him. That is why the material of this book is not arranged chronologically or logically, but as I encountered it, beginning where most modern Western people begin with Orpheus, as the bereaved lover, derived from Virgil. That is also why each chapter ends with a short passage returning to the question *What is a poet?*, with its answer redefined each time in the light of what each chapter has been considering.

It would be impossible to thank every individual who helped me to write this book, by showing me where to find what I needed, lending me books, listening, sharing ideas or the pleasure of music. I am grateful to them all (as I am to Mozart, Rilke, Pindar, the catacomb painters, and so many others who are named in these pages). The drawings are by Stephen Barlow, who worked with great resourcefulness from such disparate material; the Ince Blundell relief (page 78) was drawn from photographs taken by Ian Beech. The staff of Bristol Classical Press supported the project sympathetically from the first, with exemplary patience and expertise.

Most of all I want to thank my family, for allowing – and sometimes pushing – me to get on with it.

Introduction

Orpheus with his lute made trees
And the mountain tops that freeze
Bow themselves when he did sing.

THE opening lines of Shakespeare's lyric, requested by Henry VIII's queen in order to disperse her troubles, present a statement about Orpheus' music which is, perhaps, the only universal feature of his long-lived and multifarious legend. Greek and Roman poets had also presented this as undisputed fact: Orpheus sang, and trees and mountain tops *bowed themselves*. This is an astonishing claim, but one so familiar that we forget (and previous generations forgot) how astonishing it is. It is accepted that magicians can bend the laws of nature to make carpets fly or heroes be invisible; birds or serpents may be endowed with speech, or princes bewitched into frog form; but Orpheus has nothing to do with such enchantments. What he is doing – in all versions of his story – is not controlling the natural world by magic, but playing and singing music so powerfully expressive that the whole of creation responds to it. Rilke voices the ecstasy of tree and musician:

> Da stieg ein Baum. O reine Übersteigung!
> O Orpheus singt! O hoher Baum in Ohr!
>
> There soared a tree, O pure upsoaring!
> O Orpheus sings! O tall tree in the ear!

> (*Sonette an Orpheus*, I. 1)

Trees and stones, the vegetable and the inanimate orders of creation, are joined in almost every Orphic scene by some representatives of the animal world; wild creatures gather to listen to the music, as do trees and rocks. Again, their movement is a response to Orpheus' initiative; he does not command, but by his music invites, persuades, and wins the delighted co-operation of every kind of animal and bird. Though his songs may have words, he never speaks to the animals in any ordinary sense, and does not communicate in their language as folk-tale heroes are sometimes able to do; he communicates through music alone.

1

The response described or depicted in all versions of this scene suggests the forming of a pacific order in the natural world. Animals join together in groups (often in a circle) to listen to the music, in stillness. Species habitually hostile to one another become tame and friendly; painters and mosaicists showed them in attitudes expressing alert attention and pleasure. Trees and rocks also move to form patterned groups:

> And tokens still of that song, there are wild oaks growing at Zone on the Thracian shore, close together, which he led down in their ranks from Pieria, charmed by his lyre.
>
> (Ap. Rhod. *Arg*. I. 28-31)

Ovid makes trees of every possible variety come together to provide shade when Orpheus sits down on a height exposed to the sun (*Met*. X. 86-90). This assemblage of trees is called *nemus* (144-5), a grove of planted or consecrated trees rather than a wild forest, and the animals gathered there are called *concilium*, a council (though characteristically Ovid looks on birds with an almost Aristophanic indulgence, and they remain *turba*, an anarchic throng). In *Metamorphoses* this scene takes place in the mountains of Thrace, but Euripides had given it a still more awesome setting:

> in the forested recesses of Olympus, where once Orpheus playing his lyre brought together trees by his inspired music, brought together wild beasts.
>
> (Eur. *Bacch*. 560-4)

And the sense of purpose and order in the changes brought about by Orpheus' music is nowhere better expressed than by Bacon:

> Orpheus betook himself to solitary places...where, by the same sweetness of his song and lyre, he drew to him all kinds of wild beasts, in such manner that...they all stood about him gently and sociably, as in a theatre, listening only to the concords of his lyre. Nor was that all; for so great was the power of his music that it moved the woods and the very stones to shift themselves and take their station decently and orderly about him.
>
> (*Of the Wisdom of the Ancients*, 1609, tr. Spedding)

The power of Orpheus' music was never thought to be limited to the three realms of the natural world, animal, vegetable and mineral. Through this same power he was enabled to descend to the world of the dead and then return alive to earth. This journey to the underworld forms the second element in the Orpheus story, which is known to go back at least as early as Euripides. The husband of the dying Alcestis, in the play of that name, wishes that he had the tongue and the song of Orpheus,

> so as to bewitch Demeter's daughter, and her husband, with songs, and take you from Hades, I would have gone down.

> (Eur. *Alc*. 358-60)

The 'songs' Admetus speaks of are solemn odes or hymns, not lyrics; the moment is full of tragic feeling, even though Alcestis' story will eventually end happily. Plato wrote of Orpheus' descent to the underworld in a more playful style. Opening the discussion on the nature of love in the *Symposium*, one of Socrates' followers refers to the journey to Hades made by 'Orpheus, son of Oeagrus' (his human father, not his divine mother Calliope) who was sent back without the wife he went down for,

> because he seemed to be a weakling, being a lyre-player and not having the courage to die for love's sake, like Alcestis...

> (Plato, *Symp*. 179d)

Details of this journey to the world of the dead, and its outcome, differed from one version to another, but in ancient times it was not doubted that Orpheus' *katabasis* was possible through the same divinely granted art which enabled him to sway the world of nature. (Post-Renaissance versions often made love rather than music the power that broke down the barrier of death.)

In his journey to Hades, Orpheus was believed to have power to restore others to life, as well as to return himself. The restoration of these others was apparently not to life in this world, but to another timeless realm. Those restored, in some versions, included his wife, variously known as Agriope or Eurydice. Of these two names, Agriope seems to be the earlier, and its meaning, 'fierce-faced', 'savage watcher', seems rather inappropriate for the figure of doomed sweetness who appears in so many post-classical versions of the story. The name Eurydice is first found in the second-century *Lament for Bion*, attributed to Moschus, and the sense of this name, 'wide justice', has the effect of polarising Orpheus' wife from the band of women who, in most versions of his story, caused his death. As Agriope, she might not be alien to those Thracian women – usually thought to be frenzied Maenads, and certainly 'fierce-faced' – who attacked him even while he was singing and playing. The ambivalence of the female figure in his story persisted in some later versions, even after the name Agriope fell out of use; Eurydice was even presented as one of the many identities of Hecate or Proserpina, a goddess of death.

The link between Eurydice and the frenzied Thracians is usually of a different kind, however. If she was snatched back to Hades when her restoration was almost complete – as the version most familiar since the first century relates – Orpheus' impulse to wander in solitude in the wilderness of Thrace could arise from his grief at her irrevocable loss, and the women who tore him to pieces could be thought to resent his absorption in this hopeless love. Other versions of the story might suggest quite different reasons for the women's violence: general sexual antagonism because Orpheus had turned to homosexual love after Eurydice's death, or perhaps religious fanaticism because he was thought to have slighted their cult-god Dionysus. But whatever their motive, the story of Orpheus' death at the hands of women always included a disordered outcry which made his music inaudible, thus depriving him of his pacific power.

Orpheus' encounter with the women, unlike his charming of animals and transforming of landscapes, was localised and fixed at a single (though uncertain) point in time. It was believed to have happened before the time of Homer, and (according to some) within the lifetime of the Argonauts. The place was

> In Rhodope, where woods and rocks had ears
> To rapture, till the savage clamour drowned
> Both harp and voice.

(Milton, Paradise Lost, VII. 35-7)

From there, Orpheus' severed head floated

> Down the swift Hebrus to the Lesbian shore.

(Milton, Lycidas, 63)

After a journey of some four hundred miles, by winding river and open sea, the head was washed up on the shore of Lesbos. A shrine was erected there, dedicated to the great poet-musician, and venerated not only because it possessed the head, but also as the seat of an oracle which delivered poetic truths to mankind. It was said that these oracular messages were uttered by the head itself, which continued to sing and prophesy until it was silenced by Apollo's intervention. According to Philostratus, the god was jealous because his own oracle at Delphi had lost its supremacy.[1]

This was not the only link between Orpheus and Apollo. Orpheus was often known as Apollo's priest, and many versions assumed that this was what provoked the Thracian Maenads to attack him. Guthrie's magisterial study of Orpheus suggested that he was indeed an historical figure, an Apolline missionary who promulgated an ascetic doctrine in Thrace where Bacchic worship flourished. The hostility which led Apollo to silence the oracle at

Lesbos did not represent the permanent relation between Apollo and Orpheus, since it was Apollo who first gave him the lyre and inspired him to follow the Muses, servants of the supreme god of music and poetry.

The story of the oracular head – together with various claims that Orpheus' remains had been discovered (the cities of Dium and Leibethra both claimed to possess his bones) – brought Orpheus into historical time for the Greeks, even more reliably than the heroes of the Trojan War could be. Although the four separable features of the traditional Orpheus legend – his charming of nature, his descent into Hades, his death by dismemberment and the prophecies uttered by his head – all link him to superhuman powers, and might be interpreted in various non-literal ways, two further elements of the story as it was known in the Greco-Roman world presupposed his existence as a historical person, as few ever doubted he was. These concerned the large body of poetry and music believed to be of his composition, and the practice of the so-called Orphic rites by initiates in the mystery-cults in various parts of the Greek world. The poetry undoubtedly exists, although little that survives can be dated earlier than the fourth century AD; there is also evidence (including a great number of literary references) that the mystery cults existed and that they practised certain 'Orphic' rituals over a period of at least six hundred years. The religious formulas used by these worshippers, like the poetry read by succeeding generations, were believed to date back to Orpheus himself. The 'Orphic' poems which survive are either cosmological or mystical in content, and although their language usually makes late dating a certainty, it is quite possible that earlier works of this kind had existed and been lost.

The surviving poems and cultic formulas use language that is often obscure and intense, but their persistence in so many contexts and over so long a period indicates a religious tradition that was not merely eccentric but authentically strong in its own somewhat complex identity.

In the early centuries of the Roman Empire, this tradition could hardly remain outside the influence of Christianity, and the relation between Christian and Orphic beliefs and practices appears to have fluctuated between conflation and antagonism. The early Christian iconography of the Good Shepherd, recognisable as Orpheus the charmer of animals, is one example of the analogical linking of the old gospel and the new. Clement of Alexandria and other preachers denounced Orpheus as a dangerous rival to Christ, but the two were seen in analogy as late as the twelfth century, when the Saviour was referred to as 'latter-day Orpheus' in the Easter sequence *morte Christi celebrata.*

In the medieval period, interpretation of the Orpheus legend, and the form in which it was presented by writers and artists in many genres, developed in many surprising directions; still more so in the centuries since the Renaissance. Many of these versions are quite irreconcilable with one another or with what we know of the myth's original substance and character.

Orpheus has taken many roles in the experience and imagination of men and women over the centuries. Heroic traveller to the Beyond; paragon of faithful love; prophet, priest, troubadour, mangled victim; teacher of the alphabet and civiliser of mankind: all of these were transitory guises. The image of Orpheus as the supreme poet-musician, however, was an enduring one; whatever additional roles he might assume, Orpheus was essentially the embodiment of poetry and music. What the countless variations and developments in his story can tell us concerns the idea of artistic creativity at different times and places; his transformations confront us with the poet-musician as the bearer of values specific to Greeks, Romans, French surrealists, medieval romancers, Florentine philosophers, modern novelists. It is the range of such developments in the Orphic legend that this book will try to explore.

The link between poetry and religion was implicit in the Orpheus myth from the beginning. Orpheus was the son of a Muse, by a human father. His lyre was a gift from Apollo; he was taught to sing and play by his mother the Muse and by the great poet Linus. So the music which could sway both animate and inanimate nature, and restore the dead to life, had a divine origin, but required human discipline for its realisation. For this gift to be transmitted to future generations, it was apparently required that the poet-musician should die in a manner that had clearly ritualistic and possibly sacrificial associations.

From this Greek conception of artistic creativity, further ideas developed which were reflected in the changing versions of the Orpheus story itself. Changes and additions to the legend have always corresponded to new movements in the accepted definition of creativity and new images of the poet. In modern Europe, the poet-musician could no longer be described so literally as a channel for divine energy; other explanations had to be found for the undeniably irrational element in artistic creation, the *furor poeticus*. Again, the importance of discipline, of apprenticeship to an artistic craft, has been variously estimated; and the social role of the poet has varied widely.

This book will attempt to define some of the philosophic and psychological implications of the developments and variations in the Orpheus story up to the present time.

Notes on terms and quotations

In the case of Orpheus it is reasonable to speak either of 'myth' or 'legend', and I shall not enter into the hazards of demarcation between the two; the terms will be used interchangeably.

I have used the adjective 'Orphean' when the association is with Orpheus himself, in myth, literature, or art; 'Orphic' will refer to the religious groups generally called by that term, or to the poems attributed to Orpheus in ancient times and regarded (at least by some) as sacred.

Quotations have been given, wherever possible, in the original language as well as in English. The versions are my own, if no translator is named.

I

The Backward Glance

IN the year 1864, the Royal Academy exhibited a painting which inspired one of the keenest expressions of erotic feeling in English poetry:

> But give them me, the mouth, the eyes, the brow!
> Let them once more absorb me! One look now
> Will lap me round for ever, not to pass
> Out of its light, though darkness lie beyond:
> Hold me but safe again, within the bond
> Of one immortal look! All woe that was,
> Forgotten, and all terror that may be
> Defied, – no past is mine, no future: look at me!

The painting, by Lord Leighton, had the title *Orpheus and Eurydice*. It presented two half-length figures, male and female, in beautifully draped Greek dress. The man stands facing the spectator, eyes closed, his features wracked with anguish as he pushes aside the insistent woman, who grasps him and gazes desperately into his face. Browning's speaker, crying out for a single look from the beloved, is Eurydice, and although in collected editions of Browning the poem often has the same title as the painting, it is correctly called 'Eurydice to Orpheus'.[1] Browning's Eurydice begs for 'one look...one immortal look...look at me!', as if that glance from him will cast an enveloping light, protecting her from all that might lie beyond and outside its arc.

The language of Browning's eight lines could not be plainer, and no words in the poem betray when or where the words are being spoken. Urgency is conveyed only through the agitated rhythm and the displaced rhymes in the central lines. What kind of lovers are these? The painting actually shows part of the lyre which Orpheus carries, slung behind his shoulder and evidently forgotten; this, and his laurel wreath, suggest poetic fame, but nothing else hints at his personal identity or the occasion of his distress.[2] The lovely, clinging Eurydice could belong to any time and place. Browning has taken this deracination still further: his poem – originally 'a fragment' – includes no reference to Orpheus' instrument or song. There is no mention even of voice or touch; unlike the lovers in the painting, or even in Virgil and Ovid, neither is struggling to grasp the other. There is only the longing for a *look*, which (this Eurydice asserts) might cancel out the incomprehensible cruelty of their parting and the power of Death.

The poignancy of looks exchanged between separated or estranged lovers recurs in Browning's *Dramatis Personae* ('Too Late', for example, 'The Worst Of It', and 'James Lee'), and the emotion in 'Eurydice to Orpheus' is of the same order as the emotion in these dramatic lyrics. These poems were written in the years immediately following Elizabeth Barrett Browning's death, and it would be hard to imagine that this personal experience of deeply felt loss played no part in Browning's response to Leighton's picture.[3]

In Browning's poem, the voice is the voice of a woman who does not want to die, who clings to a sense-perception as the one vehicle of love, meaning, truth, that she knows; she beseeches her lover not to deny her this. Those who read the poem in 1864 will have been familiar with the story of Orpheus and Eurydice in the versions of Ovid and Virgil. They cannot have failed to remember what followed the moment of supreme tension depicted by Leighton: Orpheus, unable to maintain his refusal of Eurydice's plea, opens his eyes, is overcome by longing, and so disobeys the ban imposed by the gods. By looking at Eurydice he loses her a second time and – as the generally preferred version, namely Virgil's, declares – loses her for ever. In the nineteenth century, the story was taken to be a tragic one; it is the knowledge of this ending which suffuses both painting and poem with emotion.

Orpheus also had clear knowledge of what consequences his glance at Eurydice would bring; no extant version of the story states explicitly whether Eurydice herself understood this or not.[4] In Leighton's painting there is no hint of conscious seductiveness in her features or attitude; she is no Lorelei,[5] but a woman all purity and love, making a demand which her lover knows is destructive of them both. He turns away in anguish, because he is aware of another demand, a law and a dimension of love which her immediate need does not recognise. Apart from the unobtrusive lyre behind Orpheus' shoulder, this painting might just as well have been called *Aeneas and Dido*.

The Victorians did not care for Aeneas and Dido as a subject for painting or poetry. One of the reasons why they avoided it was that Aeneas did not turn round after he had set his face towards Italy, and so could not be set among true lovers such as Lancelot, Romeo, Tristan. The Victorian Orpheus turns round because his love is as all-consuming as Eurydice's, and his backward glance asserts the supremacy of a personal love which he is impelled to accept even though he knows it will destroy them both. In this form the Orpheus myth can be seen as forerunner of the great love-tragedies of modern Europe, where the woman is asserting an overriding value in their love even though it will lead to the destruction of both her lover and herself.

Since the beginning of the nineteenth century, when Keats proclaimed 'the holiness of the Heart's Affections',[6] motives of personal love had attained a newly elevated status in European life, perhaps especially in England, where the experience of falling in love began to be associated with marriage in an exclusive sense not assumed in earlier years. Young lovers in Victorian poetry and paintings are not, like the courtly lovers of the Middle Ages, taking part in a socially recognised (and sometimes passionate) diversion, but being initiated into adulthood and its loftier responsibilities. The idealisation of marriage allowed a sexual relationship to be seen as lifelong, pure, and a source of moral strength. In this search for an absolute in personal love, the woman would be thought the natural leader (public obligations belonging almost entirely to the male world). Like David Copperfield's Agnes, the ideal wife would lead her husband on to ever more selfless and devoted endeavour, her face shining on him 'like a Heavenly light by which I see all other objects...O Agnes, O my soul...pointing upward!'[7]

This is a wholly unclassical way of regarding sexual love, whether in marriage or outside it, and there are few Greek or Roman love stories that can possibly be interpreted in such terms. The story of Orpheus and Eurydice is one of these few. In daring to face the terrors of Hades in the quest for his wife, Orpheus could be seen as following a heavenly light uplifted for him by his 'soul': his disobedience when he turned to look at her face once more evoked no censure, but only sympathy, among Victorian readers. The *Liebestod* which ended their story made it the archetypal myth of tragic love, as it had never been before. The well-known painting by G.F. Watts, portraying the lovers at a moment later in the story than that chosen by Leighton, shows both figures sinking down and back into an enveloping darkness. Eurydice swoons, with eyes closed; Orpheus embraces her as she falls, and his hand seems loose on his falling lyre, which in Renaissance and medieval representations is usually conspicuously held up at every point in the underworld narrative. By allowing him to discard or forget his instrument, the nineteenth-century artist is presenting Orpheus as a lover, whose music is entirely decorative and secondary to the significant motives of action.

Ancient representations of Orpheus with Eurydice are rare. Vase painters and others more often showed Orpheus with animals, or with Maenads, or occasionally at the entrance to Hades. The most famous version of the lovers' glance, in visual terms, is the sculptured relief known as *Orpheus, Eurydice, Hermes*, used by Rilke in 1907 as the theme of one of his *Neue Gedichte*. This Greek relief, generally dated from the fifth century BC, is known from three Roman copies, of which one (in the Museo Nazionale at Naples) includes the names of the three figures forming the group. Even without the inscribed name, however, Orpheus would be plainly identified by the lyre which hangs at his left side. Hermes stands erect, slightly detached from the other two figures, though he holds Eurydice by the hand; Orpheus and Eurydice bend

Orpheus, Eurydice, Hermes. From a Roman copy of the Greek relief, probably dating from the fifth century BC. The copy is in the National Museum, Naples.

their heads as they gaze intently at one another; Eurydice's left hand touches Orpheus' shoulder, while his hand is on the draperies of her head, in a gesture which has been interpreted as a drawing back of the veil from her face. There is no sense of struggle, but rather a calm finality, in this sculpture; the work seems to belong to the tradition of Attic *lekythoi*, or *stelae*, of this period, where a husband is often seen sharing a moment of tender farewell with the wife who is leaving him in death. The farewell may also be seen to take place between other pairs within a family, or even between friends, but the husband and wife scene is frequently portrayed, and this relief very reminiscent of such memorials. As in the *stelae*, the manner of the wife's death is not hinted at. The farewell glance here shows the two lovers equally absorbed in their passion, but only too aware of all that lies about and beyond them both.

Unfortunately we have no reference to this relief in the work of any ancient writer, and it is useful to ask why we assume that the moment illustrated here should be identified as the forbidden backward glance, said to deprive Orpheus of his wife as she was about to leave Hades in his company. Virgil was certainly not describing this sculpture, or seeking to recall it, when he wrote his poignant and dramatic lines telling of Orpheus' fateful glance:

> iamque pedem referens casus evaserat omnis,
> redditaque Eurydice superas veniebat ad auras
> pone sequens (namque hanc dederat Proserpina legem),
> cum subita incautum dementia cepit amantem,
> ignoscenda quidem, scirent si ignoscere manes:
> restitit, Eurydicenque suam iam luce sub ipsa
> immemor heu! victusque animi respexit. ibi omnis
> effusus labor atque immitis rupta tyranni
> foedera, terque fragor stagnis auditus Avernis.
> illa 'quis et me' inquit 'miseram et te perdidit,
> Orpheu, quis tantus furor? en iterum crudelia retro
> fata vocant, conditque natantia lumina somnus.'

> And now he's avoided every pitfall of the homeward path,
> And Eurydice, regained, is nearing the upper air
> Close behind him (for this condition has Proserpine made),
> When a moment's madness catches her lover off his guard –
> Pardonable, you'd say, but Death can never pardon.
> He halts. Eurydice, his own, is now on the lip of
> Daylight. Alas! he forgot. His purpose broke. He looked back.
> His labour was lost, the pact he had made with the merciless king
> Annulled. Three times did thunder peal over the pools of Avernus.
> 'Who', she cried, 'has doomed me to misery, who has doomed us?
> What madness beyond measure? Once more a cruel fate
> Drags me away, and my swimming eyes are drowned in darkness.'

(*Geo.* IV. 485-96, tr. C. Day Lewis)

The moment when Orpheus halts and looks back, in Virgil, is one of instant-aneous and irreversible doom: *restitit... respexit... ibi omnis effusus labor* 'he stopped...he looked back...there all his effort was poured away'. When his forward movement and forward gaze are checked, he is not acting as a free agent but as prisoner of a *dementia* which has seized upon him and conquered his will. Eurydice speaks of *furor* as the agent which has destroyed them both.[8] The gradual progress towards daylight, in the orderly lines which described Eurydice's docile movements under Proserpina's law, is disrupted in this agitated passage, leaving Orpheus without resource and Eurydice passively swept away in encircling night.

Orpheus has disobeyed, in Virgil, because he is a lover (488), not a musician or a hero, when he moves along the way from Hades. Because of this he is incautious and liable to irrational impulse, as the traditional lovers of elegy always were;[9] and Eurydice's question, 'What is this *furor* that has seized on you?' might be answered in simpler terms than such a question could be in reference to the *furor* raging through the *Aeneid*. There, the irrational forces in human affairs, threatening all the future, are complex as well as profound; here, the single emotion of sexual passion has deprived Orpheus of judgment and (it seems) of his song. This is the force which in *Georgics* III is said to drive all living creatures 'into frenzy and fire' (244), penetrating into the bones of Leander so that he flings himself into the stormy Hellespont, to be dashed against its rocks in the darkness and fruitlessly mourned by Hero:

> moritura super crudeli funere virgo...
>
> the girl who was to die upon his cruel pyre...

(*Geo*. III. 263)

Eurydice too is *moritura puella*, a girl doomed to death, when she flees from the pursuit by Aristaeus which leads her into the serpent's path; sexual desire is thus seen as the agent of destruction in Virgil's story well before the moment of the backward glance. Aristaeus, however, does not persist in any desperate passion, and carries out acts of expiation with alacrity as soon as he knows what they ought to be.[10] Orpheus has no idea of expiation, and there is a deep ambiguity about the moral significance of his actions through-out the *Georgics* narrative. His devoted fidelity would stir sympathy in any but the heart of Pluto, whose nature is not capable of pity (470, 489); yet his disobedience was an act of madness, a moral defeat. When Eurydice fades from his sight, he grasps vainly at the air, unable to speak and overwhelmed by futile grief.

It is this scene of helpless longing that has imprinted itself on the imag-ination of readers ever since Virgil's time, including Leighton and Browning, and it is this moment of tragic doom that we have learnt to look for in any version of the Orpheus story. Because the fifth-century relief *Orpheus, Eurydice, Hermes* is exceptionally beautiful, and of a deep intensity, we want to identify it as showing the moment charged with tragic import when Orpheus looks at the wife whose face he is forbidden to see. There is, however, no warrant at all for attaching this moment to the relief, and (if we can for the moment exclude the Attic *stelae* from our minds) neither can we say for certain that the look being exchanged between these two figures must be some kind of farewell. It is a look of strong personal love, but it does not seem to express grief or fear. Hermes' hand on Eurydice's arm apparently exerts no pressure to separate her from her husband. Whatever is happening on the relief, it is not the failure of resolve and the dissolution of identity that Virgil describes.

Moving into or out of Hades, Eurydice would appropriately be escorted by Hermes as *psychopompos*, and the figures on this relief have a solemnity which might just as well suggest the handing over of the dead wife to her living husband as their actual parting. Most writers on the relief have, however, thought it to be a leavetaking, albeit a calm and expected one. Bowra believed[11] that the relief illustrated a version of the story which made Eurydice's return to life a short-term one, like the return of Protesilaus from the dead for one day only. Owen Lee suggested[12] that the sculptor's version did not allow Eurydice to move towards earth at all after she died: Orpheus was allowed to see her in Hades, but no more; his lifting of her veil was not forbidden, but uniquely granted in spite of the awfulness of looking upon the dead. These scholars (and many others) have attempted to reconstruct the older traditional story that existed before Virgil, as well as the literary version from Greece and Alexandria, conveyed to us in hints and fragments from a widely ranging number of sources. These references, diverse as they are, do not correspond at all with Virgil's version of the human tragedy.

Most of the Greek poets, and also prose writers, who mention Orpheus' attempt to restore Eurydice to life do so in somewhat oblique terms which suggest a familiar tale that had no canonical version of epic standing. In the *Alcestis*,[13] for example, what Euripides is implying in his allusion to Orpheus' descent is not at all clear: Admetus says that if he had Orpheus' gift of song, neither Cerberus nor Charon would prevent him from restoring his wife to the light of day; if Orpheus failed, then (and Euripides' words do not necessarily mean that he did) the reason seems to be connected with the terrifying powers of Hades rather than with any failure of will in Orpheus or any breaking of a tabu. However, Hermesianax in the third century plainly says that Orpheus *did* bring back his wife from Hades;[14] and the author of the second-century *Lament for Bion* ('pseudo-Moschus') hopes to win back Bion, as Orpheus did Eurydice (122-5). Isocrates in the fourth century BC, and Diodorus Siculus in the first, also imply a successful rescue of Eurydice.[15]

Plato treats Orpheus as a slightly ridiculous figure, fobbed off with a phantom instead of Eurydice because the gods did not think he deserved to have her back.[16] In the *Orphic Argonautica* (a mystical narrative in epic metre of the second or third century AD) Orpheus claims to have seen and learned things beyond death, when he went on the dark road of Hades 'for love of my wife' (42).

None of these versions, or any other before Virgil, hints at the story of the fateful glance. The earliest hint of it, apart from Virgil, is found in the prose handbook of mythology by Conon, who was contemporary with Virgil but not necessarily dependent on the version in the *Georgics*; according to this brief account, Orpheus lost Eurydice because 'he forgot the commands about her' (*Narr.* 45). The author of *Culex* (traditionally but very doubtfully believed to be Virgil) says that Orpheus lost his wife *oscula cara petens*, 'striving for dear kisses' (*Cul.* 293), implying a ban upon touch rather than sight of the beloved. Ovid speaks of a 'law' forbidding Orpheus to 'turn back his eyes' (*ne flectat retro sua lumina*, *Met.* X. 51): he disobeys, *avidus videndi*, 'greedy for sight of her' (56) but also desperately trying to grasp her in his arms.

These first-century variations on the theme of Orpheus' failure have been thought to derive from a common source, such as the Hellenistic poem postulated by Bowra. The date of such a poem need not be earlier than the first century BC, and indeed (as Bowra pointed out) its complete disappearance and critical neglect is easier to understand if it was close to Virgil's time and almost at once superseded by the *Georgics*.

Whether Virgil himself, or the hypothetical Hellenistic poet, was the first to attach the 'backward glance' incident to Orpheus' story, the motif was clearly an adaptation of the very familiar tabu on looking at the spirits of the dead, or at gods of the underworld, in any form they might assume. This tabu is very ancient, and world-wide; in Greek literature it is implicit in many references to the world of Hades, and explicit in Medea's warning to Jason:

> and do not let the sound of feet drive you to turn back, nor the baying of hounds, in case you spoil every part (of the ritual) and do not return yourself, as arranged, to your companions.

> (Ap. Rhod. *Arg.* III. 1038-41)

Apollonius' Medea has just instructed the hero to offer to Hecate a libation of honey, 'the hive-stored work of bees'. As she goes on to foretell the ordeals Jason must face in conflicts with non-human enemies, 'she gazed upon him face to face...he captivated her gleaming eyes...both fixed their eyes on the ground in shame, and then again were throwing glances at each other'. This scene presents not an already realised relationship, but the experience of falling in love, as the exchange of looks draws each of the two more deeply into a passion which Medea, and the poet, know will have a tragic end. The flashes of light and the warmth of these erotic glances are interrupted by sinister darkness with Medea's warning not to turn back when Jason has offered propitiation to Hecate (and he does not turn back, in spite of a terrifying theophany, 1221-2). Although there is no reference to Orpheus, and Jason is not descending into Hades, Apollonius is Virgil's forerunner here, in making the tabu against looking back part of a love story which turns upon the exchange of longing glances, leading to disaster.

While the possibility of such an imaginative development in the Orpheus story clearly existed in the age of Apollonius – the third century BC – all surviving versions from that period, and for two centuries after it, still speak of Orpheus bringing back his wife from the dead, with no reference to a broken tabu, and no strong emphasis on passionate love as a motive force in the story.[17] The fifth-century relief cannot be interpreted by any reference to a literary tradition that dates only from Virgil, or at the very earliest, from a Greek poet of the first century BC.

The theme of overriding sexual passion, or (in terms more acceptable to the generation of Leighton) of an all-sacrificing marital love, does not enter the Orpheus story before the late Hellenistic age; it was above all the version in the *Georgics* which released the power of romantic intensity, to reach its highest pitch in Browning's 'fragment'. But the incomparable love story that turns on the moment of the forbidden glance is only one strand in the Orpheus legend, a legend already many centuries old before Virgil used it with intentions of his own in the *Georgics*. Others before him had revealed other meanings, and among those who came after, many would continue to find still more.

When Claudio Monteverdi made Orpheus' fatal disobedience the theme of his *favola in musica* at Mantua in 1607, his choice of subject was not surprising. He was following two earlier versions of the Orpheus story dating from 1600, those of Jacopo Peri and Caccini; both musically less accomplished, and in comparison with Monteverdi dramatically shallow.[18] The story of Ariadne was an alternative that he considered: this also would have a lover's loss as its dramatic centre, but a woman rather than a man as the deprived lover. In the event, *Arianna* became Monteverdi's second opera, in the following year.

Like Browning's, Monteverdi's lovers were wholly human figures; in his *Orfeo*, the poignant music of Act IV expresses bitter natural grief. In a letter to his librettist, Alessandro Striggio, Monteverdi wrote that Orpheus' sorrow, and Ariadne's, was emotionally moving precisely because they were human beings, 'not a wind', and not (evidently) gods or disembodied spirits.[19] The preference for Orpheus over Ariadne may have been dictated partly by the voices available; but also, as with Browning, personal distress played some part: during the year when he was composing *Orfeo*, Monteverdi saw his own wife Claudia suffer from a rapid and inexplicable decline in health. She died in September 1607.

In Striggio's libretto, Orfeo's motive in turning back to look at Eurydice is never described in terms of *dementia* or of external compulsion. He looks back because he is anxious (as Ovid's Orpheus was) to see that she is really following him, and also because Love prompts him to defy Pluto's command. Love, says Orfeo, is more powerful than Pluto. Although the journey to Hades was inspired by Orfeo's trust in the power of poetry to move the gods below, it is indeed love for Proserpina which moves Pluto to grant the plea for Eurydice's release. The chorus of infernal spirits acclaim Love's triumph over the powers of Hell.

After the backward glance, however, Orfeo is denounced by these same spirits as culpably weak, and his second loss of Eurydice is seen as a just punishment. He has no defence to offer when his father Apollo also condemns him as a slave to personal passion (*proprio affetto*). The opera ends with Orfeo's meek acceptance of Apollo's wise guidance, which will lead him to fix his mind on true virtue, and so ascend to a higher life where Eurydice's 'semblance' will be found once more in the constellations of the heavens. Orfeo has already proclaimed a heavenly destiny for his lyre:

> Luogo avrai fra le piu belle
> Immagini celesti,
> Ond' al tuo suon le stelle
> Danzeranno in gir' or tardi or presti.

> You shall have place among the most lovely
> images of heaven, where the stars shall dance
> to your sound, now late, now soon.

(Striggio, *Orfeo*, Act IV, 23b)

This prophecy is made before the moral failure of Orfeo, but it seems to remain valid (the lyre is not mentioned again in the libretto). The humbled Orfeo rises, with the benevolent Apollo, to the realm of *virtù verace*, where sexual passion is evidently transcended. Monteverdi said (in the letter to Striggio already quoted) that he saw the climax of *Orfeo* as a scene of 'righteous prayer'. Because he repents of his disobedience, Orfeo's reward is in some sense compatible with Christian orthodoxy: he is transported to a heavenly life where he will be aware of Eurydice's 'semblance'.

In spite of a dénouement which without Monteverdi's music would certainly appear somewhat facile, the opera moves the listener through tragic
emotion to accept its ending as a higher resolution of conflict and grief. What
has offered the material of tragedy to Monteverdi (and to so many composers, writers, and visual artists since Virgil) is the lover's own part in causing
the second, irrevocable loss of his beloved. By giving way to a natural longing,
and so disobeying divine command, he knowingly precipitates Eurydice's
withdrawal to Hades. What might seem a meaningless act of cruelty inflicted
by indifferent gods thus becomes a moral judgment given by a higher power
who cannot be questioned.

How far the reader, or listener, could accept this judgment upon Orpheus
would depend on the assumptions made at different periods about the value
of sexual love and the autonomy of human behaviour. What, after all, had
Orpheus done but to love his own wife too dearly? Ovid's Eurydice had made
this protest, less than thirty years after Virgil's death; as she sinks away the
second time into Hades, this heroine refuses to blame Orpheus:

> iamque iterum moriens non est de coniuge quicquam
> questa suo: quid enim nisi se quereretur amatam?

> and now, dying once more, she uttered no complaint about her
> husband; for what could she complain, but that she was loved?

> (*Met*. X. 60-61)

> But as for love, man may not – or hardly – restrain it: woe, alas, woe!
> Orpheus led the way, and his wife behind him, until he reached the
> border between light and darkness. But when he stepped into the
> light he looked back at her, and instantly she was lost to him.

> (Boethius, III, Metre 12)

This passage was part of the earliest version of the Orpheus story known to
have been written in England: Alfred the Great's translation of Boethius,
dating from around 900 AD.[20] Boethius' account of the descent to Hades has
some unclassical oddities (Charon, as well as Cerberus, has three heads), but
some details are close to Ovid. The precision of 'the border between light
and darkness' where Orpheus looks back certainly recalls the Ovidian scene:

> nec procul afuerunt telluris margine summae:
> hic...flexit amans oculos.

> and they were not far from the edge of the upper
> world: here...the lover turned his eyes.

> (*Met*. X. 55-7)

In both Boethius and Ovid, the ban on turning round had been imposed
without explanation, and if it derived from a more general tabu on looking
at a ghost, or in certain circumstances at a corpse, no reason would ever have
been formulated. An irrational ban of this kind might naturally impose total
constraint within the world of the dead, but it would lose its power when the
living person re-crossed the threshold between the worlds. Orpheus looked
back, perhaps, as soon as he could.

The text of Boethius' Orpheus story, as it became known in England,
concludes with a passage of moral reflection on imperfect repentance.[21] In
Christian terms, disobedience to a divine command must be culpable. Yet
the whole tenor of the story, as Boethius told it, is sympathetic to Orpheus,
and suggests admiration for his devoted love as well as for his 'rare music'.
By his eager endurance the lover has earned the reward which is denied to
him by a cruel fate: 'The King of Hell's folk cried out, saying, "Let us give the
good man his wife, for he hath won her with his harping." ' After this praise
of Orpheus, the comment appended to the story has left many readers in
perplexity:

> These fables teach every man that would flee from the darkness of
> hell and come to the light of the True Goodness that he should not
> look towards his old sins, so as to commit them once more as fully
> as ever he did.

This comment in Boethius is uttered by the Lady Philosophy, 'forerunner of
the True Light', but her stern moralising does not make the cruelty of
Orpheus' fate (and of Eurydice's) any more tolerable to modern readers, or
to medieval ones who were familiar with both Boethius and Ovid. If Eurydice
were to be equated with sinfulness, the whole enterprise of Orpheus' descent
to Hades clearly had to be condemned; but if he were to be praised for
undertaking this journey, the project for her revival could not be an evil one
and so she could not stand for sin.

For medieval commentators, there was strong temptation to link Eurydice
with Eve, who fell into disobedience before Adam did and lured him to follow
her into the darkness of sin. This analogy is presented as a severe warning by
the anonymous author of the *Ovide Moralisé*, written about 1300, in France.
This influential work was perhaps the best-known of the many moralising
commentaries on the *Metamorphoses* produced in the early Renaissance; the
engaging woodcuts in the illustrated version of 1493 give prominence to the
serpent which bit Eurydice, causing her literal fall, just as the serpent in Eden
caused the spiritual fall of Eve. These illustrations do not depict Eurydice as
a temptress, however, but as a soberly dressed lady meekly awaiting deliverance from the jaws of hell. Orpheus has the dress of a medieval lord, and an
air of dignified detachment. What is happening here is the enactment of a

'morality' (in the medieval sense) rather than a drama of personal struggle and emotion. It would be impossible to guess that these woodcuts (and similar ones of this period) could be illustrating the same narrative as that illustrated by Leighton's painting.

Leighton and Pierre Bersuire,[22] both starting with the story as they knew it from Roman poetry of the first century, developed its moral implications in totally opposing ways. For Leighton and his contemporaries, the lovers were blameless although their longing was for the impossible. The intensity of personal emotion which the nineteenth-century poet, artist, musician, expressed so powerfully could sustain artistic structures of tragic stature precisely because they stood before a backcloth of divine indifference and inscrutability. Like Hardy's Tess and George Eliot's Maggie, the Victorian Orpheus and Eurydice are struck down by superhuman powers who care nothing for their passionate devotion or their weaknesses:

> ignoscenda quidem, scirent si ignoscere manes...
>
> (a madness) pardonable indeed, if the spirits below knew
> how to pardon...
>
> > (*Geo.* IV. 489)

The absolute value which was asserted – or at least sought for – in romantic love during the nineteenth century could be accommodated within a Christian view of life only by regarding marriage as a spiritual vocation; this, or something like it, was the experience of the Brownings. Romantic passion became the material of tragedy when it led to adultery, so that lovers glorified by their all-transcending desire were also sinful and justly doomed (as in *Wuthering Heights* and *Idylls of the King*). No just doom could be seen, however, in the final separation of Orpheus and Eurydice, and because their own religious beliefs or traditions led nineteenth-century artists, or readers, to look for justice and mercy in the ways of God, this story usually evoked expressions of intense, protesting pain rather than a tragic response in the Miltonic[23] sense. If personal devotion and erotic feeling for a wife is seen as inherently noble, it becomes hard to attach tragic guilt to the backward glance of Orpheus; indeed, there is probably no treatment of the theme since Monteverdi's which has contrived to command acceptance of both these assumptions and also to avoid a morass of emotional indulgence.

Virgil had never asserted that the doom imposed on both Orpheus and Eurydice was an act of divine justice. For him, as for Sophocles, the terror of divine power might quite irrationally turn to mercy, even tenderness, but justice was not to be looked for. *Desine fata deum flecti sperare precando* was the utterance of the Sibyl to the guiltless Palinurus, left wretchedly unburied by the banks of Styx: 'cease to hope that decrees of gods can be bent by prayer'

(*Aen*. VI. 376). In Virgil, the gods do not spare any individual because of his innocence or human worth, and they do not explain whatever *fiat* they may pronounce. In the fourth *Georgic* (and also in *Aeneid* IV), Virgil writes of his lovers with that characteristic understanding that Brooks Otis has called 'empathetic', 'entering the *psyche*' of each character,[24] but however deep this inward sympathy, there is no bending of divine decrees and no lapse into sentimentality. The idea of divine forgiveness, and indeed of divine right-eousness, is entirely absent from Virgil, and that is why Christian readers of the *Georgics* as well as the *Aeneid* have often been impelled to cry 'Can you bear this?' and cling to *sunt lacrimae rerum*, 'there are tears in things', as the one ineluctable Virgilian truth.[25]

Ovid's *Metamorphoses* presents a universe where nothing is ineluctable, and it is not surprising to find that his account of Eurydice's death and of the fateful glance is full of unexpected and ambivalent turns. For this reason Ovid's version lends itself to endless reinterpretations in allegorical or other terms, and so (like other Ovidian tales) it appealed to medieval and Renaissance readers even more powerfully than the works of 'Virgil the magician'.

The death of Eurydice is recounted by Ovid with neat objective brevity. She is 'wandering about the meadows' with a group of Naiad friends, not running headlong to escape the rapacious Aristaeus (Ovid quite surprisingly leaves out the Virgilian Aristaeus). She is introduced as *nova nupta*, newly married, which will add pathos when she dies, but does not strike the knell of Virgil's *moritura puella*, 'a girl at the point of death'. Ovid briskly continues:

> occidit in talum serpentis dente recepto

> she fell dead, with a serpent's tooth biting her ankle.

> (*Met*. X. 10)

After appropriate mourning, Orpheus goes to Hades to see whether the shades will respond to a plea for Eurydice's return. Coming before Persephone and Pluto, he launches into 'the kind of amusing *suasoria* that Ovid thoroughly enjoyed'.[26] What Ovid's Orpheus pleads for is that his wife should be allowed to live out her natural span; somehow she has died too soon, and the Fates are asked to undo their work: *properata retexite fata*, 'unweave her hurried destiny'. After appealing to the power of Love, who once united Pluto and his queen, Orpheus uses legalistic terms to plead for Eurydice's restoration:

> haec quoque, cum iustos matura peregerit annos,
> iuris erit vestri: pro munere poscimus usum.

> She too, when at the right age she has completed
> her just sum of years, shall be under your jurisdiction:
> as a gift I ask (only) the enjoyment of her.

(Met. X. 36-7)

Pluto and Persephone, acting as one, grant the return of Orpheus' wife; but they also impose a 'law': the prohibition of any backward glance until he has emerged from the valleys of Avernus (51-2).

Orpheus' first temptation to transgress this 'law' arises from the fear that Eurydice may have fainted, a thought which had not occurred to Virgil's Orpheus, though it did (too late) to his Aeneas:

> erravitne via seu lassa resedit?
> incertum...
> nec prius amissam respexi, animumve reflexi,
> quam...

> did she wander from the road, or sink down
> exhausted? uncertain... and I did not look
> back at the lost one, or turn back my attention,
> until...

(Aen. II. 739-42)

Ovid's Orpheus is then overcome by a passionate longing to see Eurydice, and so turns round:

> ne deficeret metuens, avidusque videndi,
> flexit amans oculos

> afraid that she might be weakening, and greedy
> for sight of her, the lover turned his gaze.

(Met. X. 56-7)

In *Metamorphoses* Orpheus is not (as in Virgil) portrayed as a man possessed by madness: he is a man in love, *amans*; what he feels is the simple intense desire to see his beloved, and when she is taken from him he is instantly, but quite briefly, stunned with a horror which deprives him of all personal feeling.

At this point Ovid turns from the personal sorrow of Orpheus to the subject of his song, addressed to the woodland, where there are no human listeners. The animals and birds hear a series of love stories, a miscellany[27] that is full of humour and animation. The last of these tales has a clearer relevance than the others to what will follow: it tells of the death of Adonis, leading to Orpheus' own death at the hands of the Thracian Bacchants.

Orpheus' reunion with Eurydice in Elysium, which follows immediately after Ovid's account of his dismemberment, is an untraditional ending to the story, and one for which the narrative has not prepared the reader. No Greek model existed for this (unless it were in the hypothetical lost epyllion of Hellenistic date) and the scene of the lovers in the fields of the blessed, eagerly embracing or casually strolling together, is not at all Greek in feeling. Its forerunner is the glimpse of Dido's reunion with her first husband Sychaeus, seen by Aeneas in the shadows of the Mourning Fields beside Styx (*Aen*. VI. 473-4). Virgil allows his tragic heroine to find responsive love and shared distress (*curae*) in the afterlife; Ovid's reunited lovers move with gaiety, each leading the way in turn. When Orpheus is in front, he can look round with freedom, and Ovid deftly uses the same verb which struck a knell in Virgil's story (*victusque animi respexit, Geo*. IV. 491):

> Nunc praecedentem sequitur, nunc praevius anteit,
> Eurydicenque suam iam tuto respicit Orpheus.

> At one moment he follows, as she goes before; at another he leads the way, going in front; and Orpheus looks back at his Eurydice, (doing so) now in safety.

(Met. XI. 65-6)

This translation of Orpheus and Eurydice together to the Elysian realm does not have the moral exaltation of Monteverdi's ending, but it satisfies the need which most artists have felt since the Augustan age to award some consolation to Orpheus after the heroic endeavour inspired by a virtuous devotion to his wife. Many operatic versions after Monteverdi returned to an ending closer to Ovid's, permitted by gods who (for one or reason or another) chose to relent at last. In Ranieri da Calzabigi's libretto for Gluck's *Orfeo*, first performed in 1762, the presiding god throughout the action is Amor, who calls Eurydice back to life because Orpheus' fidelity outweighs his guilty disobedience.

This happy ending, in which constant lovers are rewarded on earth by unexpected leniency from the gods, was used again by Gluck in *Alceste* and *Iphigénie en Aulide*. However, this variant of the Orpheus story was not new. Its history goes back through the secular literature of the Middle Ages (as distinct from the allegorical tradition of the *Ovide Moralisé*, though also evidently deriving from the *Metamorphoses*; even the personified Amor appears in Ovid, though not as the central figure he later became). The Middle English metrical romance known as *Sir Orfeo* – based on a Breton 'lay' and generally dated c. 1300 – ends very cheerfully with the unconditional restoration of Queen Heurodis to her devoted king (who has suffered ten years of exile and hazardous journeys to release her from enchantment).

They are crowned once more and rule 'for many years'. This fairy tale has no hint of Orpheus' disobedience, but the significant look between the lovers survives; when Orfeo enters Fairyland he sees sixty ladies riding 'as gay and graceful as birds on a leafy spray', and recognises one of them as his Dame Heurodis:

> Longingly they gazed at each other, but neither spoke a word. When she saw him in that plight, who had been so rich and noble, the tears fell from her eyes, but the other ladies forced her to ride away. 'Alas,' he cried, 'why does not death take me away? I have lived too long when I dare not speak a word to my wife and she dare not speak to me. But come what may I will ride after these ladies. I do not care whether I live or die.' At that he put on his pilgrim's mantle, and hung his harp upon his back, and went eagerly on his way. He stopped for nothing. When the ladies rode into a rock he followed them at once.

(tr. Robert Montague, 1954)

Although the Orpheus of Roman poetry – and of the nineteenth century, and much else – is primarily a lover, he still remains the musician-poet, whose nature is a paradigm for all artists. Virgil and Ovid have given rise to two quite different traditions concerning Orpheus' own poetry, and these traditions reflect their attitudes to poetry in general.

Virgil says little about any poetry or music composed by Orpheus before the loss of Eurydice, and personal grief provides the theme for all the songs after that loss. Ovid makes Orpheus a poet of much wider range. The love stories which he recounts in *Metamorphoses* X, after Eurydice's death, are often tragic, and in some cases highly bizarre. Their only common feature is Ovid's central theme of transformation (with Orpheus' own story integrated into this when the Bacchants who kill him are rooted to the ground as gnarled oaks).The transformations express the endless diversity of love, and Orpheus turns to this theme rather than the cosmological poetry of his earlier life, because he has experienced sorrow through love and has found pleasure only in the love of boys after Eurydice's loss (X. 78-85, 148-54). In Virgil, the songs composed by the bereaved Orpheus are entirely personal, suggesting a kind of poetry rare in the ancient world: the expression of wholly human emotions in actual experience. One thinks of Sappho and Catullus, but there is little else in ancient literature which can be compared, as is Orpheus' Virgilian lament, to the bereaved nightingale's *miserabile carmen* (*Geo.* IV. 514).

What then is a poet? He is a man of special emotional sensitivity, shaped by his own experiences and actions as well as from observation and awareness of the world. He has a particular talent which enables him to express human emotion in forms which bring pleasure to others. This gift is so mysterious that it is assumed to be of divine origin. What he creates can be recognised as Beauty and Truth, and what he gives to his hearers is a sense of affinity in human experience which – even when the experience is intensely painful – brings a deep personal fulfilment.

II

The Magic Flute

L EIGHTON, Monteverdi, Boethius, and many more: artists, poets, composers alike have chosen to focus on the moment of the backward glance
as the summit of intensity in the Orpheus story, the point on which events
must turn and their moral import be revealed. Since the first century AD this
has been the 'canonical form' (the phrase is Fritz Graf's)[1] of the myth 'as it
entered European consciousness'. The different endings of the story, and the
different human qualities of the principal actors, in Virgil and Ovid, seem
relatively insignificant when set against the strong tradition established by
the common narrative line of these two Roman versions.

In this tradition Orpheus was primarily a lover, impelled in all his actions
by faithful devotion to a human partner. To medieval story-tellers and
illustrators the tale will have presented a noble example of courtly love, of
ordeals undertaken for a lost lady's sake, and minstrelsy inspired by an
inconsolable sorrow. Alternatively, in the Middle Ages the backward glance
will have been interpreted as a paradigm of moral weakness, as Alfred had
made it, appending a moral to warn men of how sexual desire might lead
them to err.

The dilemma of Orpheus' overriding passion – or wavering purpose – led
to extraordinary moral and emotional convolutions in some later versions
which followed this narrative structure. One of the most ambitious (and now
largely unreadable) of these is that of William Morris,[2] written at about the
same time as Browning's poem. Morris makes Orpheus turn round because
he hears no voice or footstep behind him; he is gripped by a sudden
conviction that Eurydice is not there at all, that the gods have lied to him.
This is not so. As he turns, a white light reveals Eurydice, and

> for an instant all was well forgot
> But very love.

Almost at once darkness envelops her and a 'sickening void' leaves him
defeated and alone. It is the loneliness and 'earthly need' of the lover that
Morris unremittingly brings before the reader; and it is this craving for love
which has won mercy from the gods, but also prevented him from trusting in
them. The Argument written by Morris at the opening of the poem hedges
about Orpheus' role: Orpheus, he says,

> would yet not believe that she might not be won back again, but
> sought her where none else has dared to seek, and there *as it were*,
> compelled the gods to grant him somewhat; which nevertheless his
> own folly cast away again, and he was left to live and die a lonely
> man.

The inordinate length of Morris's version does nothing to clarify the
obscurity of 'as it were'. Orpheus' failure, for the Victorian medievalist,
ardent in pursuit of the beautiful in life as in design, was a failure to believe
in personal love as an all-subduing absolute. Hermes, in Morris, promises
happiness to Orpheus if he will believe that 'love/can never die howso the
world may move'; but if he should fail to remember

> that thou upon the steps of death art set,
> If thou shouldst deem this minute all in all
> And let such dreadful longing on thee fall
> That thou must needs turn round about to gaze
> …then thy love is weighed
> And found a light thing.

There is a chill ambiguity about the 'steps of death'; Hermes may seem to be
reminding Orpheus that he is after all a man, moving towards death as
everyone else is. The sense that each minute is 'all in all' seems close to the
experience of Browning's Eurydice. In context, however, it appears that
Hermes' 'steps of death' merely reminds Orpheus, and the reader, that the
scene is set in Hades, under the jurisdiction of its gods. Orpheus then
declares his faith in 'our lonely love', goes on through the desolation of
Hades,. and from time to time handles 'his harp, his friend', uttering songs
that tell of 'his soul's longing', until the fatal moment of doubt comes upon
him and he

> dropped his harp adown
> Scarce knowing what a change in him was grown.

All this offers neither a noble embodiment of courtly love nor a paradigm
of sexual sinfulness. It is a variant of the 'canonical' narrative which could

have taken this shape only in the milieu of the Pre-Raphaelite Movement and the utopian 'seriousness' of mid-Victorian England. Similarly, the poem 'Eurydice' by H.D.[3] – an eight-page monologue in which Eurydice reproaches Orpheus for rescuing her and then again condemning her to die – springs ineradicably from the early feminism of this century in the United States. The poem refers constantly to the theme of this world's flowers, denied to Eurydice, so that she clings instead to 'the flowers of myself...the fervour of myself for a presence'.

The 'canonical' narrative which provides the skeleton for these contorted poems, and many other versions which have carried weight in their day, is a love story of a kind not found in classical Greece. There, art and literature introduced Orpheus' descent to Hades with no emphasis at all on the theme of personal love. When Orpheus was said to descend in search of his dead wife, it may be supposed that he loved her, but in a way very different from the romantic love that could be the theme of a Breton lay, or a Renaissance opera, and still more remote from a Wagnerian death-wish or the self-scrutinising passions of the twentieth century. Romantic love is by definition non-classical, or at least non-Hellenic, and all scholars have agreed in regarding emphasis on this personal emotion as a late development in the history of Orpheus in the Greek world.

Many theories have been propounded concerning the derivation of the backward glance motif. C.M. Bowra was certain[4] that the source was a Hellenistic poem. It is also possible that the motif was originally featured in a Hellenistic work of dramatic literature, or prose fiction, where separated lovers abound (though journeys to the underworld do not). Alexandrian poetry also included the genre of romantic narrative, with endings either happy or calamitous. But even if Virgil was *not* the first to use the motif, the story is likely to have shifted direction in his version, making the pathos of bereavement a much stronger theme, and allowing Orpheus to elicit the reader's sympathy for a human experience of suffering and frustration. Virgil's Dido grew from a minor (and to our present knowledge, indeterminate) figure in Naevius, conflated with some aspects of tragic heroines such as Phaedra and Deianira, and reminiscences of Apollonius' Medea, to assume a tragic stature and a Romantic individuality that is quite unique in epic poetry. There is no reason why he should not have treated Orpheus and Eurydice with equal boldness and sureness of touch. Some parts of the scenes in Hades in *Georgic* IV were re-worked when Virgil wrote of Aeneas' journey through these regions and his last sight of Dido's shade. These doomed lovers are peculiarly Virgilian figures, and they do not belong to the world of classical Greece.

In Greek literature, references to Orpheus' journey to Hades are numerous but brief; they do not indicate how he prevailed upon the gods of Hades to release Eurydice (whether conditionally or not). Visual representations of Orpheus in Hades are very rare until the fourth or possibly third century BC, the suggested date of twelve Apulian vases which depict such a scene in detail. These vases are justly described by Guthrie as 'huge things painted in a repellent style', decorated with 'a hotch-potch' of tales about Hades.[5] Orpheus appears on them, as do Sisyphus, Ixion, and other condemned sinners, and also famous visitors to Hades such as Heracles (seen holding the chained Cerberus). Dressed in flowing robes and a Phrygian cap, Orpheus stands close to Pluto and Persephone. He holds the lyre in his left hand and is usually plucking the strings with his right. On some smaller vases he appears with Persephone and a few other figures, not always named; again, he holds his lyre in his left hand.

These vases seem to follow the general theme, though not always the iconography, of the famous fresco painted in the fifth century on the walls of the Cnidian Hall at Delphi. Polygnotus (says Pausanias)[6] showed Orpheus

> sitting on what seems to be a sort of hill; he grasps in his left hand a harp, and with his right he touches a willow. It is the branches that he touches, and he is leaning against the tree...

This lost painting, like the vases, shows Orpheus in Hades with his instrument held up for performance, or lifted like a standard which Pluto and Persephone will see before he begins to sing. The *Orpheus, Eurydice, Hermes* relief is an exception, allowing him to hold his lyre against his thigh while he touches Eurydice's veil with his right hand; but still the instrument is firmly held in his left, not slung over his shoulder or dropped to the ground.

In the Greek context, the lyre is all-important; whatever the words of his song to Persephone, he is not saying 'pity a poor lover', as Poliziano made him say, in 1480. The Greek Orpheus approaches the powers of hell as he did the realm of nature when on earth, 'striking the strings of his instrument with a master-hand'.[7] When Eusebius wrote of Orpheus in these terms, in the early years of the fourth century AD, he was presenting the figure of a musician whose skill was so masterly that he could be compared to God in his relation to the world. This supremacy could be exercised to tame wild beasts or even to change the purposes of Hades' rulers. Such power could derive only from a divine source. Thus, in the pagan myth Orpheus was said to have been taught to play by Apollo, and the instrument was believed to have come to him as a gift from Hermes. The possession of this divinely given instrument, and this divinely taught skill, is what makes Orpheus' descent unique among *katabasis*-stories, and gives it a significance which other descent-legends, such as those of Heracles and Aeneas, do not have.

In ancient Greece, Orpheus' instrument was always the lyre. While he is seen with Pan-pipes in Roman sculpture and fresco, and much later with a lute or even a violin,[8] the Greeks associated him only with the lyre or *cithara*, the stringed instrument used to accompany lyric poetry (though not the songs of tragedy, which were sung to the *aulos*, the flute). Wind instruments could obviously not be played by a singer as his own accompaniment; the lyre was entirely appropriate for an itinerant musician, being light-weight, played with the hands only, and capable of supporting or complementing the voice however the song might be improvised or repeated. It was also unique among Greek instruments in requiring animal sources for at least two of its components: the various forms of flute might be made of bone but could also be carved from wood or reeds, whereas to make a lyre, strings of gut from cattle or sheep were needed, and the sound-box was a whole tortoise shell.

To describe the lyre in these terms brings the reminder that Orpheus' music could be heard only when cattle and tortoise had died to provide materials for the singer's unique instrument. Indeed, *chelys*, 'tortoise', was said to have been the lyre's original name; the word *lyra* is first found in the work of Archilochus, in the seventh century. Though the *cithara* – a larger and more elaborate form of the lyre – was generally made with a wooden sound-box, this more professional instrument never displaced the lyre as the national medium for poetic and musical education. The music of the lyre was thought to have a serene and virile quality,[9] and was the only kind of music attributed to Orpheus in the Hellenic world. The instrument had seven strings (though Diodorus says that originally it had only four or even three)[10] and was believed to be the invention of the god Hermes, who gave or bartered it to Apollo.[11]

The story of Hermes' invention is the theme of the 'Homeric' *Hymn to Hermes*, probably dating from the late sixth or the fifth century. The instrument is devised as a plaything, on the very day of Hermes' birth. His marvellous cunning and inventiveness prompt him to discover new and expressive means of communication, and the first music sounded on this wonderful instrument is lovely and spontaneous, like the songs of young men celebrating festivals and recounting the loves of the gods (*Hymn. Herm.* 52-9).

To make this music possible, the tortoise has been scooped out from its shell and destroyed (though Hermes has addressed the animal in a friendly and even respectful manner, promising no dishonour and 'sweet song if you die'). In the *Hymn to Hermes*, the seven strings are made of sheep-gut, and the theft of Apollo's cattle is not planned to help in construction of the lyre; that takes place later, and its motive is to give Hermes a share in the savour of sacrificial meat. In Sophocles' *Ichneutae*, the *Trackers*, however, the theft of the cattle *preceded* the making of the lyre, and their skins were used together with the tortoise shell to make the first stringed instrument.[12]

Although our text of *Ichneutae* is so fragmentary, references to tortoise and cattle are closely associated and it is evident that the play's dénouement links the handing over of the lyre to Apollo with reparation for the stolen cattle. The instrument made by Hermes incorporates the nature of both tortoise and cattle. The richly-spangled tortoise, charm against witchcraft, is lifted from its pasture of lush grass by the laughing infant:

> and though it has been said that you alive defend from
> magic power, I know you will sing sweetly when you're dead.
>
> > (*Hymn. Herm.* 37-8, tr. Shelley)

In the fragmented lines spoken by Sophocles' Cyllene (the nymph who nurses the infant Hermes), the tortoise is:

> a shrivelled little creature, curved like a pot,
> with speckled hide. (295)

> It had a voice when dead although when living
> it was dumb. (293)

The tortoise was sacred to Hermes, or (says Pausanias) to Pan; the connection with Pan was found in Arcadia, where the inhabitants would not touch a tortoise or allow a stranger to take one away, although this breed, from Mount Parthenion, had especially fine shells for lyre-making. This association with Pan suggests a pure animality in addition to the apotropaic power of the tortoise, making it a creature to be shunned as well as venerated.[13]

If Apollo's cattle had also been killed to provide the lyre's strings, or for the leather strap which was apparently stretched over the 'yoke' of the instrument, their qualities might also have been absorbed into Hermes' invention, along with the earthy and magical qualities of the tortoise. In the *Hymn to Hermes*, the nature of Apollo's cattle is expressed chiefly through the intensity of his love and jealousy for them. They are 'strong' (94, 302) and even 'immortal' (71), but the poet does not amplify these epithets or add any visual detail. The cattle are valuable to Apollo, but in this poem it is important that the beauty and power of the lyre should outweigh all their worth in order to make the final agreement between the two gods seem credible. Apollo accepts the gift of reparation:

> You have sung a song worth fifty cattle; I believe that we
> shall soon come peacefully to a decision.

(Hymn. Herm. 437-8)

In the *Hymn*, these cattle are simply fine specimens made glorious by the divinity of their owner (and of the thief who takes them away). We may remember the cattle of Helios, or Hyperion, who kept large herds in Sicily, Spain, and Rhodes; his Sicilian herd was plundered and partially slaughtered by the companions of Odysseus, desperate with hunger on their troubled voyage to Ithaca (*Od.* XII). Those who committed this act were very soon drowned. In Homer these 'broad-browed' cattle are untouched by birth or death, and are tended by nymphs who are the divine daughters of Hyperion. The Sun declares (*Od.* XII. 379-83) that these cattle delight him every day as he crosses the sky, so much so that he will descend to Hades and shine only for the dead if he is not fully repaid for their loss. Such animals are clearly the subject of solemn tabu, and although the story of Helios' cattle is not usually identified with that of the beloved herd of Apollo (which would seem to belong to a later age and certainly to a different region of Greece), it seems natural to associate the sanctity and tabu surrounding Helios' beasts with the reverence shown towards Apollo's.

To create the lyre, then, Hermes had destroyed two extraordinary forms of animal life and broken a potent religious tabu. From these acts came possibilities of expressive sound never known before, bringing excitement and terror and rapture to the Chorus of satyrs in the *Ichneutae*. In Tony Harrison's dramatic exploration of what the incomplete fragment of this play might promise, for us as well as for its own time, the satyrs speculate, bewildered, on the origin of the marvellous sound:

> It could be a goat...
> It could be a cat...
> Dog's gut or hound's
> could be making these sounds...

The individual voices unite in a sinister refrain:

> Summat's been flayed
> for this sweet serenade.[14]

In *The Trackers of Oxyrhynchus*, Harrison introduces Apollo as an arrogant and ruthless deity who speaks through the mouth of a fanatical academic. Astonished at Hermes' discovery, he claims it for himself:

> This mottled tortoise, this creeping thing,
> Joined to my cattle makes dumb Nature sing.

Not only the tortoise and the cattle, but the satyr Marsyas has to die in hideous agony to demonstrate Apollo's sole mastery of the art of music. The satyrs, who enter the play to track down the thief who stole Apollo's cattle, are rejected by him once they have succeeded in their search; he exults in the transformation of tortoise and cattle to music, but warns the satyrs who aspire to handle the wonderful instrument:

> No! No! No!
> My advice is stick to being satyrs
> And don't go meddling with musical matters...
> You're satyrs, remember. You don't need lyres
> While your goat parts tether you to brute desires...
> I'm Apollo, inspirer, appreciator
> Of artist, musician and creator...
> I'm not a cowherd really. It's more me
> The sphere of music and of poetry.
> This is now my lyre and I define
> Its music as half-human, half-divine,
> And satyrs, I repeat, must not aspire
> In any way to mastering my lyre.

Trackers of Oxyrhynchus, 55

The relentless arrogance which Harrison attributes to Apollo is the motive force in many myths where he takes terrifying vengeance as Destroyer – the meaning of his name – in the form of archer, bringer of plague, dragon-slayer, master of scorching heat or blinding light or prophetic madness. The stories of Linus, Thamyris, and Marsyas show this vengeful power wielded against those who presume to rival Apollo as musical performers.

No myth ever presents Apollo as *creator* of the lyre; whether he obtained it by gift from Hermes, as the Homeric *Hymn* says, or by violent struggle, as shown in the bronze seen by Pausanias in the Valley of the Muses,[15] he was taking over the invention of another god (who, in accordance with his nature, moved on with no concern for keeping the thing he had made). Discovery was not Apollo's strength: his relation to the material world aims always at domination. So, in the *Ichneutae*, he needs the help of the Chorus of satyrs to track down his stolen cattle, which they do by scent as well as by following hoof-marks.Tony Harrison's version of the play extrapolates from the incomplete papyrus to provide a final scene where both Apollo and Hermes are superseded by the satyrs, whose resentment turns to violence:

> We're going to destroy and we're enjoying
> Destroying for the sake of destroying...
>
> No more deferential dummies from a satyr play.
> From now on MARSYAS RULES OK?...
>
> Aeschylus, Sophocles, gerroff our backs.
> We're hijacking Culture and leaving no tracks.

This is a new generation of satyrs, ready to burn the Oxyrhynchus papyri or roll them into a football.

In the Athenian theatre the role of the satyrs was limited to the short play performed as a pendant to a tragic trilogy; a subordinate but necessary part in the wholeness of dramatic celebration. Dramatist and audience alike were compelled at that point to acknowledge the gross physicality and violence which gave power to Hermes' inventiveness – and to the worship of Dionysus through the medium of tragedy.[16] Apollo stood aloof from all this, and in the forms of music and poetry directly associated with him it was possible to claim a kind of inspiration, and to strive for modes of expression that would proclaim a higher truth and reveal a purer beauty than any attained through sense-experience or the passions common to mankind.

The antithesis, even antagonism, between Apollo and Dionysus has been axiomatic for Europeans since Nietszche, and *The Trackers of Oxyrhynchus* is in that sense going over old ground. The pattern which Harrison has chosen in completing the fragmentary satyr-play (though no one supposes this the pattern followed by Sophocles) is the same as that of Euripides' *Bacchae*: those who are too high-minded to recognise the power of the orgiastic god, or of the crudely animal in humanity, find these forces turned destructively and irreparably upon them. In spite of Apollo's own eminence as Destroyer, he is not able to control these devastating outbursts of vandal energy, and his followers are warned that they walk precariously.

In this polarisation of Dionysiac, or satyric, and Apollonian, Orpheus stands on the side of Apollo. Ancient testimony is almost unanimous in relating that Apollo taught him to play and sing, and (perhaps even more significant) gave him the lyre as his instrument. He is the chosen of Apollo, his mouthpiece, some even say his son.[17] For this reason his music was always described as exquisitely melodious, endlessly beautiful in form and harmony, and able to induce tranquillity and noble aspirations in all who heard it.

Orpheus' poetry, inspired by Apollo, might also be expected to speak of
heavenly things, of divine deeds or cosmogonies, and much of the so-called
Orphic poetry that survives is of this kind. Nevertheless, Orpheus needed his
lyre in order to perform – his lyre made from a dead tortoise and the guts of
slaughtered cattle. Paradoxically, it was the music of Dionysus' dithyramb
that was performed on the *aulos*, the flute of reed. Orpheus never played on
this or any other wind instrument.

For some writers the origin of the lyre has itself been seen as the source
of Orpheus' special gift of lyric poignancy. Because it was made from
suffering and death, the instrument expressed grief and loss as no other could
do, almost as the harp in the ballad *The Two Sisters of Binnorie* plays
sorrowful music that proclaims the tale of a sister's murder even without the
harpist's intention, because it is made from the dead girl's hair (and in some
versions her collar-bone). The lyre of Orpheus is in itself eloquent of pain, a
paradigm of beauty springing from violence and death. No instrument could
be more fitting to express the endless lamentation of Orpheus the bereaved
lover, or the hope of new life for the dead brought up from Hades.

Such new life was not sought for Eurydice only. It is not clear whether the
story of Orpheus' restored wife preceded or followed his reputation as a
restorer of the dead generally. A passage in Isocrates (dating from the fourth
century BC)[18] refers to him as one who 'used to bring back the dead from
Hades', as if this were Orpheus' well-known regular practice; but it is true,
as Linforth says, that the encomiastic style might well allow generalisation
from a single incident, if the intention were to recall the recovery of Agriope
or Eurydice.[19] But even if Isocrates does not here intend to claim that others
were revived as well as Orpheus' wife, this manner of describing him, 'the
bringer-up of the dead', certainly points to the role which he assumed at a
later date as a cult hero of mystery-religion. As such a hero, he would have
many parallel figures, divine or semi-divine, such as Heracles and Dionysus,
who also had power to revive or win back the dead by various means.
Orpheus' uniqueness here lay in his use of music, and above all in his divinely
made instrument.

This use of a musical instrument is one of the usual characteristics of the
shaman entering, or returning from, his ecstatic experience of the Beyond.
The shamanist tradition – whether in Lapland, Ceylon, or North America –
may well illuminate Orpheus' role as a 'professional' rescuer of souls from a
threatening Beyond, and he has indeed been regarded as originally a shaman
living in Thrace.[20] There he would have gathered about him groups of
followers, who looked to him as a mediator between men and gods. His music
would enable him to enter into a trance and visit the world of the dead; on
returning, he would again take up his lyre and recount his experiences in
poetic form. In the course of such singing, according to this view of him, he
revealed secrets of the gods (or, as Isocrates says, told discreditable stories

about them), so that they punished him by allowing the Bacchants to tear him in pieces.[21]

If Orpheus was believed to have disobeyed a command to keep divine secrets, this ban on a particular kind of communication may have reappeared in the later Orpheus legend as a ban upon looking round at his wife. There are many variants in myth and folk-lore introducing bans of this sort: when Lot's disobedient wife turned to look back, her deliverance from Sodom instantly changed to a doom as final as the burning city's.[22] In this and other respects the re-structuring of Orpheus' journey to and from Hades, in the changed cultural world of Alexandria and the Roman Empire, is not difficult to accept. The specific limitation imposed upon his power to move between earth and the Beyond makes him subject to divine displeasure, as the shaman always knows himself to be; and the divinely given skill which fits Orpheus for his particular role in the romance of a later age may derive from his shaman-life in Thrace.

Yet the story of the scooped-out tortoise seems to have no parallel, in earlier centuries or later. Russell Hoban, in his novel *The Medusa Frequency* (1987),[23] makes Orpheus himself the destroyer of the tortoise and the maker of the lyre:

> There was an olive grove, I could feel the Hermes of it. There was a tortoise. My hand reached down and picked up the tortoise; with a hiss it drew its head in. I stood there feeling the shape of it and the weight of it in my hand and there was an idea coming to me...
>
> The tortoise was in my left hand and my knife was in my right; my idea was the tortoise-shell empty and two posts and a yoke and some strings for a kind of little harp with the shell as a sound box...I cut the plastron loose and dug the body out of the shell, ugh! What a mess and my hands all slippery with blood and gore. The entrails were mysterious. I think about it now, how those entrails spilled out so easily when I made an emptiness for my music to sound in. Impossible to put those entrails back...

Set in the context of twentieth-century London, Orpheus is speaking to a failed novelist who makes his living from *Classic Comics: ORPHEUS, Six-Part Picture Series*. The head of Orpheus, manifesting itself in various forms including a cabbage and a football, looks back over two millennia of restlessness and desolation:

> Being Orpheus was my punishment...for killing the tortoise.

To discover the potentialities of his discovery, the 'harp' of tortoiseshell, Orpheus has to lose Eurydice and through his loss become agonisingly aware of all that surrounds him or rises to meet him. On a golden afternoon,

> the flight of the kingfisher opened in the air over the river a blue-green stillness in which a dragon-fly, immense and transparent, repeated itself with every wingstroke...and as I listened to the weeping of the unseen woman... I became the tortoise I had killed. I felt my own cruel knife enter me...I suffered the many pains of death as underworld opened to me...there came a stillness and I found myself weeping by the river with the lyre in one hand and the plectrum in the other.

> (*The Medusa Frequency*, 39-40)

What remains, after the anguish of bereavement and of intolerably acute perception, is the instrument, which demands to be played. For others, poems will demand to be written, or forms realised in stone or paint; but image- making arts, verbal or visual, are further removed from the animal pain which has passed into the instrument handled by the musician. Poet and painter cannot therefore pass the gate of Hades: only the musician can do this, because he has the lyre. In medieval illustrations of Orpheus' entry to Hades, he holds his instrument before him as Christ holds the Cross and banner in representations of resurrection or the harrowing of hell; both are standards of talismanic power, a power that derives from the pain of death.

In Mozart's *Magic Flute*, composed in 1791, the hero Tamino (like Orpheus) needs a divinely given instrument to give him access to a hidden world of supernatural terrors and undefined menace. Seeking the maiden Pamina, who has been abducted by an evil demon, he receives the talismanic Flute from the three Ladies who serve the Queen of the Night. They promise that the Flute will protect him in times of danger, and will also give him power to 'change the passions of men; the mourner will be joyful, the old bachelor fall in love'. The power of the Flute is soon proved when Tamino begins to play it in thankfulness at hearing Pamina is still alive, and finds himself surrounded by a throng of wild animals, who gather to listen to the music. After long separation and many ordeals, Tamino and Pamina are united, to walk together through the region of fire and flood which represents the final experience of terror:

Wir wandeln durch des Tones Macht,
Froh durch des Todes düstre Nacht.

We move through the power of music
Gladly through the dark night of death.

It is the sound of the Flute that has brought Pamina to join her prince, just as in the sub-plot Papagena appears when Papageno remembers to play the tinkling bells that were given to him for protection by the three Ladies. Papageno, the honest and endearing bird-catcher, finds an exuberant domestic happiness with his *Weibchen, Taubchen, meine Schöne* ('little wife, little dove, my pretty') and the many children they expect the gods will send. For Tamino and Pamina the future is seen in very different terms. They are to follow the music of the Flute into the Temple of Isis (also, in the final scene, called the Temple of the Sun). There, the evil powers, the Queen of the Night and her attendants, are plunged into eternal darkness and the chosen lovers are rewarded with an everlasting crown. The reward has been won by their fidelity to divine commands; they have recognised the power of the Flute and followed its music, and also endured separation and the silence imposed by the Speakers who meet newcomers to the temple precincts.

When Emanuel Schikaneder wrote his libretto for *The Magic Flute*, he was not using classical sources; his material came principally from a German fairy-tale combined with a pseudo-Egyptian novel written originally in French. These two literary sources – interwoven with strands from several others, traditional in theatre or folk-tale – were worked into an extraordinary fabric that is unified by persistent hints and references to the rituals of Freemasonry.[24] The use of the Orpheus-structure, and the important departures from the more familiar forms of that structure, were not (it seems) due to Schikaneder himself, and we do not know how far he meant to arouse associations with the Orpheus tradition. However, the animal-charming scene and the ban on speech at the passage from one world to the other are so clearly Orphean that other parallel elements cannot be dismissed as accidental resemblances.

In the fairy tale which was the major source for the *Magic Flute* narrative, Pamina's father was a wise king who lived in the East and held a sevenfold solar orb that could reveal the secrets of nature. Once, on a lonely journey in the remote mountains of his kingdom, the king lost his way and sheltered from a violent storm under a thousand-year-old oak. From the heart of this tree he carved the Flute, which he played, finding that it led him back safely to his castle. Pamina remembers this when she commits herself to go with Tamino along the path that leads through fire and flood to the Temple of the Sun. This temple has held the sevenfold orb since the death of Pamina's father, who handed it over to Sarastro and his 'consecrated band' of initiates. If Tamino succeeds in joining this band, he too will have access to the secrets of nature.

The language of initiation in Schikaneder's libretto evidently derives in part from Masonic admission of 'the profane' into the Craft, but also from the eighteenth-century response to what had been learned of pagan mysteries, especially those of Isis. However, such mysteries were not usually associated with the Sun-god. Orpheus' devotion to Apollo was quite distinct from his supposed institution of mysteries, at Athens or elsewhere. Yet his connection with the worship of Dionysus was undoubted (a connection very variously reported, from being originator of Bacchic rites in Greece to refusing any honour to Dionysus and so incurring death by dismemberment). Those who sought Orphic initiation might discover that the traditional antithesis between Dionysus and Apollo obscured a deeper unity. Macrobius and others relate that Orpheus declared Dionysus and the Sun to be one god; the antithesis is found to be a true identity (as a fragment of Euripides, much earlier, also claims).[25] The two gods both had a home in Delphi, and it was there that Apollo was generally supposed to have overcome Dionysus in some kind of struggle for presidency. Clearly, Orpheus' initiation into Dionysiac mysteries, or his establishing of such rites for other worshippers, did not conflict with his dedication to Helios-Apollo, source of illumination and of the loftiest forms of music and poetry. The two gods might be seen as different aspects of the same divinity, but Apollo remained finally paramount, as the Sun remains at the end of *The Magic Flute*: the goal of the journey and the source of a higher life.

At the beginning of the opera Pamina has been snatched away by a powerful evil Demon, who crept into the cypress grove where she was sitting. 'By his power to change himself into every conceivable shape' (the three Ladies say), the Demon abducted Pamina so that she fell into the hands of her mother, the Queen of the Night, whose professed love for her daughter concealed a jealous and evil spirit. When Pamina chooses to follow her lover with courage and resolve, the power of the evil mother is broken and Pamina can proceed from Persephone's realm, to be accepted in the Temple of the Sun.

This dénouement is a wholly unexpected one in the Orpheus tradition: not only does the lost girl return from the realm of darkness, but she shares the decisive moves made by her lover and will go on to live in partnership with him when they have both received enlightenment in the temple. This is much more than the conventional happy ending of the *Singspiel*. As Pamina and Papageno assert, the love between male and female will exemplify the divine truth and the cycle of nature:

Mann und Weib, und Weib und Mann,
Reichen an die Gottheit an.

Man and wife, and wife and man,
Reach up towards the Deity.

This contradicts the belief of Pamina's father (and, earlier in the opera, of Tamino) that woman is too weak and imperfect to attain to the higher spiritual life; *this* Eurydice enters a new kind of Elysium, as an equal partner with her lover.

In spite of this new dénouement, Mozart's Orpheus story is thoroughly classical in many ways which perhaps neither he nor Schikaneder considered; classical authenticity was certainly not their aim. The elegance and humour, the marvellous diversity and warmth of *The Magic Flute* belongs to eighteenth-century Vienna, to Schikaneder's *Freihaustheater*, and above all to Mozart. But the clarity and the stern moralism at the centre of this opera derive from its Greek origins. The lovers attain their happiness and their enlightenment because they resist all temptation to disobey divine commands, and because they have the Flute to guide them through the darkness of the underworld. Although the love between man and woman is exalted, as no Greek ever exalted it, Mozart and Schikaneder did not fall into the trap of sentiment which closed around Morris and Watts.

From the time of the Renaissance onwards, Orpheus had been shown as winning his lost bride (and, in the usually preferred version, once more losing her) through the intensity of his love rather than the power of his music. In opera especially, he was increasingly the lover rather than the divinely gifted musician. At first sight this may seem a paradoxical feature of the developing operatic form, but the emphasis in Italian opera was always on the virtuoso voice and its power to express human emotions. The instrument carried by Orpheus thus became no more than a decorative, perhaps vaguely symbolic, attribute. (Although Monteverdi's Orpheus thanks his 'almighty lyre' for melting the heart of Pluto, and promises that it will be taken up to heaven, his own final ascent is granted by his father Apollo as a reward for 'true virtue', and the instrument is not mentioned again.) For the first time in the history of opera, Mozart made Orpheus' lyre more important than his voice. So he becomes again, as in Greece, the dedicated worshipper of the Sun-god, able to make sublime music because he has the Flute and because he can show love for his bride without losing his humble obedience to the divine will.

What is a poet? He is a man who has received a special talent, a gift from a divine power. This talent may be symbolised by a musical instrument made from an animal body or from some form of plant life. The gift sets him apart and enables him to reach levels of consciousness not accessible to the majority of mankind. Through his poetry he can communicate with super-natural as well as human beings, and so he can act as an interpreter of divine things.

Poetry may therefore offer to its readers experiences that are spiritual rather than emotional, and can guide men towards a life of deeper awareness and personal discipline. A recurrent hope is that through poetry men may also recover elements of experience that have been lost.

III

The Healer of the Soul

IF the Flute given to Tamino was able to change the dispositions of men, making them more open to goodness and heavenly delight, it would be following the pattern set by Orpheus' lyre; from earliest times this was said to soothe the wild passions of its hearers and bring them to ways of peace and religious devotion.

This traditional Orphean power is a strong motif in the *Argonautica* of Apollonius Rhodius, written in the third century BC. His Orpheus, sailing with the Argonauts, constantly gives guidance to the heroes about the direction they should take, about sacrifices to be offered, about rites of expiation or the averting of evil; and when strife breaks out among them as they are preparing for the voyage.

> Orpheus... lifted up his lyre in his left hand, and began a song...
>
> (I. 494-5)

He sings to the quarrelsome heroes about the origins of the earth and the stars, their separation 'after deadly strife', and the earliest gods. When the song is over, the Argonauts bend forward eagerly, still intent to listen even though the song has ended:

> such a charm of song he left within them.
>
> (I. 515)

The divine music has entered into the listeners so that their impatience and impulse to anger has wholly vanished. They pour libations to Zeus, then sleep, and next morning set sail, rowing together to the sound of Orpheus' lyre. The sea surges and sparkles, and the rowers' arms shine in the sun like flame:

on that day, from heaven all the gods watched the ship, and the strength of the heroes half-divine.

(I. 547-8)

A rather abstract account of Orpheus' civilising music is given in Horace's *Ars Poetica*:

silvestres homines sacer interpresque deorum
caedibus et victu foedo deterruit Orpheus.

Before men left the jungle, a holy prophet of heaven,
Orpheus, made them abhor bloodshed and horrible food.

(Hor. *Ep*. II. 3. 391-2, tr. Rudd)

How Orpheus 'made them' turn away from bloodshed, Horace does not say, but the verb *deterruit* makes his intervention a single and effectual one, and it was because of this, Horace goes on to say, that he is thought to have been able to tame raging lions and tigers. The poet's approach to men in their primitive days was like Orpheus' approach to animals; he did not reason with them or explain, but won their consent by the charm of his song. So too Tyrtaeus and Homer 'sharpened the courage of men to enter battle'. Several specific social and religious institutions are attributed to the influence of early poets, but it is these changes of disposition which Horace makes parallel with the taming of animals and even with Amphion's lyre raising the stones of Thebes to form the city walls. If men gave up slaughter and promiscuity and instead began to live by written laws, this was because their impulses were changed and the ordered pacific life became what they wanted. The authoritative guidance given by Orpheus and the other early poets is not teaching in the sense of instruction or discipline, but rather the gift of a transforming experience which is accompanied by pleasure and a sense of gratitude:

sic honor et nomen divinis vatibus atque
carminibus venit.

That is how heavenly bards and their poems came to
acquire honour and glory.

(II. 3. 400-1)

The effect of music upon the listener's emotions and disposition had been amply discussed by Greek philosophers, as Horace was no doubt aware. Aristotle observes that the different musical modes are suited to express different attitudes,[1] and that rhythms also have different characters, such as steadiness, liveliness, or refinement. These qualities inherent in the music are aroused also in the listener, making music a powerful educational medium (Aristotle's chief concern, in this passage of the *Politics*). Its effectiveness in training the young derives from the pleasure which, Aristotle repeatedly states, music 'very naturally' brings 'to all men', part of their instinctive endowment. Thus children can learn to find pleasure in the experience of socially valuable emotions such as fortitude and steadfastness, if they hear and practise music of the appropriate kind from their earliest years.

According to Aristotle, such imitative character-development is not the only means by which music operates upon the listener. There is a further experience (he carefully limits this to *some* musical modes and *some* especially susceptible persons) which leads beyond a merely sympathetic response to 'a calming and restorative effect...a release of emotion accompanied by pleasure'. Aristotle compares this sense of relief and well-being to the physical effect of a purge, as he does when discussing the effect of tragedy on an audience (*Poetics*, VI). The kind of music which can act in this way is described as that which encourages action or offers inspiration – in particular 'religious melodies' which arouse pity, fear, and a sense of exaltation. To a lesser degree, he goes on to say, all listeners can share in this experience of 'purging'. The result is analogous to the medical result of a purge: a better condition of inward health.

Mental health had long been associated with harmony: 'some saying that the soul is a harmony, and others that it possesses the attribute of harmony' (*Pol.* VIII. 5, 1340b). When Plato speaks of music as an essential part of education from the earliest age and throughout life, he frequently refers to a 'harmony in the soul', which can be realised by familiarisation with music that is harmonious and so inherently pleasing to the human ear. Both Plato and Aristotle emphasise the value of the rhythmical element in music, and its ability to express qualities that can arouse a response in the life and personality of the listener.

Plato asserts more decisively than Aristotle is willing to do that music derives from a heavenly source and is naturally pleasing to mankind for that very reason. Just as the sense of sight was given to man 'so that we might observe the orbits of reason which are in heaven, and apply them to the revolutions of thought in our own souls', so too sound and hearing were bestowed by the gods to allow men to realise in their souls the divine pattern of creation:

> Harmony, since its motions are akin to the changes in our own souls, has been given by the Muses to the man who, using his mind, seeks their help, not for an irrational pleasure, as is the fashion now, but

to help us in ordering and assimilating to it the discordant motions of our souls. And again, rhythm was given to us from the same source, and for the same purpose, to help us in dealing with what is unmeasured and chaotic in the minds of most of us.

(Plato, *Timaeus*, 47d-e)

The divine intention explains why music is so peculiarly effective in 'charming the souls of children while still young and tender', to grow in wisdom and every kind of virtue: 'for the gods say the best life does in fact bring most pleasure' (*Laws* II, 664b). The divinely intended order is naturally preferable, as health is preferable to disease, but mental harmony is as liable to disturbance as physical; so discords will need to be resolved, not once but many times in a human life, by attention to music (and poetry) that is truly harmonious and rhythmical. The whole educational programme of 'music and gymnastic' in the *Republic*[2] (both terms used in the widest sense) is based upon this view of what music is and how it acts upon the soul.

For Plato, the idea of 'harmony in the soul' would be realised as a hierarchic order in which the different human functions would serve the purposes discerned by the highest of them – the power of reason. Emotional impulses of every kind needed to be trained to accept a subordinate position. Because music so clearly possesses an intellectual structure as well as emotional expressiveness, its appropriateness as a means for such training was always evident. This made it easy to see Orpheus (or any other highly gifted musician) as a figure of religious enlightenment, a 'holy prophet' leading men towards spiritual health. Orpheus had truths to proclaim, as well as emotional enrichment or purification to bestow.

Belief in the healing power of Orpheus' music persisted into the Middle Ages and beyond: Christine de Pisan, writing in France in the early years of the fifteenth century, confidently cites him as an example of the assimilation of psychic states to the harmonic order of music, as described in Plato's *Timaeus*:

> tant melodieusement faisoit sons a la harpe que par les proporcions des accors tant a point ordenez il garissoit de pluseurs maladies et les tristes faisoit estre ioyeux.

> (Orpheus) made such melodious sounds on the harp that by the perfectly ordered proportions of his harmonies he cured several maladies and made sad men happy.

(Christine de Pisan, *La Vision*, fol. 32r, 1405)

Equivalence between Orpheus and David, the Psalmist who brought peace of mind and spiritual health to Saul, had been accepted long before Christine de Pisan's time. David's music had power over 'evil spirits', who were said to trouble the king and cast him into deep depression:

> and it came to pass, when the evil spirit from God was upon Saul, that David took an harp, and played with his hand; so Saul was refreshed, and was well, and the evil spirit departed from him.
>
> (1 Sam. 16:33)

And it was obvious to a Byzantine exegesist of the seventh century that Orpheus and David should be classed together as divinely inspired poets and musicians:

> for however much Orpheus smote his divinely tuned lyre, so much more David, seeing the glory of the heavens as they stretched from the height to the depths of creation, sang out about them.
>
> (George of Pisidia, *Hexameron*)

George was a Greek, 'keeper of the records' at Sta Sophia. He willingly assumes knowledge and (in some sense) acceptance of the Orpheus legend, so that David can be set in parallel with this familiar figure; whereas for Cassiodorus, about a century earlier, in Italy, it is David who commands acceptance, and Orpheus is given credence only reluctantly, because the two figures so clearly analogous:

> If we do not speak of Orpheus' lyre and the song of the Sirens on the ground that they are fabulous, what shall we say of David who delivered Saul from the unclean spirit, by his redeeming melody?
>
> (Cassiodorus, *Introduction to Divine and Human Readings*)

Jewish as well as Christian scriptures in the medieval period illustrated David as harpist surrounded by deeply attentive listeners who often included animals: the scenes are unmistakably Orphean.[3] In a famous Jerusalem mosaic of the sixth century, now in the Archaeological Museum, Istanbul, the lion (or at least the bear) is seen to lie down with the lamb; a satyr and a centaur also appear to be under the control of the musician in the Phrygian cap who must be Orpheus but could not fail, in Jerusalem, to call to mind the acts and the power of David. This example is thought to be part of a Jewish tomb. There are many other representations of the divinely gifted musician, where a crowned Orpheus or a Hellenised David shows a conflation of the two singers who subdued savagery and disorder in both men and beasts.[4]

The music of the poet-singer, in both Greek and Hebrew traditions, has the effect of Milton's 'flutes and soft recorders' upon the fallen angels; from fretful rage and 'looks/downcast and damp', the vast gathering of Satan's followers assumes an ordered strength, responding to the music's

> power to mitigate and swage
> With solemn touches troubled thoughts, and chase
> Anguish and doubt and fear and sorrow and pain
> From mortal or immortal minds. Thus they,
> Breathing united force with fixed thought,
> Moved on in silence to soft pipes that charmed
> Their painful steps o'er the burnt soil.

(Paradise Lost, I. 556-62)

The resolution and coherence shown by the fallen angels at this moment sustains them through the orderly conclave of Book II, until Satan departs to look for Earth and the angels disperse 'each his several way'. Like Apollonius' Argonauts, or the 'people that know the joyful sound' in the Psalmist's song of celebration,[5] the followers of Satan (even though they are enemies of God) respond to the divinely inspired music by acting peaceably, in unity, and with zest.

In all these accounts of response to the music and words that come from the divine source, the musician – David, Orpheus, or the unnamed musicians of Milton – is fulfilling the function which T.S. Eliot defined[6] as the task of all art: he is bringing the hearers to 'a condition of serenity, stillness, and reconciliation'. And this he does by 'eliciting some perception of an order in reality'. The state of peaceable, active calm is possible because it corresponds to a state of calm creative power in the suprahuman world, and it is made accessible through the divinely given medium of art.

Music of such power must seem to belong to a realm beyond the experience of this world, and to arise from knowledge and vision which the ordinary person, however gifted, cannot possess. As the one chosen to bring such gifts to men, Orpheus the Healer is an insufficient icon. The story of his journey to the world beyond the grave conferred on him another status, one which David could not parallel.

It might seem that Elysium, or something like it, should await the hero-musician at the end of his journey through Hades. Heracles and Aeneas had attained apotheosis, after similar journeys, and the ancient tradition concerning Orpheus had constantly spoken of an elysian realm as his final home.[7]

In the fifth-century painting by Polygnotus, described by Pausanias, and again in the vision of the afterlife as seen by Virgil's Aeneas, Orpheus appears, enjoying a timeless state of blessedness. However, these scenes in Elysium are not related to Orpheus' perilous journey into Hades as a living hero, and are not described as being his reward earned for merit during his lifetime. He is in Elysium as a divinely gifted teacher, venerated and followed by the souls of the good. Nowhere is there any account of ordeals or purification to be undergone by Orpheus himself before entry to the heavenly realm. The parallel between Orpheus and Tamino does not hold here. In ancient myth the purification and ascent to blessedness are experienced not by Orpheus himself but by his followers, those who were delivered from Hades, or the threat of Hades, by the hero-musician.

Orpheus as initiate, struggling and enduring on his path towards a higher life, is not a figure of the ancient imagination; this was never an exemplary icon, as far as our surviving evidence shows, even for the Orphic initiates who used his name and the hymns and formulas associated with it. The image of Orpheus as a pilgrim, striving for his own salvation, seems to originate with Boethius in about 500 AD. Such an interpretation of the *katabasis*-story would certainly accord with medieval ways of thought, and it is not surprising to find it developed, for example, in the twelfth-century commentary on Boethius by Guillaume de Conches.[8] Orpheus, for Guillaume, represented the searcher after heavenly truth, whose *sapientia* (intellectual enlightenment) alone could not sustain his purpose; natural desire, *concupiscentia*, in the person of Eurydice, distracted him from the hard path and left him at the mercy of tormenting impulses. In Henryson's words, 'a woful widaw hamwart is he went', and no heavenly realm awaits him unless we allow a different choice as a possibility at the earlier crux of the story. Henryson's *moralitas*, appended to his version of 'Boece', sets this alternative before the reader:

> Bot Orpheus has wone Erudices,
> When our desire with reson makis pess,
> And sekis up to contemplacioun,
> Of sin detestand the abusioun.[9]

This ending remains an abstract consideration. Unless the backward glance story was discarded altogether, there could be no positive outcome for Orpheus' journey in terms of spiritual pilgrimage. His story could be a didactic allegory, bleakly admonishing the waverer, but it could not take him to Elysium.

A good *moralitas* such as Henryson's would find many to relish it, but in the same age a love story with supernatural dangers and a happy ending was also likely to win enthusiastic readers and to be remembered. The tale that is told in *Sir Orfeo* was very easily developed in the courtly and even romantic manner of the later Middle Ages. A happy-ever-after conclusion to such a story could also be allegorised as standing for truly ever-after bliss in heaven, for both the lovers; and in that case Eurydice could not be seen as a temptress or distraction. Bitten by the serpent, an immediately recognisable image of evil, she was a wounded and weakened victim as she struggled towards the light. Without the strength and devotion of Orpheus as he lifted up his lyre and dared to enter Hell, she could not reach the light of day, still less the joy of Heaven.

The interpretation to which this kind of story-telling would lead is allegorical in a sense entirely opposite to Henryson's: Eurydice would now represent the human soul, whose nature is wounded by the serpent in Eden. This soul can be healed and brought to salvation only by the love and the descent and ascent of the divine Orpheus, the Christ. The equivalence of Orpheus and Christus is made in Bersuire's commentary on Ovid, and became much more familiar, in the early Renaissance and afterwards, than the Boethian reading of the myth. Bersuire did include this alternative allegory, in which Orpheus stood for wayward mankind, losing his soul through inattention to divine commands, but the 'prefiguration' of Christ in Orpheus is the reading that he upholds.[10]

This prefiguration had, by the fifteenth century, almost entirely replaced the traditional identification of Orpheus with David. When the *Ovide Moralisé* first appeared, about 1300, Orpheus' lyre was described as 'truly the harp by which David, God's helper, gave aid and comfort to Saul'. The prose summary of this work, a century later, displaces David:

> By Orpheus we must understand the person of our Lord Jesus Christ...who played the harp so melodiously that he drew from Hell the sainted souls of the holy Fathers who had descended there through the sin of Adam and Eve.

The lyre, or 'harp', of Orpheus is uplifted at the mouth of Hell in many medieval illustrations of Eurydice's rescue, just as Christ lifts up the Cross in the traditional iconography of the Harrowing. The equivalence of lyre and Cross is implied in the earliest extant parallel between Orpheus' saving descent and the redemptive descent of Jesus. This is found in the twelfth-century Easter sequence *Morte Christi celebrata*:

> Homo, gaude si reductus
> consoletur tuus luctus
> dulci sono, cithara...
>
> Israhelem in Egypto
> Pharaone circumscripto

serpens salvat eneus;
sponsam suam ab inferno,
regno locans in superno,
noster traxit Orpheus.

O Man, rejoice if your grief be turned back and consoled by a sweet sound, the cithara...

The brazen serpent saves Israel in Egypt, with Pharaoh made powerless; our Orpheus has brought his bride from Hell, setting (her) in a heavenly kingdom.[11]

Among Renaissance philosophers the lyre was understood as a symbol of music's power to arouse emotion, or (as in Cusanus of Trier, for example) of the divine element in human nature, which might override natural law. The correspondence between lyre and Cross persisted, however, and became a powerful theme in Calderón's two Autos called *El divino Orfeo*, of 1634 and 1663. In this drama Orfeo carries a harp made in the shape of a cross, and called *La citara de Jesus*.

Along with the Orpheus-Christus identification, medieval writers and artists also suggested analogy between Eurydice and Eve. Whether the figure of Aristaeus appeared in the scene or not, the serpent that bit Eurydice's foot almost always did. Here was clear fulfilment of the prophecy given to the serpent in Eden: 'he (the offspring of Eve) shall bruise thy head, and thou shalt bruise his heel' (Gen. 3:15). Illustrators frequently showed the serpent attacking Eurydice at one side of the picture, with Orpheus leading her from Hell's mouth at the other, just as Fall and Redemption would appear in parallel manuscript panels or window lights. The double image continues in Renaissance paintings also. The small glowing painting by Titian, now at Bergamo, shows a very young Eurydice turning in alarm to look at the dragon, almost her own size, that bites purposefully at the back of her ankle; at the other side of the picture a much smaller Eurydice struggles to follow the hurrying Orpheus, and their clothes are flying in the wind as they pass an open cave-mouth of billowing smoke. Dating from the mid-sixteenth century, the painting uses no specific religious symbolism, and its warmth and delicate sensuality suggest the Orpheus story of Poliziano rather than the Middle Ages or even Ovid. The moment depicted is that of the backward glance, and already Eurydice seems to be straining against an unseen force that pulls her backwards. The ending will be sorrow, not triumph. None the less, the iconography of 'Eve fallen-Eve restored' remains, and creates the painting's structure. It lingers after this date in literature also: for example, in Phineas Fletcher's *Christ's Victorie and Triumph* (1610) when he writes of Eurydice as a second Eve 'by a serpent slayne'.

Fragment of a relief known as *St Peter in the guise of Good Shepherd*, from the catacomb of St Sebastian, Rome.

Although the *morte Christi celebrata* is the earliest example we have of direct correspondence between Orpheus' *katabasis* and the Harrowing of Hell, the Orpheus-Christus analogy in a general sense is much older. The evidence of fresco paintings in the catacombs at Rome and elsewhere proves an iconographic equivalence in the earliest Christian centuries. In the catacombs of Rome, Naples, and Syracuse, the Good Shepherd appears as one of the regular subjects for wall-painting, and has two iconic forms, both closely related to well-known pagan precedents: the figure of the Shepherd with lamb or ram (or even sometimes kid) carried across his shoulders illustrates with clear and touching directness the parable of the Lost Sheep sought and found by the loving Saviour; the second figure is the seated Shepherd, surrounded by the flock who lift their heads to hear the voice which they recognise (Luke 15:4-6, John 10:14-16). The first of these icons unmistakably follows the image of the sculptured *kriophoros* ('ram-carrier') of the sixth century BC from the Athenian Acropolis, an image itself derived from much older models which go back to Hittite tradition. It was regularly used, at least up to the sixth century, in sculpture as well as painting. The second Shepherd of the catacombs has an equally clear ancestry, and his forerunners are the representations in sculpture, fresco, coins, and vase-paintings, of Orpheus surrounded by animals, both tame and wild, who lift their heads to hear his music.[12]

The traditional pagan form for this subject showed Orpheus at the centre of the design, seated on a rock or a hillock, as in the Hades-scene described by Pausanias. He does not lean on a tree, however, or touch any branches: both his hands are occupied with his lyre, which he is actually playing, while the animals perch or rest close around him, often with head turned towards the sound. Most surviving examples of this type, in whatever medium, date from the first century AD or later, and so are not much earlier than the catacomb paintings; however, the famous wall-painting at Pompeii cannot be later than 79 AD, and a bronze mirror illustrated in Eisler's *Orpheus* appears to date from the fourth century BC or earlier.[13] Kern also spoke of a Boeotian vase in his possession which he believed to date from the seventh century,[14] much earlier even than the scenes of Orpheus' death which are a more popular subject than the animal audience in the early period. The existence of this Orpheus-type, indeed its general familiarity at the time, explains the presence of the lyre in the hands of the seated Good Shepherd in the catacomb paintings as well as the pipe often carried by the standing one. (The traditional figure of the piping shepherd in pastoral poetry would also make this image seem a natural one.) The Good Shepherd of the New Testament is never described as making music, but the musician of the catacombs clearly maintains the Orpheus-role and also that of the Saviour who feeds his flock like a shepherd. Along with compositions that reproduce the pagan icon in every detail (for example, the *arcosolium* painting from the catacomb of Domitilla in Rome, set in biblical context by the figures of Micah and Moses, above left and right), there are scenes where the same musician-figure is playing to an audience made up only of sheep (in the catacombs of St Callistus and of Peter and Marcellinus).[15] Finally, the same figure is seen seated among the sheep, but with no musical instrument: in the fifth-century mosaic in Galla Placidia's mausoleum at Ravenna, for example, the Good Shepherd holds a tall cross in his left hand, while his right is outstretched across his body, in the lyre-playing position; but this hand extends to caress the uplifted head of a sheep.

Elsewhere in the Domitilla catacomb a painted ceiling makes Orpheus and the animals the central octagonal image in a *tondo* design, surrounded by pastoral scenes which alternate with biblical ones. These represent Daniel in the lions' den, the raising of Lazarus, David poising his sling, and Moses striking the rock from which water was to spring for the thirsting Israelites. These are not (as some of the Orphean animal-scenes appear to be) intended to evoke biblical reminiscence in a general way, by recalling paradisal tranquillity or the prophecies of Isaiah in which the lion was to lie down with the lamb. The biblical scenes chosen here are all well understood enactments of deliverance through divine power. In taming the animals shown in the centre panel (eight of them, ranging from leopard to rat, and numerous birds), Orpheus must be exercising a liberating or restoring power analogous to that which freed Daniel, Lazarus, and the people of Israel. He does not simply *gain mastery* over the animals, as if he were a snake-charmer: the lions and wolves and rats in these Orphean scenes *undergo a change*, as did the Argonauts and the fallen angels of Milton; their ferocity becomes noble strength, their rapacity a healthy vigour, and all their animal passions, which for Platonists and Stoics alike would represent diseases of the soul, are transmuted to their salutary counterparts by the healing music.

The bringer of such spiritual liberation and health must, in the early Christian age, have appeared to possess either divine grace or magical powers. The perplexity of a devout Christian is seen in the writings of Clement of Alexandria, on other Greek myths and cultic heroes as well as the Orpheus story. In his *Stromata* (*Miscellanies*) of about 200 AD Clement speaks of 'Orpheus the theologian' as one who (like Plato) 'prepared the way' for the Gospel. Such Greek teachers were at this time declared by Clement to be prophets in direct line of descent from Moses. The status of Orpheus is not the equivalence with Christ which we find many centuries later in the *Morte Christi celebrata*, but that of 'prefiguration', as a divinely sent fore-runner who was to show the nature of the Christ to come. This position was not easily maintained, as Clement's (apparently) later *Protrepticon* (*Exhortation to the Greeks*) makes clear. This work was a reply to the attack on Christianity by the Platonist Celsus, also of Alexandria, in which he declared Orpheus more worthy of worship than Jesus Christ. The vehemence of

Clement's reply is itself a witness to the continuing potency of the Orphean *figura*:

> A Thracian, cunning master of his art (he also is the subject of a Hellenic legend) tamed the wild beasts by the mere might of song, and transplanted trees – oaks – by music...
>
> How, let me ask, have you believed vain fables, and supposed animals to be charmed by music, while Truth's shining face alone is looked on with incredulous eyes?...To me that Thracian Orpheus seems to have been a deceiver ...enticing men to idols...But not such is the song of Christ, which has come to loose the bitter bondage of tyrannising demons. It alone has tamed men, the most intractable of animals; the frivolous among them answer to the fowls of the air, deceivers to reptiles, the irascible to lions, the voluptuous to swine, the rapacious to wolves. The silly are stocks and stones... Behold the might of the new song! It has made men out of stones, men out of beasts. Those that were as dead, not being partakers of the new life, have come to the true life simply by becoming listeners to this song.

It seems that Orpheus as 'cunning master of his art' might soon be regarded as a possible rival to Christ in attempting to gain power over men's souls. This is vividly shown in the unique 'crucifix amulet' which was formerly in the Berlin Museum. This seal-cylinder, made of haematite, showed a crucified figure, identified by the inscription, ΟΡΦΕΟΣ ΒΑΚΚΙΚΟΣ, Orpheus Bacchicus; above the cross was a crescent moon and an arch of seven stars. The seal (which was destroyed, or lost, during the Second World War) was generally thought to date from the third or fourth century AD.

In modern times the crucifix is likely to be seen as an image of religious orthodoxy, but this was far from true in the early Christian centuries; if used by Christians at all, it must have been among small groups who possibly inclined to syncretist doctrines associating Christianity with pagan mystery-cults. (There are no images of crucifixion in the catacombs.) It may be that the maker of the crucifix amulet hoped to possess a talisman of multiplied potency by conflating Orpheus, Jesus, and Dionysus as saviours.[16] In addition, he invoked moon and stars in order to contribute some astrological power which we cannot now define. The seven stars are similarly shown above the head of a *kriophoros* on a terracotta lamp of the third or fourth century. Seven stars are also seen in the hand of the figure 'like unto the Son of Man' in the Revelation of St John (1:16), and in Gnostic literature seven stars represent the seven planetary archons who rule the regions of the universe and, in astrology, the different functions of the human soul. The figure of Orpheus could easily be drawn into (what seems to us to be) the

The crucifix amulet, formerly in the Staatliche Museen, Berlin

indiscriminate syncretism of this period. The Berlin seal evidently belongs
to the world of magic as well as to some religious movement.

The association with magic is strongly suggested also in a tradition of
Orphean imagery which at first sight seems thoroughly mundane: the pavement mosaics of the Imperial period in Roman Britain, Gaul, and Africa. By
far the largest number of Orpheus floors is found in Britain, particularly in
the South West of England. In the fourth century, a workshop at Corinium
(Cirencester) produced a distinctive design for Orpheus pavements, with
animals surrounding the musician as centre of the composition. This is not a
variant of the traditional scene already described, as in the catacomb frescoes
or on coins. The figure of Orpheus in these mosaics is usually standing alone
in a central circle; sometimes he is accompanied by a small dog. The other
animals and birds appear on a circular band, or two concentric bands, where
they are not resting but slowly walking in a processional manner. There are
rare examples of leopards and other animals leaping along, but usually the
movement appears solemnly quiet.

Floor design in mosaic undoubtedly lends itself to formal patterning, but
it is not the availability of materials that has dictated such drastic change from
the traditional iconography of Orpheus with animals. Asymmetrical designs

for non-Orphean pavements in Britain include chariot-races, jumping dogs, dolphins, and various scenes from mythology. The artist(s) who originated the Corinium type of Orpheus pavement did not aim at evoking the kind of 'paradisal' image seen at Pompeii and in the catacombs. Here, the animals respond to Orpheus not merely by listening, but by ceremonial movements which trace a circular pattern. Although the central figure of Orpheus does not walk, his cloak is lifted by a wind and he seems to share the onward movement of the animal circle. His flashing eyes and floating hair might be those of the poet-singer in 'Kubla Khan': 'weave a circle round him thrice...'

Key-pattern or guilloche circles, or the interlocking squares used at Woodchester and elsewhere, certainly do not in themselves bear any magical significance, but they are fitting frameworks for elements of design that do. The iconography of the floor at Littlecote, Wiltshire, includes stylised suns and opening blossoms, and heraldic animals who appear to be supporting a chalice (as well as the animals encircling Orpheus). This floor, for an unheated hall leading to a further room with three apses, seems to have been

The centre of the mosaic pavement at Woodchester, near Gloucester.

laid for a religious meeting place or initiation-chamber rather than for a hall
or dining-room in a villa. A recent interpretation of this mosaic suggests that
Orpheus here acts as an intermediary between Apollo and Dionysus, and
that he was believed to effect transformations in men and animals by imparting divine energies through his sacred music and verses.[17] These
transformations might be feared, but also desired, as the building of a
meeting place such as this must indicate.

Even more remarkable than the Littlecote mosaic was the Orphean 'Great
Pavement' found at Woodchester, near Gloucester. This very large and
elaborate floor, of expert workmanship, had several concentric circles within
a square, and an interlocking square at the centre where the figure of
Orpheus might be expected to stand. Instead, an octagonal star pattern is set
inside the interlocking squares, and a number of fish swim between the centre
and the first band of animals and birds.[18] Water nymphs appear in the
spandrels of the design, and the outer band enclosing the animals takes the
form of an acanthus scroll springing from a bearded face, thought to be
Neptune. The emphasis on water-creatures supports the conjecture that a
small pool or fountain may have stood at the centre of the whole floor, where
we might have looked for Orpheus. Instead, he is seen directly above the
Neptune-head, standing, but not quite upright; his legs suggest a leap to the
ground, though he appears to be actually playing his three-stringed lyre. His
dress is boldly patterned and his Thracian cap is studded with spots of colour,
or possibly stars. To make his leap he has broken through the octagon that
encloses the fishes, and the first of the concentric circles.

It is hard to believe that the position of Orpheus, in this extraordinary
pose, was simply the result of a demand for a pool or fountain at the centre,
pushing the lyre-player outwards. Orpheus springs across the boundary
between swimming fish and the tame creatures in the first band, and seems
poised to take another step into the band of the wild animals; he would come
then to the Neptune-head (or is this a vegetation-god?),[19] where human
features are an unusual – perhaps unique – addition to an Orpheus design.
Trees and leafy twigs also appear in the two animal bands, so that all the
orders of creation are included, with Orpheus not standing apart but moving
with easy mastery between them.

When Horace wrote of Orpheus' lyre as commanding beasts, trees, and
water, he went on (as other Roman poets almost invariably did) to recall the
stillness that fell upon Hades as the music began:

> tu potes tigres comitesque silvas
> ducere et rivos celeres morari;
> cessit immanis tibi blandienti
> ianitor aulae
>
> Cerberus...

You (the lyre) have the power to lead tigers, and forests in their company, and to halt swift-flowing streams; when you beguiled him, the dreadful watcher at the gate drew back – Cerberus...

(Hor. *Od.* III, II, xii-xvii)

The perfect *cessit* represents the instant response of a single movement when Cerberus hears the sound; in the next stanza Ixion and Tityos laugh, and the Danaids' jar stands still (*risit, stetit*) as if by enchantment. (The same effect is obtained in another ode on the power of music, II. 13, by the use of present tense verbs, *demittit, recreantur*, when Cerebus lets his ears drop and the snakes in the Furies' hair relax.) The details of the underworld scene are close to those in Virgil's story of the *katabasis* (*Geo.* IV. 481-4); he too uses instantaneous perfects (*tenuit, constitit*) to describe the suspension of all movement not only for Cerberus (*stupens* in Horace) but for all the mansions of the underworld (*stupuere* in Virgil). For water, and for the dwellers in Hades, the magic immobilises, while for trees it bestows the power of movement, and for wild beasts it commands obedience.

The idea of Orpheus as magician was familiar to Euripides; in his *Cyclops* one of the satyrs suggests Orphean magic as the most effective way of overcoming Polyphemus:

but I know a spell of Orpheus, a really good one, so that the stake will step of its own accord into his brain, to set fire to the one-eyed child of Earth.

(Eur. *Cycl.* 646-8)

The context of the satyr-play makes this magic a thing of excitement and gaiety rather than alarm; again, when the Chorus in *Alcestis* long for a way to overcome Necessity (and so recover Alcestis from the dead), they think of Orpheus' magic only as something which might have brought a hope of healing and liberation:

some enchantment on Thracian
tablets, which Orpheus' voice inscribed.

(Eur. *Alc.* 966-9)

The scholiast on these lines refers to Heracleides of Pontus, a philosopher who said that in his time, the fourth century BC, tablets containing some of Orpheus' writings were reputed to exist somewhere on Mount Haemus.[20] The poems were quoted or mentioned by a great many writers in the early Christian centuries, with credulity or with antagonism. Specific reference to magical verses appears in the writings of Athanasius, in the fourth century:

he denounces 'old women who for twenty obols or a glass of wine will churn out a spell of Orpheus for you'.[21] From Euripides to Athanasius is a span of more than seven hundred years; yet the tradition of Orpheus as beneficent magician appears to have been unbroken, for that length of time and more.

Hostility to cults and practices that were simply or mainly magical, even if always beneficent, was inevitably present in philosophic circles, and followers of the monotheistic religions of the Eastern Mediterranean, Judaism and Christianity, were particularly forceful in their condemnation. The willingness of Christian believers such as Clement (in his earlier work) and Eusebius, a century later, to allow analogies between Orpheus and the Saviour is surprising when one considers their general rejection of superstitious belief in the 'Thracian wizard'. But just as Orpheus was re-clothed in the Christ-role by visual artists, and re-cast by poets as a 'prefiguration', so too he was made the mouthpiece of a re-interpreted monotheism by an anonymous writer, probably of the second century AD, and probably a Jew living in Alexandria. This was the author of the *Testament of Orpheus*, a poem of forty-one lines,[22] written in hexameters which imitate the diction and style of Homer. Orpheus is the speaker throughout, and he claims to be revealing a truth that will bring 'dear eternity' to those who attend to it. He is addressing a Greek, Musaeus, but the message is for all men, and calls on them to turn from old beliefs to new awareness of the single divine 'pattern of the universe':

> for I will utter true things. Do not deprive yourself of dear eternity,
> by proclaiming what was in your heart in the past. Looking towards
> the divine word, give attention to this, directing the intellectual
> casket of the heart...
>
> from the height he brings all things to pass and sets them in order.

>   (*Testament of Orpheus*, 4-7, 39)

This truth proclaimed by Orpheus declares the universal power of the 'One, self-begotten' who 'commands the beginning, middle and end'. His 'tracks' on the earth are visible to Orpheus, but not to his listeners, who need revelation from the inspired prophet before they can perceive the means of salvation. The tradition was (and this story had existed for three centuries or more when the *Testament* was composed) that Orpheus in his youth had travelled to Egypt, where he was taught by Moses and as a result rejected Hellenic polytheism; from then on he instructed his followers to worship one God only.

A considerable body of literature, addressed in a proselytising spirit to the Greeks of North Africa and the Levant, is known to have appeared among the Jews of Alexandria during the early centuries AD. Eusebius, commenting on the *Testament*, quotes the comment of an Alexandrian Jew, Aristobulus: 'Plainly I think that through all this *Testament* is the power of God'. The fervent monotheism and the zealous devotion expressed in the poem makes it acceptable to the pious Jew; he excises the name of Zeus, but the name of Orpheus is not excised – in fact it does not seem to have been unwelcome either to Jews or to Christians.[23]

In the opening words of the *Testament*, Orpheus addresses those who are permitted to receive his message. The unitiated are excluded, but it appears that they are *profani* of their own choice, since the universality of God's purpose is emphatically asserted throughout the poem. It is possible, says this Orpheus, to become aware of God through the intelligence, to observe his 'tracks' on the earth, and to 'approach by thought', with concentration and self-control. The reward of this spiritual discipline is nothing less than 'dear life' or, in the sense that *aeon* is used in Plato's *Timaeus* and in the Septuagint, 'eternity'. The part played by Orpheus himself in bringing this gift to mankind is not that of magician, or musician, but rather that of a religious visionary and teacher:

> listen...I will show you, when I see clearly...

Of all pagan heroes Orpheus was the most likely to act as spokesman to the Greeks for Semitic monotheist spirituality. The story of his descent into Hades to deliver the dead, and the power of his song to bring healing and peace to troubled souls, fitted him for the role of religious leader among the Gentiles. Still greater claims had been made for him by some, long before the *Testament*. His connection with Greek mystery-cults was ancient, and in some sense he was seen as an authoritative founder of such worship. One of the clearest assertions of Orpheus' part in bringing the mystery-revelation to mankind is found in the *Rhesus*, attributed to Euripides. The Muse who mourns for Rhesus claims (962-73) that Persephone will grant him release from Hades, because he was a friend of Orpheus, who 'showed' the torch-processions of the mysteries to the Athenians. The Eleusinian Mysteries remain obscure in many ways, but we know that they offered some kind of immortality to their initiates. This is explicit in the work of every writer who refers to Eleusis, from the Homeric *Hymn to Demeter* in the sixth century BC to the epitaphs written for initiates and hierophants eight hundred years later. The words of Sophocles, as recorded by Plutarch, make the promise in plain unqualified terms:

Thrice happy are those mortals who see these mystery-rites before they depart to Hades. For to them alone it is permitted to have true life on the other side.

(Plut. *de aud. poet.* 21f)

The 'true life' of which Sophocles speaks is to be gained by 'seeing', and what the initiate will 'see' is the ritual which, according to the author of *Rhesus*, was first 'shown' by Orpheus. The man whose name had always signified poet and singer was also the revealer of religious truth, holding the secret of spiritual peace and even of eternal life.

What is a poet? He is a man of religious experience whose creative gift enables him to communicate spiritual truths to men. His poetry can bring deliverance from spiritual death, bringing his hearers to a new knowledge of their divine Creator, who gave him this special power. In this way souls that have been disordered can be healed, and the human relation with God may be restored when it has been impaired.

In aesthetic terms, the poet may be seen to fulfil a Saviour-role analogous to that of Jesus Christ. This is the fruit and indeed the purpose of music and poetry, direct gifts from God to mankind.

IV

Eternal Life

R ADIANT light and exquisite music are the most constant elements in the various representations of Christian Heaven, and this tradition goes back much earlier, to Jewish scriptures and pagan literature alike. Eternal life can be imagined only in a world of rich abundance, where the air glows with supernal light and is resonant with harmonies unheard on earth.

The most famous account of the pagan Elysium is perhaps that of Virgil, as his Sibyl guides Aeneas past the terrifying region of Tartarus, to leave the Golden Bough as an offering at Persephone's gateway and enter the realm of the blessed:

> his demum exactis, perfecto munere divae,
> devenere locos laetos et amoena virecta
> Fortunatorum Nemorum sedesque beatas.
> largior hic campos aether et lumine vestit
> purpureo, solemque suum, sua sidera norunt.
> pars in gramineis exercent membra palaestris,
> contendunt ludo et fulva luctantur harena;
> pars pedibus plaudunt choreas et carmina dicunt.
> nec non Threicius longa cum veste sacerdos
> obloquitur numeris septem discrimina vocum,
> iamque eadem digitis, iam pectine pulsat eburno.
> hic genus antiquum Teucri, pulcherrima proles,
> magnanimi heroes, nati melioribus annis,
> Ilusque Assaracusque et Troiae Dardanus auctor.
> arma procul currusque virum miratur inanes.
> stant terra defixae hastae, passimque soluti
> per campos pascuntur equi. quae gratia currum
> armorumque fuit vivis, quae cura nitentes
> pascere equos, eadem sequitur tellure repostos.
> conspicit, ecce, alios dextra laevaque per herbam
> vescentes laetumque choro paeana canentes
> inter odoratum lauri nemus, unde superne

> plurimus Eridani per silvam volvitur amnis.
> hic manus ob patriam pugnando vulnera passi,
> quique sacerdotes casti, dum vita manebat,
> quique pii vates et Phoebo digna locuti,
> inventas aut qui vitam excoluere per artes,
> quique sui memores alios fecere merendo.
> omnibus his nivea cinguntur tempora vitta.

When this had been done, their duty complete towards the goddess,
They came to the region of joy and the pleasant green spaces,
Abode of the blessed, and the groves of the fortunate souls.
Here a more generous air clothed the fields with a dazzling
Light; they knew their own sun and their own stars.
Some of them exercised on a grassy playground,
Competing at games and wrestling on yellow sand.
Some beat with their feet in a chorus and sang as they danced.
There Orpheus, singer of Thrace, in a flowing robe,
Accompanied them on the seven strings of his lyre,
Striking them now with his fingers, now with ivory pick.
Here was the ancient race of Teucer, most handsome
Descendants and great-hearted heroes born in happier times,
Ilus, Assaracus, Dardanus, founder of Troy.
From a distance he marvelled to see their arms and chariots,
Empty of men; their spears stood fixed in the ground;
Their horses, released, pastured here and there through the field.
For the pleasure they took in chariots, arms, while alive,
Their interest in caring for glossy horses, remain
When their bodies are laid in the earth.
He looked at the others
To right and to left on the grass as they feasted and sang
A joyful paean in chorus, there in the fragrant
Laurel grove where the great river Eridanus rolls
Through the woods to the upper world.
Here was a band
Of men who had suffered wounds while fighting for country;
Some who were priests and chaste while their life remained,
And others loyal seers who spoke things worthy of Phoebus,
Some creative in arts which enrich man's life,
And others whose merit had made men remember them.
All of them wore a white fillet around their temples.

(Aen. VI. 637-65, tr. L.R. Lind)

Antecedents for this passage in Greek literature are well known. The closest parallel comes in a fragment of Pindar, whose 'sense of celestial glory'[1] sheds radiance over so many scenes of human life as well as the abode of the gods and the home of the blessed dead:

For them shines the strength of the sun below, while here the night lasts, and in meadows bright with roses before their city the land is shady with the incense-tree and laden with gold fruit. And some with horses and wrestling take their pleasure, some with draughts, some with lyres; and beside them all blossoming wealth flourishes, and a scent spreads continually about the lovely region, of those who mix all kinds of incense on the altars of the gods, in a far-shining fire.

(Pindar, fr. 114; quoted by Plutarch, *Cons. ad Apoll.* 35)

'Some take their pleasure...and some...and some' became a conventional pattern in lyric poetry, both Greek and Latin, describing diverse human pursuits in ordinary life.[2] Virgil has been accused of bad taste, or imaginative poverty, in adopting this form to describe the dwellers in his Elysium. The radiance and the natural freshness of his picture have always won assent from readers of the *Aeneid*, but some have felt that Virgil reached an impassable barrier when trying to devise activities suitable for eternal life. An endless athletic festival might seem as limited in interest as the repetitive harp-playing or cloud-floating of a crudely pictured Christian Heaven.

Writers and artists after Virgil were, however, powerfully influenced by this passage; they have regularly accepted the wrestling and the chariots, along with the light and the music – and the presence of Orpheus. The iconography of a fourth-century illumination in a Virgil manuscript,[3] which follows this description very faithfully, became traditional in other media: the scene shows groups of figures walking in a wooded landscape, while others, naked, exercise or dance on grass beside grazing horses, with weapons and armour lying close by. Above, to the left, Aeneas holds up the Golden Bough at the entrance to a small hut which represents Proserpina's doorway. From the upper right-hand corner, Orpheus watches them as he touches his lyre with his right hand; he wears long robes and Thracian cap, and sits on a rock in the traditional pose seen in the catacombs. Orpheus is the only figure identified in the picture by name, ORFEUS, beside his head. His position in the design makes him preside over, as well as accompany and give direction to, actions which in themselves might seem miscellaneous and lacking in purpose.

Virgil's own explanatory comment on the lines that mention horses and chariots is carefully lucid:

> quae gratia currum
> armorumque vivis, quae cura nitentis
> pascere equos, eadem sequitur tellure repostos,

whatever delight they took in chariots and arms when they were
alive, whatever attention they gave to rearing sleek horses, remains
the same, following them when they are laid in earth.

(Aen. VI. 653-5)

The pleasures pursued by the blessed are the outcome of their earthly lives.
What determines their activities in Elysium is the strength of their personal
feeling for the pursuits they choose, so that they do not move on to a uniform
future, but are identified by their love of horses, of exercise, of music, or
'skilful discoveries'. *Gratia* and *cura* are words of strong emotional attach-
ment. Although no emotional relationships are seen to exist between those
in Elysium,[4] the *impulses* of emotion have not been destroyed in the souls
that enter there. The soldiers, priests, poets, and all the nameless ones whose
goodness admits them to Virgil's Elysium, are not re-made in a new image:
the eternal life which they enjoy is a life of growth in which they severally
become *more themselves.*[5]

In Virgil this experience of individuation takes each soul towards his next
incarnation in a long cycle of deaths and re-births. Through repeated incarnations the soul is purified until (in the words of Anchises' discourse to
Aeneas in Elysium)

> longa dies perfecto temporis orbe
> concretam exemit labem, purumque reliquit
> aetherium sensum atque aurai simplicis ignem.

> When time's cycle is completed, the long day has taken away the
> ingrained pollution, and left a pure heavenly awareness, and the fire
> of the unmixed upper air.

(Aen. VI. 745-7)

Virgil's version of the doctrine of reincarnation derives from a number of
different sources, in which the tradition of Orphic literature had an important place, not always clearly definable.

When Plato introduced the subject of reincarnation into his *Phaedo*, it
was as an 'ancient story' recalled by Socrates (*Phd*. 70c) to support his belief
in a future life beyond the death that would so soon be coming to him. The
story of rebirth is associated with 'those who established the mysteries for us'
(69c), another periphrasis for 'those connected with Orpheus' who, in the
Cratylus, are said to have put forward the doctrine that the body is the prison
of the soul.[6]

While Plato was willing to allow a mild ridicule of Orpheus' journey to
Hades, in the speech assigned to Phaedrus in the *Symposium* (and much
more serious criticism, in the *Republic*, of the itinerant 'evangelists and

prophets' who sold Orphic 'initiations'), the doctrines of rebirth and of spiritual purification are not treated with irony anywhere in Plato, and their Orphic association is not doubted. The figure of Orpheus, as seen in mythological narrative, was no more appealing to Plato than those heroes or giants whose stories had to be excluded from the ideal republic because their scenes of violence and passion could only do harm to the young. Plato distrusted traditional Hellenic myth and, equally, the stories of Dionysus, of the Titans, and of a theogony apparently non-Hellenic in origin, which the Orphics seem to have adopted and developed, perhaps as early as the sixth century. He preferred to use myths of his own, myths whose unique strangeness and clarity have asserted themselves so powerfully for all readers that incidental ironies and touches of fantasy slip past any defences. So in the astounding Myth of Er, when the throng of souls awaiting rebirth are told to choose what their next incarnation will be, the moment is utterly solemn, for 'everything is at stake', and yet there is laughter in it as well as pity and amazement.[8] The first example of a soul's choice, in Plato's narrative, is that of Orpheus: Er sees him 'choosing the life of a swan; in hatred of womankind, because of his death at their hands, his soul was not willing to be born of a woman'. Other souls choosing animal incarnations from similar motives of bitterness included Agamemnon and Ajax, curious companions for the pacific Orpheus, who (as in the *Symposium*) is credited with no particular insight, or any other gift. Yet this ironic presentation of the traditional hero does not preclude a completely serious acceptance by Plato of eschatological doctrines held by the Orphics. 'Soma-sema', the body-tomb equation, was generally known to be one of these doctrines, and reincarnation was linked with this as a means of progression towards final escape from the cycle of corporeal existence. Whether Plato became familiar with such beliefs chiefly from Orphic literature or from personal contact with groups of Orphic believers, it is impossible to determine. The term 'Orphic' was loosely applied to almost any kind of group holding a belief in some kind of personal immortality, and Plato was not concerned to identify the sources of his thinking. But the line of descent, from the Orphics to Plato to Virgil, has not been questioned.

Equally clear in Virgil's account of the afterlife is a Pythagorean strain, which is most strongly heard in the discourse of Anchises on the one sustaining Spirit immanent in all forms of the temporal creation. The terms used are Stoic, and the doctrine comes to the Roman reader through familiar Stoic categories as well as familiar language. Anchises speaks of the human soul as a spark of divine fire, *aurai simplicis ignis*, trapped during earthly life in a 'blind prison' where it is stifled and polluted by the passions of fear, desire, grief, and delight. The prison metaphor we have already met in Plato. Anchises' classification of emotional impulses is Stoic, but the idea of gradual purification and liberation from passion through expiatory suffering is not. Although Virgil allows Anchises to speak of souls 'hung up to the winds', 'washed under a whirlpool', or cauterised of their sins, what remains after their purgation is an 'ethereal sense' only, an apparently non-material being unlike the unimaginably fine but still corporeal soul posited by the Stoics. It is this non-material soul which, in Virgil, can attain to a state beyond the cycle of rebirth, and beyond even the shining meadows of a visually imagined Elysium.

Such an antithesis between soul and body – also between light and darkness, stillness and motion, unity and multiplicity – was for the Pythagoreans the principle underlying the life of the universe. Systematic and above all mathematical exposition of this world-view was a development from the teaching delivered by Pythagoras himself to his followers in the sixth century BC. However, the dualist cosmology which these developments presupposed, and the belief in moral purification as the individual's road to eternal life, were certainly older than Pythagoras. Burkert has written of the 'transformation in the concept of the soul' which took place over the sixth and fifth centuries BC[9]; but the Attic dramatists associate such beliefs with various sources, with Eleusis or with the ascetic disciplines known as 'Orphic', as well as with philosophic ideas drawn from their contemporary Anaxagoras or from the earlier thinkers of Ionia.[10] The Pythagorean teaching was only one attempt – a supremely lucid and relentless one – among many endeavours in the sixth and fifth centuries to find a religious rather than purely intellectual formulation that would satisfy longings for immortality. Orpheus had always been a visitant – whether as guide, magician, or exemplar – in poetic or visual representations of the afterlife. His presence in Platonic or Pythagorean contexts was never felt to be incongruous. If Pythagoras was said to have published some of his writings under the name of Orpheus,[11] and if Pythagorean and Orphic disciples followed similar disciplines in many aspects of personal life, there is a sense of continuity and perhaps confusion, but certainly no conflict, between the two modes of religious expression and practice.

What came to Virgil through Pythagorean channels was undoubtedly in large part Orphic, as was much of what he derived from Platonic sources. The fabric of Virgil's *katabasis*-poem was woven so closely with strands drawn from many philosophical and literary sources that separation of Pythagorean from Orphic became even more difficult after the writing of the *Aeneid* than it was before. The vision of eternal life which Virgil's epic enshrines is uniquely rich, influencing all the later eschatological literature that survives from the ancient world. It commanded wide consent at once, influencing later generations not by offering imagery for esoteric writings or practice, but through the mainstream of Christian literature (above all through Dante). But this does not mean that Virgil's own sources, and his own experience, were necessarily confined to what might be called mainstream in his own time. Plato and Pythagoras, both incorporating much that was Orphic, were clearly familiar to him; but we do not know what he may also have owed directly to Orphic literature now lost, or to the practices of Orphic groups who would meet to worship, to discipline themselves, and to prepare themselves for death, in the hope of life beyond the grave.

To talk of 'Orphic groups' at all immediately raises questions; and our information about the mystery-cults or the meetings of disciples known as 'Orphic' is so haphazard that all accounts must be tentative. References to these groups in ancient literature range from Herodotus in the fifth century BC to Neoplatonist writers eight hundred years later. None of these references ever clarifies the sense of the term 'Orphic', as distinguished from other kinds of religious practice offering a hope of personal immortality. Linforth enumerates eight major deities whose rites were linked with Orpheus' name in various parts of the Greek world, and a great many cults in which no single deity was worshipped, but the rituals or at least the words prescribed for hymns and prayers were attributed to Orpheus. (The *Orphic Hymns*, thought to date from the second or third century AD, include verses addressed to 'the eighty-six deities' worshipped at a place presumed to be Pergamum.) Some mystery-cult gods had close and obvious links with Orpheus; Dionysus and Persephone are the clearest examples. Others, such as Rhea (in Phrygia) or 'the goddess called Megale, the Great One' (at Phlya in Attica),[12] have no apparent connection with the Orpheus legend.

In this multiplicity of cultic practices it may seem reasonable to conclude, with Linforth, that there were never any specifically Orphic mysteries or groups of people, and that the name 'Orpheus' was used as a convenient title for the supposed founder of the whole system of mystery-rituals, of *teletae* or initiation-rites, and of incantations. 'Orphic', for Linforth, was simply a term for any kind of personal religious faith or discipline, especially if its doctrine included belief in personal immortality: 'The things associated with the name of Orpheus...form, not a unity, but an aggregation.'[13]

Linforth's learned and persuasive study did not lead Guthrie to change his opinion that the Orphics were a very distinct group, 'a small band of religious devotees with...an unusual and original message to deliver'.[14] Guthrie was inclined to believe that there was a historical Orpheus (as some more modern writers such as Böhme have also thought), and that the exclusiveness of the Orphic sect was maintained not only by ceremonial means but by the transmission of doctrines and formulas that did derive, finally, from this historical founder. This view does not mean (as Guthrie and others who accept it have recognised) that Orphic belief and practice could remain at all times distinct from other religious and philosophical movements such as the Pythagorean or the Platonist schools.

Initiates of an exclusive sect do not provide accounts of their experiences and beliefs for the general reader. Accounts by others of what the people called *Orphici* said and did are not hard to find, but they are fragmentary and often vitiated by credulousness or malice. Some characteristics of these groups do, however, seem well attested.

Membership was for individuals, and – as far as the evidence suggests – required no qualification except a willingness to undergo initiation and accept the rule of life imposed on all disciples. This was an ascetic discipline which included vegetarian diet and perhaps some sexual abstinence. Other prohibitions seem to carry respect for animals to surprising lengths: the Orphic was forbidden to wear wool inside a temple, or to be buried in a woollen garment.[15] Traditionally recognised crimes such as murder, perjury, robbery, were forbidden, as well as many less obvious sins which brought ritual defilement. Even apart from such actions, the Orphic believed he was polluted by an original taint inherited from man's forefathers, the Titans. These sins and defilements could be expiated by a life of purity and by regular participation in the Orphic *teletae* (Theophrastus, in the fourth century BC, makes his superstitious man go along every month with his children and wife, or his children's nurse, to receive ritual purification at the hands of the *Orpheotelestai*).[16] These *teletae* are named by Aristophanes as the first gift conferred on mankind by Orpheus; the second was the teaching of non-violence.

Orpheus taught you rituals, and to keep away from slaughter.

(*Frogs*, 1032)

In this passage the speaker is Aeschylus, master of tragedy, majestically defining for the Athenian audience what a poet's work should be. In his list of poets, Orpheus stands first, followed by Musaeus, Hesiod, and Homer; all four revealed knowledge and skills that are precious to men, but the *teletae* have first place among the gifts that authentic poets have brought to men 'from the beginning'. This speech (which seems to express the view of the comic poet himself, as well as the judgement he attributes to Aeschylus) is echoed by Plato and Demosthenes, by the author of the tragedy *Rhesus* and, four centuries later, by Horace.[17] It is because Orpheus instituted the *teletae* that Virgil can introduce him into Elysium without naming him, as *Threicius longa cum veste sacerdos*, 'the Thracian *priest* in his long robe' (*Aen.* VI. 645), accompanying on his seven-stringed lyre the dancing and singing of the blessed spirits. This music is not simply one of the pleasures enjoyed in Elysium, but is itself sacred and ritualistic.

Plato's scornful reference to the *Orpheotelestae*, as travelling evangelists and spell-mongers, implies that the *teletae* consisted of two elements: ritual acts such as offerings and 'the accompanying feasts', and the use of incantations drawn from sacred writings attributed to Orpheus and Musaeus. Orphic rituals[18] included sacrifices, but not of animal victims (the offerings are not described by any author). Some kind of dramatic representation seems to be implied in the hostile references to mystery-rites by Clement of Alexandria and Arnobius, and in the more detached references by Macrobius and Diodorus; all these writers speak of Bacchic myth, and particularly the dismemberment of Dionysus, as elements in Orphic cult.[19] These writers range from the first to the fourth century AD, and all write of the mystery-cults as contemporary practice, esoteric but long established, and likely to be familiar by repute to all readers.

Ritual purification would be an expected part of the preparation required of anyone taking part in religious acts; this is not peculiar to the esoteric branches of Greek religion. The code of personal morality imposed upon the Orphic disciple was also consonant with the customary worship of the Olympians, though ceremonial requirements were generally more significant than moral ones. What was wholly untypical in the practice of the Orphics was the obligatory use of sacred texts, believed to be composed by Orpheus himself.

The collection of poems known as the *Orphic Hymns* contains more than eighty pieces, most of them less than thirty lines long; the metre is the hexameter, said to be Orpheus' own invention.[20] Some scholars have dated these poems as early as 200 AD, but they appear to originate at various periods and a considerably later date has been more generally accepted. Each of the poems is addressed to a god, or an abstract power such as Nature or Justice; praise of the divinity is followed by prayer for the special blessings associated with the power invoked. Sometimes the deity is entreated to appear in gracious form before the initiates. This invitation, addressed collectively to over seventy divinities, also forms the conclusion of the longer poem which prefaces the collection. This poem is addressed to Musaeus and instructs him to 'learn the solemn sacrificial rite, the prayer that is surely most excellent of all'. These opening words of the collection surely indicate that the poems were put together as a single book for a ceremonial or at least didactic purpose.

Musaeus acts as amanuensis to Orpheus at the beginning of the *Testament*, as in the *Orphic Argonautica* and also in the *Rhapsodic Theogony* of much earlier date. It is in this sense that Musaeus is regularly called Orpheus' 'son'. Orpheus is never said to *write* poetry, but only to sing it, and his compositions are handed on by writers who have learned them by ear. In the moment of composition, Orpheus was said to be *entheos*, 'in a state of divine possession'. This phrase comes from a fragment of unknown authorship, probably dating from the first century AD; Orpheus there composes hymns while in an ecstatic state, and Musaeus (who is never described as experiencing divine possession) 'sets them right as he writes them down'.[21] The text goes on to speak of mysteries established by Orpheus, and then to tell of Persephone's abduction and the wanderings of Demeter. It is implied that the mysteries established by Orpheus are those of Eleusis. The *Orphic Hymns* again associate Musaeus' intermediary role with the revelation of religious cult-lore. The *Orphic Argonautica*, however, is a mythological narrative where Orpheus himself is the speaker, dependent on inspiration which he prays to receive from Apollo. This inspiration is described as 'a destructive frenzy, wandering in the air', which hurls Orpheus out of the body into the broad heaven; and it is because of this experience that he can reveal to Musaeus things unknown before, as he claims he previously revealed the story of Persephone and his own descent into Hades:

> Now since a destructive passion, wandering in air, cast (me) away into the broad heaven, and left my body behind, you shall learn from my utterance all that I concealed before.

> (*Orph. Arg.* 47-9, cf. 1191-3, 40-1)

It is notable that all three narratives – Persephone, the *katabasis* of Orpheus, and the quest of the Golden Fleece – tell of perilous journeys which bring the traveller to realms outside the bounds of ordinary life. In the *Orphic Argonautica*, Orpheus claims that he was able to guide the Argonauts because he had already travelled to the regions of darkness and terror 'beyond the world's end'.

The receptive attitude of Musaeus the intermediary is paralleled, as Linforth pointed out, by the scenes on two Attic vases, on some Etruscan mirrors, and on several Hellenistic gems, showing a young man writing on tablets while he watches and apparently listens to the severed head of Orpheus which lies on the ground before him. (The head is named on one of the mirrors.) These scenes may suggest a vividly literal, indeed somewhat frightening, understanding of Euripides' reference to the 'voice of Orpheus' as the writer of a charm on Thracian tablets.[22] The voice of Orpheus speaks – whether in his lifetime or after his death – and the visible writer of the poetry, or performer of the music, is no originator, but at most a responsive servant of the creative power.

In the *Orphic Hymns*, the guidance of Orpheus is needed not for a journey but for the encounter with deities, feared even while desired. The *Hymns* appear to be intended for ritual use by groups of worshippers, who call themselves *mystae* and invite the gods to reveal themselves at the celebration. The language sometimes echoes what we know of Dionysiac and other cult-rituals. For linguistic and other reasons it seems likely that this hymn-book originated in Asia Minor, and was used at the precinct of Demeter at Pergamum.[23] It is also very likely that other hymn-books, now lost, existed before the Imperial age and in other places as well as Pergamum. The tradition of Orphean poetry was very old; quotations are found in Plato, long before the Neoplatonists began to use early cosmological poems such as the *Rhapsodic Theogony* as sources for sayings capable of Neoplatonist interpretation.[24] These theogonies are known in immense disorderly detail. Like the *Hymns*, they are written in hexameters, and (with the exception of Hesiod's *Theogony*) they are presented as the compositions of Orpheus, addressed to Musaeus, his 'dear child', who is told to receive all he hears as a revelation from Phanes, the first-born of the gods.[25] Poetry of this kind was generally known as the 'sacred words', and as its author Orpheus was called not 'poet' but 'one who speaks of the gods'. Plato speaks of the old *theologoi*, like himself true myth-makers, with a profound respect underlying his note of ironic urbanity:

> Do not therefore be surprised if in treating at length of many matters, divine powers and the origin of the whole universe, we do not find it possible to submit accounts that are worked out with precision and in every way and in every direction consistent one with another...We must be persuaded by those who have spoken in the past, who were, so they said, the sons of the gods, and may be assumed to have had clear knowledge about their own parents. We must not therefore disbelieve the children of the gods, although they spoke without convincing strict demonstrations, but must follow custom and take their word...
>
> (*Timaeus*, 29c, 40d)

Plato's emphasis on divine parentage as credential for the *theologos* may suggest a reason why Orpheus became known as a son of Apollo, in spite of the strong tradition that his father was Oeagrus, a king (or again, some said a river god) in Thrace. His divine descent on his mother's side was never in question: she was Calliope or possibly Polyhymnia, certainly a Muse. His son or disciple Musaeus could be identified as divinely born, by his self-explanatory name.

Both hymns and theogonies were sacred literature used by cult-members as a group. Another kind of verse, of which we have several examples from South Italy, Crete, and Rome, was written for individual initiates and was intended to assist them when they passed through death in the hope of finding eternal life beyond the grave. These hexameter fragments (all are in Greek, including the example from Rome) are inscribed on the famous gold plates which have been discovered at various times since 1835, in graves of persons evidently believed to be going on a journey from earth to a life beyond. Only one of these persons is named, Caecilia Secundina, in the grave at Rome, which dates from the second or third century AD. Although the same phrases recur, the other examples are much older, perhaps seven centuries older. The graves are invariably simple, containing nothing of value except the gold of the plates. These are very thin, and have been closely folded or rolled – in one example, inside a small case strung on a gold chain, as a necklace. This might have been worn when the owner was alive, as well as after death. Strikingly similar objects have been found in many other places, including one which can be seen in the Segontium Museum (Caernarvon). This, like other examples, has no specifically Orphic phrasing, but seems to carry a magical invocation, with the words 'protect me'. The plates in the graves may also have been intended to protect the wearer from evil in this life, as well as to assure safe passage after death.

In 1934 Guthrie wrote that 'a whole literature has sprung up' around these plates, and this literature is of course much larger nearly sixty years on. The interpretation of these strange verses will remain controversial. It has generally been assumed, however, that there is at least an element of the Orphic in the beliefs and attitudes they imply. The name of Orpheus is never mentioned in them, though Persephone is, and also Eukles (Pluto) and Eubouleus (Dionysus?).[26]

The wording of the plates varies: some phrases appear on two or more of them; all include words supposed to be spoken by the soul of the buried initiate, addressed to the 'guardians' whom he will meet when he arrives in Hades. Two of the plates begin with lines of instruction given to the soul; the unnamed speaker is a benevolent guide, ready to prompt the solitary *mystes* as he approaches Persephone's realm:

> but as soon as the soul has left the light of the sun,
> to the right...
> Hail, hail, as you take the right-hand road...
>
> (Plate from Thurii, now at Naples; Kern, fr. 32f)
>
> you will find to the left of the House of Hades a spring,
> and beside it a white cypress, standing by.
> To this spring you should not approach at all.
> But you will find another, from the Lake of Memory
> cold water flowing forth...
>
> (Plate from Petelia, now in British Museum; Kern, fr. 32a)

The soul is instructed to ask for a drink from the Spring of Memory and (in all the plates) is promised some form of blessedness, after suffering thirst and other hardships or penalties. Some of the verses promise apotheosis as a right earned by a suffering 'child of Earth and starry Heaven'. (Caecilia Secundina is to become divine 'by law'.) The fullest expression of this aspiration is found on three of the plates from Thurii, now in Naples:

> From the painful circle of heavy grief I have flown,
> To the desired garland I have moved on with swift feet,
> Beneath the bosom of the mistress, underworld Queen,

I have sunk.
And now as a suppliant I have come to holy Persephone,
That she may graciously send me to the seats of the Hallowed.
'Happy and blessed one, a god shall you be instead of mortal.'

(Murray's reconstruction; Kern, fr. 32c-e)

Apart from the phrase 'seats of the Hallowed', there is no suggestion that the promised future life is to be lived in any spatial dimensions. The journey is described visually – the forked road, the two springs, the cypress – but beyond that there is no hint of anything resembling Virgil's scene of the meadows clothed in light. It is an *inward* change that the blessed soul will experience; he will attain a new identity, a divinity which has always been his by right, since he is a 'child of starry Heaven', and can say to the gods, 'I am of your blessed race.' In his earthly life he has been compelled to expiate sins which excluded him from the life of the blessed: this expiation – at the end of a series of incarnations – he now claims to be complete, and he regains his true identity in the divine life beyond the known dimensions of time and space.

The mourners who placed these gold plates beside the bodies of the dead at Petelia and elsewhere clearly hoped that their souls would be assisted by them on the difficult journey to Hades. They also believed that their dead friends had a right to such help, that they were qualified to move towards divinity and to make the right choice when the waters of Memory or of Forgetfulness were placed before them, to the right and the left. This could be true only if these were the graves of initiates, who might be considered to have achieved their final reincarnation.

Rohde (418) thought that the different wording in the references to the future life on some of the plates might correspond to 'different stages of the process of redemption'. We have no real evidence for such gradations in status, or even for any formal recognition of entry to the Orphic or other esoteric discipleship. It may be that no one ever called himself an 'Orphic' at all (though it is true that the graveyard marked out for those 'who have taken part in the Bacchic rites' at Cumae suggests an acknowledged status). No statement of membership of such a cult appears on any tombstone, though the worshippers of Adonis, Cybele, and some other non-Olympian deities were identified in this way at their death. The only sign of such formal membership has been discovered in recent years at the town of Nikolayev (Borysthene, or Olbia, on the Black Sea coast), a Greek colony founded from Miletus. The bone tablets which have been found at various places scattered about the town (not in graves) look like membership tickets; the uniformity of their size makes them as convenient to carry as a modern bank card, but not convenient to wear night and day as a good luck charm, like a ring or an amulet on a chain. The tablets are inscribed with abstract nouns in antithetical pairs: Death/Life, Truth/Falsehood, Peace/War. They also feature the three letters DIO, in one example running into the word ORPHIC as if to suggest that the active opposites of Death/Life, and so on, might be reconciled by union between the two divine beings.[27]

The boldly scratched BIO – ANATO – BIO, 'Life – Death – Life', seems to proclaim the faith of these Olbian Orphics in the sequence of experiences expected by the initiates in South Italy: from this life, through death, to an eternal life different in kind from what we know on earth. Orpheus, and sometimes Dionysus, could guide men to such a life. Euripides, in *Hippolytus*, includes derisive reference to Pythagorean and to Bacchic practice conflated with the Orphic, and it is possible that all three were mingled at Olbia.[28] When Hippolytus is mocked for his 'lifeless diet' (authentically Pythagorean, however inappropriate in this drama), and for his celebration of 'Bacchic rites', these charges are joined to a veneration of 'the smoke of many writings' in which Orpheus is taken as king (*Hipp*. 952-4). The conflation of these three elements will not have sounded absurd to an Athenian audience, and although Hippolytus in the play is not preoccupied with the journey beyond death, he is a man obsessed by a longing for purity and for some kind of communion with the divine. Hippolytus' devotion to Artemis is expressed with something of the fervour which animates those of the *Orphic Hymns* addressed to Eros or Helios.

The reason why Hippolytus, with his single-minded worship of Artemis, might still be plausibly supposed to choose Orpheus as his 'king' must lie in the nature of his religious attitude rather than any particular link between Artemis and the mystery-cults. Euripides' Hippolytus, like the worshippers of Dionysus in the *Bacchae*, longs for a direct personal knowledge of the divinity, which can be accorded to him only for a moment, when he is 'at the gates of the lower world' (1447). To share in the life of gods could only be possible, for the Greek, by going through death. Socrates, in the *Apology*, speaks of 'the common belief' that those who die continue to live 'elsewhere', facing a judgment which might – if they have lived well on earth – bring them to a place happier than our world, a place we might all long to reach: 'for what would you not give to converse with Orpheus and Musaeus and Hesiod and Homer?' (*Apol*. 41a). If any group of men could be assumed to have reached this Elysian life, it was always taken to be the poets, with Orpheus foremost among them. Poets might meet the gods in earthly surroundings, as Hesiod claimed to have done, but they might also be pictured as sharing in divine feasts, thus conversing in a heavenly realm. This idea was introduced by Tacitus, five centuries later, in his *Dialogus* (Orpheus and Linus are specifically mentioned) to support the argument that poetry is a higher form than rhetoric. Orpheus could be at home in the Elysian world and could act as guide even in the final transition to the divine life to be won after a soul's last incarnation. No other hero in legend could do this; Orpheus, always given the title of hero, was the only one who never killed or even held a weapon. He was thus uniquely fitted to offer eternal life to men.

It was through participation in the *teletae*, which included Orpheus' religious formulas and sacred songs, that the soul of the believer might hope for safe passage in his journey through successive incarnations to the divine life beyond. Only in this way could anyone ensure that the experience of repeated incarnations would not be a mere extension of existence in time, but a purificatory succession, for the expiation of sins both personal and collective, and the heightening of consciousness above the level of ordinary mental life.

When the painters of the vases found in South Italy depicted Orpheus in the underworld, they showed him in the act of playing his lyre, and standing by the entrance to an elaborate portico. Inside, Pluto and Persephone are conversing, apparently unaware of Orpheus' presence. On one of the vases, Orpheus seems to be followed by an unnamed group, man, woman, and child; on another, he is playing to one attentive listener, an old man who holds a scroll in his left hand. These vases do not illustrate the Elysian scene of Orpheus and the blessed ones, as described in Virgil, and the images are still more remote from the story of Eurydice. Both good and bad characters are labelled, as are the Judges of the Dead, Aeacus, Triptolemus, and Rhadamanthus. The presence of these judges is the most obvious difference between the work of this Apulian painter, or painters, and the famous fresco by Polygnotus at Delphi. The former's stronger emphasis on moral judgment in the afterlife, together with the appearance of a fountain to the left of Pluto's gate, where the soul of the Petelian was told he would find the Spring of Lethe, perhaps suggests that the painter in South Italy, some two centuries after Polygnotus in Greece, had some familiarity with a more developed Orphic eschatology. It is hard to avoid the identification of the unnamed family group, the old man with the scroll, and other anonymous figures who appear to be guided by Orpheus on other vases (not always showing Pluto's palace), as initiates or persons seeking initiation and guidance from the musician who can teach them the saving *teletae*.

Hanging from the roof of Pluto's portico on these vases, or in one case hanging in the air and balanced under the hand of a seated boy, are a number of four-spoked wheels and other circular objects, which do not correspond to anything described in any ancient accounts of the underworld. The association with the Orphic 'wheel of birth' suggests itself; but on the gold plate from Thurii the soul is saying 'I *have flown out of* the sorrowful circle' as he approaches Persephone, whereas on the vases these circles seem to await him as he arrives. What the initiate longs to approach, at this moment, is the undefined *stephanos*, the garland to which he has 'come with swift feet'. The word could bear the meaning 'crown', as it was offered to guests at a banquet, or to victors in athletic contests. It could also mean an encircling defence, even an adornment like the 'garland of fair children' which is the pride of Euripides' Heracles (*HF* 839). No one on the vases is offering any of the circles to the new arrivals in Hades (or doing anything else with them); but since almost every item in these paintings is disconnected from every other, no importance can be attached to that. On one of the vases, a circular object at the central point under the roof of the portico is so thick that it resembles neither wheel nor garland, but perhaps a drum or a large padded cushion; again, no one in the crowded scene appears to be interested in it. If the wheel is a natural symbol for endless repetition, the circle is also a natural symbol for eternity or wholeness.

A surprising parallel to these hanging circles is seen on the remarkable marble relief generally known as *Orpheus Among the Satyrs*, which was formerly in the collection held by the Blundell family at Ince Blundell Hall, Lancashire.[29] The relief is thought to be a Roman copy of a Hellenistic original (which may have been a painting). The scene is a woodland. A seated lyre-player faces a group of naked satyrs, who all appear to be listening and waiting (though one is also holding his foot, in the position of the famous *spinario*). The foremost of them holds out his hand to the lyre-player, as if to

The marble relief known as *Orpheus among the Satyrs*, formerly at Ince Blundell Hall, Lancashire, now in the Reserve Collection of the Liverpool Museum.

receive something, or possibly making some offer. A much taller satyr, at the right, lifts up his arm in a solemn gesture.

So far this work might seem to illustrate the familiar theme of Orpheus as tamer of wild creatures: a fragment of Lucan's lost poem *Orpheus* speaks of *fauni silvicolae*, 'Fauns who dwell in the woods', among his listeners, and it was *silvestres homines*, 'people of the woodland', who according to Horace[30] were taught by him to turn from slaughter and animal food. Alternatively, the seated figure with the lyre might represent Apollo, with the satyrs (as in the *Ichneutae*) fascinated by the sound of the newly discovered instrument. However, the upper half of the relief introduces three figures of a very different character, one male and two female; these are draped forms, only partly visible as they look down on the scene from behind projections which may represent rocks, or clouds, or even the branches of trees. Between them, high above the musician and the satyrs, is a circle, which shows traces of some pattern or image too worn to be identified. (The whole relief has suffered damage, apparently by water, as well as being broken at several points.) The figures in the lower half of the relief do not seem to be aware of what is above them, but those in the upper half appear to be watching, with arms extended to unify the whole composition. One of the female figures reaches towards the circular object in the sky, but as the hand is worn away the gesture is hard to interpret.

These upper-level figures are too strongly integrated in the design to be satisfactorily described as Ashmole described them, 'local nymphs or demi-gods looking out from among the rocks'. The contrast with the haphazard space-filling on the Apulian vases is extreme. Michaelis thought that the round object was originally held in the extended hand of the central watcher, and supposed it might be a tympanum or a mirror; Ashmole gave it more significance, as an *oscillum* hanging from the branch of a tree and marking the wood as sacred. Peterson (and Kerenyi) believed it to be the moon.[31] The resemblance to the four-spoked wheels and other circles on the Apulian vases is clear, though the position of this circle, in the sky, may suggest the desired *stephanos* rather than the wheel of pain and grief. Whether it represents the moon or a *stephanos* (and these are the only alternatives that seem convincing), it clearly belongs to the same order of being as the three half-figures who watch from the upper level of the relief, apparently poised in the sky.

The whole scene has frequently been identified as an initiation-ceremony, the assumption being that the relief was originally placed in a building where Orphic *teletae* were performed. If that is so, those to be initiated must be the three satyrs (one is only faintly visible in the worn condition of the marble) who stand facing Orpheus. The three figures above would seem to corres-pond to these three, either as guardian spirits, guides who were appointed to take charge of each man (or satyr) on earth and in the journey beyond, or possibly representing the three postulants in their more exalted state after initiation. Plato speaks of guiding 'supernatural beings' as familiar in common belief,[32] and they might well be thought (by 'Orphics') to be present at the rite of initiation for their charges. They might also be seen as holding up a symbolic *stephanos* as prize for the aspirant who passed to immortality. It is hard, however, to suppose that such a garland, or crown, would not be an individual prize; why are there not three circles? More acceptable is Peterson's theory that the circle in the sky represents the moon. The outstretched hands would then be pointing to it, not holding it. Plato's derisive reference to itinerant spellmongers suggests that they claimed Orpheus and Musaeus, authors of their wares, as 'descendants of the Moon and the Muses' *(Rep.* 364e). The appearance of the moon in the sky above the seated Orpheus might serve to reinforce his authority. It might also be seen as the future home for any number of initiates, as their final abode or (as in Plutarch's account) as an intermediate stage between the final incarnation and the return of the soul to the cosmic source of light.[33]

The belief in a future life on the moon, or some other planet, is attributed to Pythagoras by Iamblichus,[34] and a bolder version of this idea was current as early as the fifth century, when Aristophanes made a comic slave ask:

> Isn't it true then, what they say about the air,
> that we *become* stars, whenever anyone dies?

> *(Peace,* 832-3)

Plato developed this popular idea in his *Timaeus,* where the Creator is said to have made souls 'equal in number to the stars, and assigned each one to a star', from which every individual would go to earth, and to which he would return after his human life followed by purification and the final recovery of his true nature in blessedness *(Tim.* 41d-e). We may have here a principal source for Virgil's insistence upon the uniqueness and diversity of the personalities who find themselves in his Elysium. In Pythagorean thinking, this recovery of the true nature could be achieved only after successive lives in many forms (and this may be the reason why the seekers after initiation are shown on the Ince Blundell relief as satyrs, not men). The final condition, for those released from further incarnation, seems to have been regarded not as a return to any all-absorbing universal Spirit, but as realisation of fuller consciousness and a more richly developed personal identity.

If the *teletae* needed to admit men to the beginnings of this fuller consciousness were believed to be the gift of Orpheus, whether in Pythagorean context or within the cult-worship of some god quite outside Orphean legend, it would be natural to find music as well as formulaic poetry as part of the ceremonial. No such music survives, but music is often mentioned as part of Eleusinian ritual, and we can assume that it was important in other mystery-celebrations. Lucian also mentions dancing as an important part of cult-worship.

> I may say that it is impossible to discover any ancient *telete* which did not include dancing; clearly because it was Orpheus, Musaeus, and the best dancers of that time who established them.
>
> *(de Saltatione, 15)*

What kind of dancing this was, no source tells us. The formal solemnity implied in most references to the *teletae* suggests that these dances did not resemble the frenzied movements of the Maenads in Bacchic ecstasy. They were perhaps more like the dances used in the spiritual disciplines of Sufism, or those described in the apocryphal *Acta Johannis* (95) where Christ sings to a circle of disciples and tells them: 'Everyone who does not dance does not know what happens...Listening to me during the dance, you look at yourselves. Everyone who dances understands what I am doing.' The link between Christ and Orpheus is as clear in this image of the singing Christ, who has taken on Orphean attributes, as it is in the Good Shepherd figure or in the harrowing of hell.[35]

Music and all its related arts, gifts of Orpheus, are thus seen as divinely imparted means of admitting men to a heavenly realm, restoring a relation with the gods that has been impaired, and even allowing them to attain the life of eternity. This view, linked in ancient times with the belief in reincarnation, was revived in the Renaissance among thinkers who could readily reconcile it with a Christian understanding of death and Judgment. Pico della Mirandola, in the fifteenth century, described the *Orphic Hymns* (which he believed were Orpheus' own compositions) as 'hieroglyphic' communications for the use of initiates. The truths to be realised through initiation, in the view of Pico and others of his time, concerned the nature of love as a supra-sensual and supra-intellectual experience. Poetry and music were thought to reveal the path to such experience and so to a spiritual wholeness which would fit the soul for immortality.

Because the men of the Renaissance had inherited the tradition of Orpheus the lover and the rescuer of Eurydice, they had to attempt a reconciliation between two very different hero-figures, which the Greeks were never called upon to make. The love-story was insignificant in the Greek world when compared with the powerful image of Orpheus the bringer of the *teletae*, the mediator, perhaps magician. Even if Virgil's version of the Eurydice-story was not original, it had no wide currency in the Greek world and could not be older than the Hellenistic age. Neither does it seem to have been compelling for Manilius, in the generation immediately following Virgil: he speaks of Orpheus as drawing a response of tears from Pluto, but going on to triumph over death, with no mention of the backward glance.[36]

In Renaissance Italy, however, any account of Orpheus had to embrace both Orphean images, and this was done by a somewhat softened version of the medieval condemnation of Orpheus' disobedience to divine commands. Orpheus looked back at his wife, said Lorenzo de' Medici, because he had failed to realise the true meaning of the supra-sensual love. His desire to *see* Eurydice was so strong that he lost faith in the divine purpose and (like the Orpheus ridiculed in Plato's *Symposium*) gave way to a craven impulse which could only debar him from the felicity of those who learned truly what love is. In spite of this fatal act of weakness, Orpheus was still perceived in the age of the Renaissance as a guiding figure in the spiritual quest which so much preoccupied the Italians of Pico's generation and the century following. The fervent belief in the value of art – of music, drama, poetry, and the newly emerging form of opera, which united them all – served to enhance the Orphean image at a time when the surge of secular, often erotic, literary and artistic exploration might easily have overwhelmed the figure of the spiritual guide who spoke in the idiom of a religion long dead.

Music and the arts that relate to it have been part of religious ritual in many cultures all over the world, and the words, sounds, and movements used in these rituals have been objects of awe, believed to be revealed by the divine will and powerful in themselves to effect spiritual transformations. What then is a poet? He is an enunciator of sacred mysteries, to be approached only through ceremonial means and by privileged persons. Only the initiated can rightly respond to a mystery; and for those who are initiated, poetry may bring about states of heightened consciousness and fuller awareness of the divine.

In the Orphic tradition, poetry aids the soul's release from temporal and spatial bonds, and even from the cycle of reincarnation. The esoteric knowledge gained through initiation reveals the true meaning of poetry and music, and allows the disciple to attain the prize of eternal life.

V

The Music of the Spheres

WHEN the soul of the Orphic initiate arrived at the entrance to the House of Hades, the gold plates told him to beware of the water springing up on his left. Only from the cold spring flowing on the right should he accept a drink to quench his intense thirst. This spring on the right is said to flow from the Lake of Memory, and the one on the left we can identify as the Spring of Lethe, 'Forgetfulness'.

The Spring of Lethe was a threat also to the souls who awaited judgment in Plato's Myth of Er. When these souls had made the choice of their next incarnation,

> they encamped by the Forgetful River, whose water no pitcher can hold.[1] And all were compelled to drink a certain measure of its water; and those who had no wisdom to them drank more than the measure. And as each man drank he forgot everything. They then went to sleep, and when midnight came there was an earthquake and thunder, and like shooting stars they were all swept suddenly up and away to be born. Er himself was forbidden to drink...
>
> (*Rep*. X. 620e, tr. Lee)

Er was forbidden to drink because he was chosen to return in the same body as before from the world of the dead, so that 'the tale would be preserved from perishing'. Otherwise his experience would turn to nothingness, like the memories of 'those who had no wisdom', swept away into rebirth. To attain release from the cycle of reincarnation, the soul needed the water of Memory, which would prevent dissolution of its past life and so of its identity.

This insistence on the importance of memory is Virgilian[2] as well as Pythagorean. Although Virgil does not introduce the Spring of Memory into his account of the after-world, he does show the throng of souls waiting by the waters of Lethe, which they will drink before returning to earth in a new incarnation. This drink, Virgil suggests, will poison volition within the soul,

83

> scilicet immemores supera ut convexa revisant
> rursus, et incipiant in corpora velle reverti.

(*Aen*. VI. 750-1)

Conington's 1870 translation, often seeming so inappropriate now in rhythm and diction, here catches the sense of wilful disaster in the fate of the unthinking:

> That earthward they may pass once more
> Remembering not the things before,
> And with a blind propension yearn
> To fleshly bodies to return.

Forgetfulness will not only remove old purposes from the mind and obliterate perception of the spiritual realm which is its true home, but will introduce a positive desire for return to earthly bondage and corruption.

The tradition of the two springs persisted in Greece, and not only in accounts of *katabasis*; Pausanias, in the second century AD, said that anyone who consulted the oracle at Lebadeia in Boeotia was required to drink 'the water of Lethe' before descending into the cavity where he would receive answers. This was to make him forget 'all he had hitherto thought of'. He then had to drink 'the water of Mnemosyne', to ensure remembrance of all he would see and hear from the oracle. When he came up again from this mimic *katabasis*, he was questioned on what he remembered.[3]

The discipline of memory-exercises was said to be part of Pythagoras' own teaching, a tradition perhaps reflected in his reported patronymic Mnesarchides,[4] 'son of one who remembers the beginning'. The Pythagorean disciple was required to recollect at the end of each day every detail of what he had seen and done. The recollection-exercise was gradually extended to include recall of experiences over periods longer than a day, progressively training the memory so that eventually the disciple would be able to review the whole of his life at will.[5] No extant text explains exactly why these exercises were thought so valuable, but clearly the training was intended to equip the disciple for the moment after death when, in Plato's words, 'everything is at stake'. By developing powers of memory and clear judgment, he would then be able to reject the water of Lethe, and so return more rapidly and securely to the heavenly life that was his before birth.

That the soul had experience of a pre-natal life, recoverable through mental discipline, was a central Pythagorean doctrine, most readily accessible to us through words attributed to Socrates by Plato. The fullest expositions are in the two Dialogues *Meno* and *Phaedo* (the latter given more personal immediacy by its setting, in prison on the day of Socrates' death). Socrates introduces the belief in personal immortality as something asserted by 'men and women who understand the truths of religion...priests and priestesses who make it their business to account for the functions they perform', and also by 'divinely inspired' poets such as Pindar. The 'men and women who understand the truths of religion' sound like the *Orpheotelestae*, but Plato is not specific here. It is notable that he names religious and poetic authorities for the doctrine, but not any earlier philosophers such as Pythagoras or Empedocles. What follows this passage (*Meno* 81, tr. Guthrie) presents the subject of recollection in a form that goes beyond what is related of the Pythagoreans; this is the specifically Platonic *anamnesis* that could recover pre-natal experience:

> So the soul, since it is immortal and has been born many times, and has seen all things both here and in the other world, has learned everything that is. So we need not be surprised if it can recall the knowledge of virtue or anything else which it once possessed. All nature is akin...seeking and learning are in fact nothing but recollection.

There are two kinds of knowledge which Plato presents, here and in other Dialogues, as examples of what is recoverable by *anamnesis*. These do not concern material details of previous lives, though any daily memory-exercises might have to include such ordinary matters. The knowledge rescued from oblivion consists either of abstract qualities – beauty, justice, courage – or mathematical relations – evenness, equality, triangularity. Although the first of these two kinds of knowledge is more often seen as characteristically Platonic, being consonant with the whole system of Ideas, or eternal Forms,[6] it is the second kind, the mathematical, which receives closer attention and exemplification in Plato's Dialogues. In order to prove that 'seeking and learning are in fact nothing but recollection', Socrates goes on from the passage quoted above from the *Meno* to conduct an educational experiment with a slave-boy. The matter of the experiment is the understanding of geometrical principles, demonstrated by examining squares and their diagonals drawn on the ground before the boy's eyes. The understanding of problems put to him by Socrates dawns in the boy's mind without any imparting of information, so that it can be called 'the spontaneous recovery of knowledge that is recollection' (*Meno*, 82-5).

The emphasis on mathematical knowledge as an innate and recoverable possession, brought by each human soul from pre-natal experience, clearly relates to a tradition that was Pythagorean, though not necessarily as old as Pythagoras' own generation.[7] What might be retained from the world beyond this life was believed to be a part of eternal truth, a truth not so much moral, finally, as intellectual; pre-existent truth was expressible in mathematical relations, which revealed its essential being as no visual image or form of language could ever do.

Pythagoras, or his followers, declared that 'all things are numbers', and asserted that numbers had special identities: the even and odd, the 'square' and 'oblong', and the abundant tetraktys, composed of one, two, three, and four. The intricate developments of this thinking were not simply fanciful, and did not tend to magic. The claim was, as Heisenberg has asserted in this century,[8] that 'mathematical structures are actually deeper than the existence of mind or matter'. Because this is so, plant growth and crystal formations, for example, will exhibit unchanging patterns which can only be expressed in numerical terms, such as the Fibonacci Series of numbers. 'Numbers are the language of nature', in Bronowski's words,[9] the language of geometry, of astronomy, and of physical sciences which seek out the relations underlying changing light or changing sounds.

For the Pythagoreans, sound in the form of music was above all else a mode of revelation through which the human mind might perceive eternally potent truths.This affirmation rested on Pythagoras' discovery of the numerical relationships between sounds which are harmonious and pleasing to the human (or at least to the Western) ear. The vibrations of a string plucked at precise points on its length were heard as corresponding to the intervals of the musical scale, with exact and satisfying regularity. Pythagoras (it was said) had also observed that a blacksmith's hammer produced different notes on an anvil, proportionate to the weight of the tool that was used. The intricacy of the interrelationships thus revealed within the world of humanly produced and plotted sound – of music – was so exhilarating that it seemed to open doors which had artificially separated physical science from psychology and from metaphysics. If such proportions existed unchangeably in the production of sounds, they must be present in the universe as a whole. They must be discoverable in the order of the planets, and also within the soul of man.

From this urgent impulse to find inner coherence in the whole range of orders in creation – the physical, the astronomical, the psychological, and the unmodifiable order of mathematics – there developed a system of thought which is hard for us to recover in its ancient form, but clearly traceable in the wide-ranging 'correspondences' of the Middle Ages and in much speculative as well as mainstream critical writing of the Renaissance. The Pythagorean number theory connected arithmetical and geometric entities (for example, a point in geometry was another form of the number one) and it thus became possible for philosophers to relate the study of the material universe, including living beings, to the study of mathematics. The account in Aristotle's *Metaphysics* gives us the most intelligible surviving version of Pythagorean doctrine:

Since all things seemed in their whole nature to be modelled on numbers, and numbers seemed to be the first things in the whole of nature, they supposed the elements of numbers to be the elements of all things, and the whole heavens to be a musical scale and a number. They collected and fitted into their scheme all the properties of numbers and scales they could show to agree with the attributes, the parts, and the whole arrangement of the heavens.

(Metaphysics, 985b 27)

The whole heavens were believed 'to be a musical scale and number', since there were thought to be seven planets, each carried round the earth on a crystal sphere; each produced in its orbit one note of the musical scale, the pitch becoming higher in proportion to the distance from earth. Plato's awe-inspiring vision of the Spindle of Necessity, in the Myth of Er, elaborates this scheme and adds a siren to each orbit, carried along and uttering a note of steady pitch, all of them making up the scale. Aristotle, not dealing in myths or visions, remarks that moving bodies on the earth produce sounds, and so, 'when the sun and moon and stars, so many in number, and huge in size, are moving at very great speed, it is incredible that they should not produce extremely loud noise'. The Pythagoreans, he adds, believe that 'the speeds of the stars, judged by their distances, are in the ratios of musical harmony, and so they assert that the sound of the stars is concordant' (*De Caelo*, II. 9).

This was the *musica mundana*, the Music of the Spheres, a theory of momentous import for two thousand years or more. For the men of the Renaissance, it pointed the way to a new evaluation of music itself, related to ideas that were metaphysical rather than mathematical. While medieval thinkers had believed that proportion and numerical relationships proceeded from God, and so held the secret of beauty in music as in the visual arts and natural forms, Ficino in the fifteenth century insisted on correspondences between musical and psychological experience, as well as between music and the movement of the planets. While Boethius had applied standards of 'proportion' to music, so that its merits could be judged by purely mathematical criteria (and indeed judged more perfectly, he maintained, by students of musical theory who did not depend on their ears for perception), Ficino believed that music had to be performed and heard in order to reveal its true being. Music, for the Renaissance artists and thinkers, brought a revelation of cosmic order, authentic because of the mathematical truths underlying its rhythms and harmonies, and authoritative for mankind because the human soul might find its own true nature mirrored there. Through music, the soul might be refreshed by contact with the *spiritus mundi*, the essential being of the universe. Not refreshed only; Petrarch, Valla, and other fifteenth-century humanists write fervently of the many functions of music when it addresses the soul: to inspire, guide, instruct, purge, entertain. Music is a language natural to the human heart and mind, these humanists say, and this is because music is not only a mathematical vehicle for truth – it expresses the whole range of human passions and human knowledge, just as it expresses the cosmic order and the transcendent being of numbers.

The early Church Fathers liked to draw the analogy between music and the divinely created order of nature, without troubling very much about the numerical correspondences that had seemed so exciting and significant to Pythagoras' disciples. They also set very clear hierarchic boundaries. Athanasius, in the fourth century, exalts the performer by showing him as comparable, but not akin, to God:

> Just as a musician, tuning his lyre and skilfully combining the bass and the upper notes, the middle and the others, so the wisdom of God, holding the universe like a lyre, draws together the things in the air with those on earth, and those in heaven with those in the air, and combines the whole with the parts, linking them by his command and will, thus producing in beauty and harmony a single world and a single order within it.

The comparison was deeply congenial to Christian thought all through the Middle Ages; centuries after Athanasius, the same terms are used by Honorius of Autun:

> The universe is ordered like a cithara, in which there is a consonance of different kinds of things, like chords.

> (Honorius, *Lib. XII Quaestionum*, 2)

By 'a consonance of different kinds of things', the medieval thinker meant the composition of physical elements which produced the order of nature, in correspondence with a metaphysical order willed by God. The function of the poet or musician was analogous to the work of God in so far as his work followed the divine patterns that he was able to discern. Essentially, the medieval poet or musician was – like the visual artist – a craftsman whose skill and knowledge enabled him to copy the cosmic order of God's creation.

Such a definition had classical antecedents. The analogy between God the Creator of the cosmos and the lyre-player who could produce order in sound was used by the Platonist Theon of Smyrna, who sets the Pythagorean image of the *musica mundana* in the context of the *Hymn to Hermes*:

> When Hermes was a boy, they say he invented the lyre, then first going up into the heavens and passing the planets, he marvelled aloud that from the swing of the planets there came forth a harmony similar to that of the lyre which he himself had constructed.

> (Theon, *Expos. rer. math. ad legendum Platonem utilium*, ed. Hiller, 142)

Hermes was, however, not merely a musician; he was also a god. When the neo-Platonists and other speculative thinkers of the Renaissance (including some whose primary interest was musical theory) began to revive the tradition of the Music of the Spheres, they revived also the idea of the musician, or poet, as a creative agent of divine status or at least divine descent. While the medieval theorists had spoken of all the arts as imitations of God's creative activity – so that literature, for example, could offer 'similitudes' and 'fables' rather than truth – the humanists believed the poet to be a vehicle of revelation, directly inspired by God. Aquinas[10] was scornfully dismissive of the Muses, and of Orpheus; but only half a century later Dante was writing of poetic creativity as an experience of illumination still fitly described in pagan terms:

> O diva Pegasea, che l'ingegni
> fai gloriosi...
> illustrami di te.

> O Pegasean goddess (Muse of the Hippocrene fountain),
> you who make glorious men of genius...
> illuminate me with yourself.

(Paradiso, XVIII. 82-5)

At this point Dante is speaking of his own poetic vocation, but the sense of dependence on direct inspiration from a divine source embraces the other poets or musicians introduced into the *Divine Comedy*. Dante's treatment of Virgil throughout the *Inferno* and *Purgatorio* makes him also a responsive channel of divine truth (as far as his unbaptised condition will allow), rather than a servant of God, working in analogy with the one Creator. In Dante, the poet-musician of the classical world begins to be restored to his old rank, as divinely gifted, and himself something of a numinous figure. It is appropriate to find Orpheus, and Linus, among the great statesmen and philosophers of pre-Christian ages who are seen 'suspended' in the serene light of a 'fresh green meadow' in Limbo (*Inf.* IV. 110-44). This is the Elysian landscape of the *Aeneid* once more, and those who are seen there are living in a realm not heavenly perhaps, but one that is filled with a light of revelatory knowledge and joy.

The many philosophic circles known to have met regularly in the sixteenth century in Italian centres of culture (the Camerata at Florence and the Accademia degli Uranici in Venice are two examples) returned frequently to the figure of Orpheus and to the question of his true identity and status. Ficino and others believed that Orpheus had been the teacher of Plato (perhaps with Pythagoras as intermediate), so that he could readily take a place in the deliberations of philosophers. The early operas on the Eurydice story were composed at this time, also in North Italy; Orpheus' power to move the rulers of Hades and to reverse the doom of death, at least for his wife, could not be forgotten. The philosophers – or dilettanti – of this time were much concerned also with Orpheus' relation to Apollo, either as disciple, illuminated by the divine radiance, or – in the genealogy often preferred in the Renaissance – as son. The planetary diagrams published in this period show (as they had done in the Middle Ages) Sol at the centre of the universe, with the other spheres controlled by the reigning figure of Apollo. These seven planetary spheres corresponded to the ruling planets of astrology, but also to the notes of the musical scale.[11] As Apollo's son, or favoured disciple, Orpheus was uniquely fitted to reveal or (the more frequently used metaphor) 'unleash' the power of music, which was also the harmony of the universe itself.

> For there is a musick wherever there is a harmony, order, or proportion; and thus far we may maintain the musick of the Sphears; for those well-ordered motions, and regular paces, though they give no sound into the ear, yet to the understanding they strike a note most full of harmony.

> (Thomas Browne, *Religio Medici*, c. 1635)

The intellectual pleasure of unheard music would not seem as fulfilling to many, perhaps, as it evidently was to Browne. An Orpheus was needed – magician, or prophet, or saviour – to untwist

> all the chains that ty
> The hidden soul of harmony

> (Milton, 'L'Allegro', 143-4)

Ever since the earliest references to the Music of the Spheres, the question had been asked: why does no one hear it? Aristotle provides an explanation in natural terms (though this is presented as part of the whole theory attributed to 'some thinkers'; Aristotle does not say that he believes in the supernal music at all). The explanation he records is that

> the sound is with us right from birth and thus has no contrasting silence to show it up; for voice and silence are perceived by contrast with each other, and so all mankind is undergoing an experience like that of a coppersmith, who becomes by long habit indifferent to the din around him.

> (*de Caelo*, II. 9, tr. Guthrie)

This theory did not generally convince. What demanded explanation, as well as the planetary silence to the human ear, was the almost universal recognition of rhythm and harmony as beautiful and satisfying when they were produced by men, using instruments made to produce them. 'Recognition' was felt to be the fittest way of describing this experience. Macrobius, writing in about 400 AD, reverts to a Platonic *anamnesis* for the explanation of this:

> Every soul in this world is allured by musical sounds...for the soul carries with it into the body a memory of the music which it knew in the sky, and is so captivated by its charm that there is no breast so cruel or savage as not to be gripped by the spell of such an appeal.

Macrobius here is writing a commentary on Cicero's *Dream of Scipio*, the visionary conclusion to a political treatise. He adds a notable comment of his own:

> This, I believe, was the origin of the story of Orpheus.
>
> *(Comm. in Somn. Scipionis*, II.i.vii)

So almost a thousand years after Pythagoras, the figure of the divinely inspired musician demands his place in a somewhat prosaic writer's consideration of the traditional theme of the cosmic music. Orpheus is needed here because he alone has the gift to make music which can admit its hearers to knowledge of eternal truths, manifest in the cosmic order.

Charles Kingsley's novel *Hypatia*, a tour-de-force somewhat uncongenial to modern readers, presents the Alexandrian philosopher Hypatia in the fifth century AD as lecturing to a largely hostile audience on the timeless truths exemplified in human experience on earth. The most famous and the most moving passages in the *Iliad* are expounded as allegory, or symbolism, setting forth the great doctrine of *anamnesis*. Hypatia speaks, quoting her mentor (and Porphyry's) Abamnon Magister:

> For well said Abamnon the teacher, that 'the soul consisted first of harmony and rhythm, and ere it gave itself to the body, had listened to the divine harmony. Therefore it is that when, after having come into a body, it hears such melodies as most preserve the divine footsteps of harmony, it embraces such, and recollects from them the divine harmony, and is impelled to it, and finds its home in it, and shares of it as much as it can share'.
>
> (Kingsley, *Hypatia*, 1853, Ch. VIII)

Recognition of the divine harmonies of the universe is possible, through hearing inspired music. But why is it so difficult? Why do men require a divinely favoured mediator? The Christian thinkers of the Middle Ages found an obvious answer: man was cut off from the heavenly harmony by his own sinfulness. So Erigena in the ninth century argued that sin should be defined as a dissonance that originated in the misuse of free will (and would finally be re-incorporated in the universal harmony). This theory of cosmic harmony, based on the laws of number, had neo-Platonic sources (going back to Origen, but perhaps more often known in medieval times through Cicero's *Somnium Scipionis*), but was fully integrated into mainstream Christian doctrine. Milton, essentially traditional though often boldly unorthodox, again and again returned to the theme of heavenly harmony and of man's alienation from this eternal music through his own sin.

If human sin had closed men's ears to the divine music – and, to evoke another range of imagery equally powerful in the history of heaven and salvation, also closed their eyes to the divine light – it was easy to realise why any true tales of journeys to the Beyond, man's true home, must be 'preserved from perishing'. Orpheus, with his instrument of power, and his perception of the cosmic harmony, might create music and poetry that could lead to man's restoration. His compositions could be secured in the memory of their hearers and so lead souls back to heaven:

> io su cetera d'or cantando soglio
> mortal orecchio lusingar talora,
> e in questa guisa a l'armonia sonora
> de la lira del ciel piu l'alme invoglio.

These words are sung by La Musica, at the opening of Monteverdi's *Orfeo*.

> With my lute of gold, it is my custom to sing,
> beguiling mortal ears, so that under this guise
> I can impel their souls to the sonorous
> harmony of Heaven's lyre.

La Musica is offering not pleasure but redemption. Although Monteverdi's hero is the 'poor lover' stricken by cruel Fate, and daring all for love, he also appears as the powerful icon of the Healer of the Soul, indeed of the Redeemer. To Calderon in 1663, it seemed appropriate to speak of Orfeo as conductor of the Music of the Spheres. He could take this part because he had the power to purify men's souls, by commanding their deep attention to the heavenly beauty of his song. The Orpheus of the Renaissance, and of the following century, is once more the Christ-figure of the catacombs and of the early Middle Ages.

———— ◇ ————

> From harmony, from heavenly harmony
> This universal frame began.

Dryden opens his ode *A Song for St Cecilia's Day*, 1687, with a confident assertion of Pythagorean cosmic harmony as the originating – not merely the sustaining – force at the heart of the universe. Extant cosmogonies from the Greek world, whether deriving from Hesiod or from Orphic sources, do not describe the process of creation in this way. Dryden's own sources were partly classical, partly biblical. He continues with a vivid and elegantly written passage proclaiming Music's creative control of the primordial atoms, leading to a repetition of the first two reassuring lines:

> When Nature underneath a heap
> Of jarring atoms lay,
> And could not heave her head,
> The tuneful voice was heard on high,
> 'Arise, ye more than dead!'
> Then cold, and hot, and moist, and dry,
> In order to their stations leap,
> And Music's power obey.
> From harmony, from heavenly harmony,
> This universal frame began.

The combination of Democratean 'jarring atoms' with an idea of elemental separation which seems to derive from Empedocles, and a Pythagorean conviction that 'the whole heaven seemed to be a musical scale and a number',[12] would create no intellectual difficulties for Dryden or his readers, who were habitually prepared to juxtapose much more disparate parts of classical culture. The poem continues with a series of verses, each demonstrating with some virtuosity the particular power of one instrument to arouse its own emotional response. The climax comes with the figure of Orpheus, leading savage mankind:

> and trees uprooted left their place,
> sequacious of the lyre.
> But

(and Dryden needs no more transition than 'But' to move into Christian imagery)

> bright Cecilia raised the wonder higher;
> When to her organ vocal breath was given,
> An angel heard, and straight appear'd
> Mistaking Earth for Heaven.

The Pythagorean Music of the Spheres has led painlessly to the angelic choir traditional in a Christian heaven since the Revelation of St John. In the Grand Chorus which concludes Dryden's ode, the movement of the planets is again said to have begun in response to music, and the spheres themselves join in the hymn of praise to God.

This hymn of praise as the Creator sets the universe in motion echoës the singing of the morning stars and the shouts of joy raised by the angels when God determines the measurement of earth's foundations in the Book of Job (38:5-7). Like William Blake when he made his magnificent watercolour drawing to illustrate this passage in Job, Dryden can readily integrate items of classical thought and classical mythology with his biblical theme and the Christian occasion of the poem. (When Addison in his hymn *The Spacious Firmament* addressed the same theme, fifty years after Dryden, he discarded all overtly classical elements and answered Aristotle's doubts with a majestic austerity:

> What though in solemn silence all
> Move round the dark terrestrial ball...
> In Reason's ear they all rejoice,
> And utter forth a glorious voice;
> For ever singing as they shine,
> 'The Hand that made us is divine.')

Dryden's 'St Cecilia Ode' was following the manner – and in part the theme – of Milton's much more ambitious 'Nativity Ode' (1629). Milton also had recalled the singing of the Sons of Morning

> while the Creator great
> His constellations set,
> And the well balanced World on hinges hung.

This song at the dawn of creation is equalled only by the song of cherubim and seraphim heard by the shepherds on the eve of the Nativity, a music so sweet that human listeners and the air itself are rapt with pleasure, and Nature believes that she will be supplanted by this harmony uniting Heaven and Earth. Milton is not at this point evoking the idea of the Last Judgment (as Dryden did at the close of the *St Cecilia's Day* ode) but turning entirely to a pagan framework:

> Ring out, ye crystal spheres!
> Once bless our human ears,
> If ye have power to touch our senses so;

And let your silver chime
Move in melodious time,
And let the bass of heaven's deep organ blow;
And with your ninefold harmony
Make up full consort to the angelic symphony.

For, if such holy song
Enwrap our fancy long,
Time will run back and fetch the Age of Gold...

The heavenly music has been unheard by men since Adam's fall left them afflicted with 'speckled Vanity' and 'leprous Sin'. To imagine a reversal of Time in order to restore the Age of Gold is dismissed as an impossible fantasy: the Redeemer must die and the whole earth come to judgment before men can hear the music of the creation. There is no hint of any possibility of recovering perception of the heavenly sound, or of the truths which it expresses, by any kind of Platonic *anamnesis*. In his university *prolusion* on the theme of inspiration, Milton had already written of Plato 'that best interpreter of Mother Nature' and of the 'doctrine of the unheard symphony of heaven and of the melody of the spheres'; the whole theory of 'the heavenly harmony' is, Milton assures his academic audience, to be understood in an allegorical sense,[13] as we understand oracles or poetic utterances. There is to be no recovery of the heavenly music by recollection of a pre-natal life. Nevertheless, he goes on to imply that the music does exist:

But if our souls were pure, chaste, and white as snow, as was Pythagoras' of old, then indeed our ears would ring and be filled with that exquisite music of the stars in their orbits; then would all things turn back to the Age of Gold.

Men might then be innocent as birds and hear as birds can:

It is in order to tune their own notes in accord with that harmony of heaven to which they listen so intently, that the lark takes her flights up into the clouds at daybreak and the nightingale passes the lonely hours of night in song.

Again and again, Milton returned to the Music of the Spheres, with longing for:

The heavenly tune, which none can hear
Of human mould with gross unpurged ear.

These words are spoken by the Genius of the Wood, in the brief pastoral 'Arcades'. Being non-human, he can hear 'the celestial Sirens' harmony' and sing after its pattern, compelling 'the low world' to a joyous measured movement. His song exerts an Orphean power over the world of nature, and breathes sweetness into the souls of men. The Genius of the Wood appears again in the closing passage of 'Il Penseroso', bestowing 'ecstasies' through music, and both in this poem and in its companion 'L'Allegro' Orpheus himself is called from Elysium to revive the music that touched Pluto's heart. But this is all aspiration and 'high-raised phantasy'. The glorious music of the 'Sphere-born harmonious sisters, Voice and Verse' is most intimately drawn into Milton's own verse in the dazzling 'At a Solemn Musick' of 1630.

This sublimely assured address to the 'sisters', Poetry and Music, is a prayer proportioned like a sonnet: sixteen lines of invocation and petition, twelve of self-dedication and aspiring praise. The self-dedication, we note, is offered for 'all creatures', not for the poet as speaker; it is 'we on Earth' who long to hear the heavenly music, 'we' who have sinned and marred the 'perfect diapason'. While the thought is Orphean – Voice and Verse have power

Dead things with inbreathed sense able to pierce

– the hope of renewing the universal song depends on a generalised return to God, who may

ere long
To his celestial consort us unite,
To live with him, and sing in endless morn of light.

This radiance and all-embracing harmony are true marks of the joyful realm where the blessed have always been set for the fruition of eternal life. In Milton's heaven, however, no individuals are named and the experience of redemption is presented as a collective one. This is very different from the Orphic tradition, and also from what English poets looked for when they sought the heavenly music and light a hundred years after Milton's death. Milton was willing to mingle pagan and biblical narratives, even to parallel his new-born Christ with 'the mighty Pan', but he does not, in the Nativity Ode or anywhere else, attempt to express or describe the redemptive work of Christ in the soul, or its progress towards eternity. His poetry does not concern itself with describing the experiences of Orpheus' listeners and disciples as they attended to his music. Still less does Milton concern himself with whether they learned to remember all that Orpheus had revealed to them.

Milton's Music of the Spheres, although it inspired such majestic poetry, could finally draw the soul no further towards heaven than the words of

Lorenzo do in the magical scene at Belmont which ends *The Merchant of Venice*. The moonlight, and the music heard in Portia's garden, are full of sweetness; Lorenzo addresses his bride as 'sweet soul':

> Sit Jessica; look, how the floor of heaven
> Is thick inlaid with patines of bright gold:
> There's not the smallest orb which thou behold'st
> But in his motion like an angel sings;
> Still quiring to the young-eyed cherubins;
> Such harmony is in immortal souls;
> But whilst this muddy vesture of decay
> Doth grossly close it in, we cannot hear it...

Lorenzo goes on to speak (as Cornford remarked)[14] like a student of the Paduan Faculty of Astronomy and Music. The power of music, he says, is observable in the behaviour of 'unhandled colts' who are subdued by its sweetness.

> Therefore the poet
> Did feign that Orpheus drew trees, stones, and floods,
> Since nought so stockish, hard, and full of rage
> But music for the time doth change his nature.

'For the time'. There are men who have no music in their souls, and so all their affections are 'dark as Erebus'; they are like Caliban, the 'thing of darkness', who cannot be illuminated or purified even by the 'sounds and sweet airs' that fill Prospero's magic isle. However, Shakespeare affirms (here and in many other plays and poems) that poetry and music draw most men towards a fuller awareness of beauty, and of the vastness of things. The poet or musician himself is inspired by an external force that comes from a divine source. For the men of the Renaissance, this was the secret of 'the Planet-like musicke of Poetrie' (the phrase is Sir Philip Sidney's). But of how the poet draws his hearers towards this divine fount, and what his own experience means, Shakespeare tells us no more than Milton. In Shakespeare's case, the dramatic form constantly invited him to turn away from such personal expression or analysis; Milton would find similar constraints on subject matter in *Paradise Lost* (and he wrote even less on personal redemption in *Paradise Regained*). In the earlier poems, where the form offered no discouragement to the personal, Milton held back for reasons which may have been theological as much as inward.

——— ◇ ———

'Light unsufferable' was Milton's phrase, at the opening of the 'Nativity Ode', to signify the Second Person of the Trinity. The Sun himself hides at the coming of this unbearable light, and the stars gaze fixedly until God himself dismisses them at morning; in a globe of circular light, the angels harp 'in loud and solemn quire'. As the Sun rises, and the singing ends, the poet is able to point to the Virgin and Child, seen in humble but majestic setting:

> But see!...
> And all about the courtly stable
> Bright-harnessed Angels sit in order serviceable.

This concluding passage of the Ode breaks through Milton's reticence and carries a weight of enthusiasm, in the Greek sense, as few other parts of his work can be felt to do. (The invocation to Urania, in *Paradise Lost*, VII, is one of those few).[15] Through his verse Milton proclaims an order of earth and heaven, made visible to him as the 'Heavenly Muse' responded to his invocation.

The sense of illumination, of a radiant light not of this world, is traditionally, perhaps invariably, part of the poet-musician's experience when he attains awareness of the Music of the Spheres. The experience is described as one of recognition rather than discovery; nowhere more simply and earnestly than in Wordsworth's ode 'Intimations of Immortality from Recollections of Early Childhood' (1807). Throughout this poem there is music – the songs at wedding and funeral, the birdsong and the bounding of lambs 'as to the tabor's sound' – and the poet is impelled to 'raise the song' in celebration of all his experiences of awe, questioning, 'shadowy recollections'. But the central image is that of light: the sunshine and moonlight of ordinary life, and the other light, the 'visionary gleam', perceptible to the child, who recognises 'whence it flows' but has to travel further away from it every day he lives on earth. The rare moments of *anamnesis* for which Wordsworth raises his song of thanks are recognised by him as imperishable truths,

> Which, be they what they may,
> Are yet the fountain-light of all our day,
> Are yet a master-light of all our seeing.

In 1936, more than a century after Wordsworth's 'Immortality Ode', G.K. Chesterton again spoke of a light which was forgotten but could be rediscovered 'at the back of our minds...a forgotten blaze or burst of astonishment at our own existence'. Although he regarded this emotional experience as accessible to all men, it was especially the task of the poet (in the widest sense) to enlarge awareness of this 'submerged sunrise of wonder'.[16] Chesterton used the startling metaphor of digging to describe the search for this light, a metaphor whose incongruity he no doubt realised and wanted (though the fact that the search is subterranean is *not* incongruous in an Orphean context).

Wordsworth did not speak of going underground. What he believed he must do was to shun abstract thought, and attend with humility to the butterfly, the worm, the meanest flower that blows. A passage from *The Excursion* vividly exemplifies this attentiveness of the poet, together with the response it draws from all the things of nature. At this point in the poem the Solitary who is sunk in depression turns for guidance to the Sage, who perceives that theoretical discourse will not help him, and instead assures him of hope to be grasped by 'the imaginative Will':

> Your discourse this day,
> That, like the fabled Lethe, wished to flow
> In creeping sadness, through oblivious shades
> Of death and night, has caught at every turn
> The colours of the sun. Access for you
> Is yet preserved to principles of truth,
> Which the imaginative Will upholds
> In seats of wisdom, not to be approached
> By the inferior Faculty that moulds,
> With her minute and speculative pains,
> Opinion, ever changing!
> I have seen
> A curious child, who dwelt upon a tract
> Of inland ground, applying to his ear
> The convolutions of a smooth-lipped shell;
> To which, in silence hushed, his very soul
> Listened intensely; and his countenance soon
> Brightened with joy; for from within were heard
> Murmurings, whereby the monitor expressed
> Mysterious union with its native sea.
> Even such a shell the universe itself
> Is to the ear of Faith; and there are times,
> I doubt not, when to you it doth impart
> Authentic tidings of invisible things.

These 'authentic tidings', the Sage declares, may come from the air, from the sound of water, from a bird, from any 'Form of nature', and these natural beings will *teach* the attentive soul. Because the lessons mentioned include 'duties' and 'philanthropy', it is easy to smile at Wordsworth as primly sententious; but he is not setting forth 'Parables from Nature', like Mrs Gatty's. The life and the processes of nature, which the Wordsworthian

disciple learns to know, bring a wisdom and liberation from confining bounds
of earthly life. The soul can then find its true identity:

> So build we up the Being that we are.

In English poetry of the nineteenth century, Wordsworth's disciples were
few. It is not surprising that Elizabeth Sewell's study *The Orphic Voice* turned,
at this point in its chronological survey, to the literature of Germany and
France. Lyric poetry in those countries did not lose sight of the reciprocal
relation of the poet with living things as one which could illuminate the poet's
soul and make his work a channel of spiritual truth.

This understanding of poetry's being and function also extended, in
France particularly, to the nature of the visual arts. The preoccupation of
French painters in the nineteenth century with light, and with new and (in
purpose at least) profounder modes of perceptual experience, led to attempts to define 'pure painting' in terms of revelation or heightened consciousness. The figure of Orpheus emerges in French art and French writing
of many kinds towards the end of the nineteenth century, as a bringer of light,
revealing the mystery of creation.[17] This is the Orpheus of the *Rhapsodic
Theogony*, who is made to sing of the universe and its beginnings, of Proto-
gonos the first-born, who was also Phanes 'the revealer', the bringer of light.
By 1912, Orpheus had been chosen as patron for a somewhat disparate group
of painters[18] who were concerned with the exploration of 'internally coherent
structures' in their subjects. The name 'Orphism' was attached to the movement not by the painters themselves but by the poet Apollinaire, whose own
work, especially in the often cryptic collection *Alcools*, spoke in revelatory
tones; his poems were to be shafts of light in the mysterious dark of creation,
treasures won by subterranean exploration.

Apollinaire, and the Symbolists who were his forerunners, are remote
indeed in themes and style from Wordsworth, but all are united in their
experience and understanding of how poetry comes into being and what a
man must do to make it possible. The Orphic line continues not in English
poetry, or French, but in the work of Rilke, from *Neue Gedichte* onwards.
After Rilke moved to Paris in 1902, he began to write with a new concreteness
and objectivity, insisting on attentiveness and craftsmanship in the spirit
which he says he learnt from the sculptor Rodin. French poetry as well as
French painting and sculpture clearly influenced his move towards detachment and economy of style during the years in Paris (and he was writing in
French as well as in German at this time). The aim which he struggled to
define and to realise becomes more and more clear in Rilke's letters, over
the years, until his death in 1926. He writes in 1915 of his sense of poetic
vocation, experienced with sudden intensity on a visit to Spain:

for there the outward things themselves – tower, mountain, bridge – instantly possessed the unparalleled, unsurpassable intensity of the inner equivalents through which one would have wished to portray them. Appearance and vision everywhere emerged in the object, as though an angel who encompassed all space were blind and gazing into himself.

(Letter to Ellen Delp, October 1915)

Rilke's Angels, presences who come directly from God (he never doubts this), fill him with terror:

> Jeder Engel ist schrecklich.

> Every Angel is terrible.

(Opening words of *Duino Elegy* II; repeated from *Elegy* I)

They command him to attend to 'the object', and their command is as essential to his poetry as his own diligence and honesty. The Angels come 'to vouch for the recognition of a higher degree of reality in the invisible' (*Briefe aus Muzot*, 337).

The poets of earlier ages had also depended on intermediary powers who could guide, remind, sharpen, perhaps rebuke. Their traditional form was familiar to Wordsworth, and Goethe, though they had grown grey and dim compared with the bright glimpses caught by Pindar. They were the Muses, Daughters of Memory.

The poet is one who knows eternal truths, of which he is aware through recollection of pre-natal experiences which most men have wholly forgotten. Recovery of these experiences is possible, to greater or lesser extent, for those who hear and attend to the poetry or music which has come into being through such recollection.

The truths apprehended by the poet concern the creation of the world and all living beings, and the mathematical and musical relationships on which the creation rests. Poetic forms, like spatial ones, can express underlying harmonies not perceptible to ordinary consciousness, and so quicken awareness of the divine life which animates the universe.

VI

The Daughters of Memory

IN the early books of *The Prelude* Wordsworth records particular experiences of his youth which drew his mind on to an apprehension of 'the invisible world' as his own soul's native element. These experiences are described with a fidelity to nuances of perception and emotion that is assiduous, some would say even laborious; and they are experiences of natural surroundings, as the boy knew them in his actual life. To discover the mill-race at Cockermouth, the 'glimmering lake' of Winander, trees and winds, and the tussocked pathways of Cumberland fells, was – as Wordsworth remembered it – to encounter living presences which communicated knowledge of timeless truths. From

> meadow, grove, and stream,
> the earth, and every common sight,

he would receive awareness of another reality beyond the 'common'.

This awareness was the only theme, at the time when Wordsworth wrote *The Prelude*, that could find expression in his verse (heroic narrative and 'philosophic song' having proved impossible for him). He repeatedly defines his source of poetic energy as a power within external nature which restores to the poet a pre-natal knowledge that has been forgotten in the forlorn life of 'the world'.[1] The 'presences of Nature' are acclaimed because they have

> Impressed upon all forms the characters
> Of danger or desire; and thus did make
> The surface of the universal earth
> With triumph and delight, with hope, and fear
> Work like a sea.

> (*Prelude*, I. 471-5, 1850 version)

102

Wordsworth again uses this image of surging water, as the element that brings forth natural forms stamped with emotional identities, in the sixth book of *The Prelude*, when the soul receives from the 'visiting' of Imagination a flash from the 'invisible world', and a

> beatitude
> That hides her, like the mighty flood of Nile
> Poured from his fount of Abyssinian clouds
> To fertilise the whole Egyptian plain.

(VI. 613-16, 1850 version)

Again, this experience may be felt as a 'mild creative breeze' promising the breaking up of winter frost (I. 41-54, 1805 version) and allowing Wordsworth to enter into 'the holy life of music and of verse'.

In attributing such revelatory power to particular places and natural forms, Wordsworth is not simply following the ancient tradition which venerated sacred springs or trees, for example, as channels of inspiration for the poet. Tides of emotion had 'worked' powerfully for earlier poets of Greece and Rome and England, who often associated their creative impulse with named places or specific natural phenomena, but they had not believed that this powerful swell was flowing to them from 'the surface of the universal earth'. Human beings, as much as natural things and creatures, had been springs of inspiration for these earlier poets, but all alike furnished such inspiration by the indwelling of powers that were non-material and non-human. These powers, on which the ancient poets felt themselves dependent, were described in mythological terms precisely because they were not 'presences of Nature' at all. It was Apollo and the Muses, not the Castalian spring or the slopes of Helicon, that revealed to the ancient poet the truths that his verse would convey to men.

Wordsworth certainly recognised the power of the non-material and the non-human (and he would at most, perhaps all, periods of his life have been ready to acknowledge the Christian God as supreme and universally active), but he had no impulse to distance the 'presences' he felt in nature by associating them with any mythological forms. Almost invariably, Wordsworth's intimations of timeless reality, of immortality, came to him directly from the things of nature, stirring him to excitement, apprehension, and above all, joy.[2] This immediate emotional response, he says, was later recollected in tranquillity[3] and then – when conscious memory prompted a revival of the original emotion – the experience could issue in true poetry.

This sequence (emotional experience – recollection – conscious direction of the revived emotion) released Wordsworth's creative powers without the need for any intermediary figure such as the traditional Muse who had been invoked to inspire Pindar, Virgil, or Milton. Although in his short poems Wordsworth does occasionally refer to 'the Muses' in traditional terms (even as late as 1830, 'my weak Muse' appears, needing the support of a caged turtle dove), this sort of language is usually avoided as part of the false classical poetising which had vitiated old heroic themes for him. The sonnet 'Though the bold wings of Poesy...' (published in 1842, and written possibly much earlier) imagines Poesy as leaving the clouds and mountain tops, 'well pleased to skim the plain', pausing to watch

> The least small bird that round her hops,
> Or creeping worm, with sensitive respect.

Bird and worm are seen here not merely as proper subjects for poetry, but as prompting 'deep thoughts' and the exercise of 'divine' creative function. No Muse is needed to guide the poet here.

It is true that the living creatures which hold attention and release emotion in Wordsworth's poems include human beings as well as mountains, flowers, or 'creeping worms': children, wayfarers, friends of both sexes, and some fictional characters such as Emily in 'The White Doe of Rylstone'. These human beings do not carry any weight that can be called archetypal or mythological, with one exception: the Lucy of the five short poems, all dated 1799, which introduce a note that is tragic in a human sense and also assert a relation with the timeless.

Lucy is presented in these poems as a human girl who is chosen by Nature to grow in 'silent sympathy' with natural forces. She will share the leaping of the fawn, the dance of the rivulet, even the rage of the storm. Trees will bend for her, and she will feel, with Nature,

> an overseeing power
> To kindle or restrain,

having an inward knowledge and finding 'both law and impulse' in Nature herself. When Lucy died, says Wordsworth, she left a memory only; she passed into the natural world, not simply dead but

> Rolled round in earth's diurnal course
> With rocks, and stones, and trees.

The two Lucy poems just quoted are included in the group called 'Poems of Imagination'. Read in their light, the three which are 'founded on the Affections' take on a different resonance. The first of these three recalls a sudden fear of Lucy's death which 'slides' into her Lover's head as the moon suddenly drops behind her cottage roof. In the second, Lucy is compared with 'a star, when only one is shining in the sky'. Both poems link her life with singular moments in the working of the planetary system. Again, while Lucy's humble outward life is that of a country girl spinning 'beside an English fire', she lives in a hidden place,

> among the untrodden ways
> Beside the springs of Dove,

like one of those Naiads whom Wordsworth rejected as poetic types of a natural source of inspiration,[4] or like Hesiod's Muses on Mount Helicon 'dancing on soft feet by the dark-blue water of the spring'. Lucy's death, closing her senses so that she becomes part of the unconscious natural world, also closes the doors of awareness for Wordsworth himself so that he loses the direct apprehension of universal joy and is no longer able to make

> A present joy the matter of a song.

> *(Prelude,* I. 47, 1850)

Whether Lucy was an actual person or not[5] has no importance for the interpretation of Wordsworth's expression of this personal loss. The poems on her death speak of the same kind of experience as the deprivation expressed later in 'Intimations of Immortality', when it seemed to him that a glory had passed from the earth. What remained to him, as 'fountain-light of all our day', was 'a shadowy recollection' and the joining of himself *in thought* to the spontaneous delight of birds, lambs, infants, and the spring landscape in which they lived. By the time he wrote the 'Intimations Ode' (1803-6), Wordsworth no longer looked for inspiration in 'present joy', but rather in

> Meditations passionate from deep
> Recesses in man's heart, immortal verse
> Thoughtfully fitted to the Orphean lyre.

> *(Prelude,* I. 231-3)

It was this source of inspiration, fitful and austere as it was, that sustained him through the composition of his longer and more ambitious works written after the age of thirty.

The almost tortuous opening of *The Prelude* brings the poet's experience of inspiration home to his reader. The exclamation of the first line 'Oh there is blessing...' welcomes a gentle breeze as both natural and perhaps supernatural,

> A visitant that while it fans my cheek
> Doth seem half-conscious of the joy it brings.

> *(Prelude,* I. 2-3)

The joy is almost instantly questioned and discussed; a sense of fretful bafflement postpones the real beginning of the poem for 270 lines, until recollection of the 'bright blue river', the Derwent he knew in infancy, prompts vivid evocation of the naked five-year-old basking and plunging and basking again 'all a summer's day', in the 'seed-time' of his soul. The remembered scenes from boyhood which follow this passage realise with compelling sureness the aim Wordsworth had defined for himself, to express in the fullest and most faithful terms the quality of actual – and ordinary – experiences, without poetic diction or the apparatus of classical imagery and mythological reference. Any archetypal figures entering his poetry must do so through incidents of real life, and in the most homely guise: the 'Girl who bore a pitcher on her head', struggling against the wind by the 'naked Pool' of *Prelude* XII, the drowned man trawled up by grappling irons in *Prelude* V, and Lucy herself, 'a violet by a mossy stone'. In this poetic world, the archetypal Muse as Milton – and Pope, and Horace – had invoked her, could have no place.

This almost total absence of archetypal figures gives Wordsworth's poetry a singular plainness, but his descriptive accuracy is not pursued for its own sake. The reader is never allowed to forget that the meanest flower, or the creeping worm, offers a key to the invisible world of Being. The intensity of vision is like that of William Blake:

> To see a world in a Grain of Sand
> And a Heaven in a Wild Flower

> *(Auguries of Innocence)*

Sixteen years before Wordsworth wrote the Lucy poems, Blake had already found the traditional Muses unfit to inspire poets of his generation.

> Whether on Ida's shady brow,
> Or in the chambers of the East,
> The chambers of the Sun, that now
> From ancient melody have ceased;
>
> Whether in heaven ye wander fair,
> Or the green corners of the earth,
> Or the blue regions of the air
> Where the melodious winds have birth;
>
> Whether on crystal rocks ye rove,
> Beneath the bosom of the sea,
> Wandering in many a coral grove;
> Fair Nine, forsaking Poetry;

How have you left the ancient love
That bards of old enjoyed in you!
The languid strings do scarcely move,
The sound is forced, the notes are few!

(To the Muses)

For Blake, the image of the 'fair Nine' clearly has not lost its power to charm, but ultimately he finds them wanting. The earlier verses of the poem, with their vivid luxuriance ('the chambers of the East, the chambers of the Sun', 'the green corners of the earth, the blue regions of the air'), already suggest that Blake's dissatisfaction with eighteenth-century convention in poetry may not lead in the same direction as Wordsworth's did. In his annotations to Reynolds's *Discourses to the Royal Academy* – written in or about 1808 – Blake defines further the fatal debility which he believes has overtaken the Muses: art and poetry have been corrupted in his time by the intrusion of 'Reasoning', of 'Generalising', and of 'Bacon's Philosophy', with the 'Opinions of Newton and Locke'. All these aberrations, leading artists to stifle inspiration, Blake traces to 'the Greeks' calling the Muses 'Daughters of Memory'. What is needed, for him, is not the dismissal of such archetypal bringers of poetic truth, but their regeneration. The first step was to discard the Greek and Roman models so much admired by eighteenth-century artists and writers, and with them the idea Blake attributes to Reynolds, that 'Genius may be Taught'. When each man began to attend to his own genius and to the genius inherent in 'the forms of all things...which by the Ancients was call'd an Angel and Spirit and Demon',[6] a New Age would dawn in which men would be true to their own imagination and live with a new consciousness of eternity.

At the time when he wrote *Milton* (1804-8), Blake was confident that the New Age must come, and that not only individuals but nations would attain a new life, casting off rational demonstration together with all those who

mock at Eternal Life,
Who pretend to Poetry that they may destroy Imagination
By imitation of Nature's Images drawn from Remembrance.

In this New Age, he says, 'all will be set right...and the Daughters of Memory shall become the Daughters of Inspiration' (Preface to *Milton*).

It was because the Muses were traditionally *teachers* of the poet that they were known as Daughters of Mnemosyne, Memory, 'queen of the Eleuthe-rian hills' who bore them when Zeus lay with her for nine nights 'going up into her sacred bed, far away from the other immortals'. This account of the Muses' birth comes from the earliest – and longest – description of them, in the first hundred lines of the *Theogony*, traditionally ascribed to Hesiod, a passage which M.L. West has censured for 'prolixity and repetitiousness'.[7]

Hesiod tells us in his first four lines that the Muses live on a mountain, near a spring, that they dance, and that they are associated with Zeus. This provides the setting for the narrative of Hesiod's own encounter with the Muses and the account of the kingly leader who has also been favoured by them and so shares the poet's power to influence men for good. Though repetitious, the whole passage holds the reader's attention with its insistent delight in the recurrent image of the dancing or bathing nymph-like Muses, the light and airiness of their mountain home, and the unqualified sweetness of their gift. There is a feeling of awe too, in their association with the gods, and a mysterious element when the poet speaks of them going abroad 'by night, veiled in thick mist'. The region which is their home is accessible only to immortals; but 'one day', the poet says, with no anticipatory phrases, 'they taught Hesiod glorious song'.

The following passage describes the meeting between Muses and poet, a meeting that might seem more like an alarming visitation than a lesson; the Muses speak in a minatory style:

> 'Shepherds of the wilderness, wretched things of shame, mere bellies, we know how to speak many false things as though they were true; but we know, when we choose, how to utter true things.' So said the ready-voiced daughters of great Zeus, and they plucked and gave me a rod, a shoot of sturdy laurel, a marvellous thing, and breathed into me a divine voice to celebrate things that shall be and things that were aforetime; and they told me to sing of the race of the blessed gods that are eternally, but always to sing of themselves first and last.

> (*Theog.* 26-34)

In this way, with wonder and submissiveness, Hesiod comes under the patronage of the Muses. What he has received from them is a *holy* gift; it brings to mankind both pleasure and the end of strife. Their gift bestowed on the favoured political leader also benefits all men; he will have the power to make 'straight decisions', uttered with 'unfaltering declaration' and 'gentle arguments'. These gifts come from the Muses because their universal know-ledge enables them to tell poets and statesmen of things they could not otherwise know. With this information they also bestow good judgment and a fluent command of words.

Muse and poet are depicted in this relationship of instructor and disciple in many sculptures and vase paintings;[8] she speaks or sings, while he listens and occasionally writes. Like Hesiod when the Muses handed him the staff of laurel, the poet-musician is represented as entirely passive when he receives the Muse's message. This is true also of accounts given by Greek lyric poets such as Bacchylides and Alcman, who speak of themselves as mouthpieces of the Muse; their own personalities do not seem to enter into their experience as poets; all initiatives rest with her. Even so, the tone used by Greek poets when speaking of the Muse has individual variations. Some poets address her with reverence, others in outbursts of praise and devotion. There were, of course, a number of Muses, not just one,[9] and their diversity would naturally relate to the diverse branches of the arts which each one favoured as patron. But a poet will often speak of 'his' Muse as having her own qualities, her own temperament, not included in the recognised character of Calliope or Erato or whoever his presiding Muse may be.

This personal character is especially marked among Roman poets, who sometimes seem to be using the Muse-image simply as a convenient and picturesque way of referring to 'my poetry' or 'myself as poet'. When Horace declines to write on the theme of Rome's military greatness and says 'the Muse has chosen me to write sweet songs of the lady Licymnia, to tell of her bright-sparkling eyes' (*Od.* II. 12. xiii), we could quite fairly paraphrase this as 'I enjoy writing verse on frivolous subjects more than on themes of war'. The Muse can be a poetic formula for personal inclination: Horace finds her *procax* (wilful, saucy) one day and *pervicax* (headstrong) another; Propertius can call his Muses *graciles* (slight), and Pope asserts that his is not 'venal or ungrateful'.[10] For the poets of the eighteenth century, the Muse has indeed – as Blake lamented – shrunk to a mechanical device incapable of bearing any emotional weight or taking initiative in the poet's work.

Even in Roman times, however, the reverence professed towards the Muse still has a serious tone in many passages; there are solemn invocations as well as playful rebukes in Horace, and Virgil – whose major work is naturally less personal in expression – uses in the sixth Eclogue the almost hieratic phrase *non iniussa cano*, 'I sing only as I am bidden'. The Muse decides on the poet's theme and manner of composition. She can command a man to write about anything, because she *knows* everything and can give him the knowledge he needs. The poet may ask for knowledge of a whole branch of science, as Virgil does for astronomy:

> me vero primum dulces ante omnia Musae,
> quarum sacra fero ingenti percussus amore,
> accipiant, caelique vias et sidera monstrent,
> defectus solis varios lunaeque labores...

But first and foremost, for me, let the sweet Muses, for whom I bring offerings, overwhelmed by deep love for them – let them receive me, and show me the paths of heaven, and the stars, all the eclipses of the sun, and the moon's labours...

(Geo. II. 475-8)

When Demodocus at the court of Alcinous tells the story of Troy's fall, which neither he nor any of his hearers has seen or heard of, Homer puts a significant comment in the mouth of Odysseus: 'Either the Muse taught you, the daughter of Zeus, or Apollo. For very correctly you sang of the path of the Achaeans, all that they did and suffered, and all the toils of the Achaeans, as though you had been there somehow yourself, or had heard from another.'[11] The Muse would also guide the poet to find the right words for what he described and to arrange them in rhythmical form to charm the listener's ear. All this she would do, because it was her nature to rejoice in all forms of beauty and (provided men remained properly docile and receptive) to love mankind.

The experience of contact with the Muse, a separate being who is at the same time interior and inescapable, is expressed by Hesiod as a vision, by Callimachus and Ennius as a dream.[12] These poets – and Archilochus, Ovid, Milton, and many others – found that such an experience of contact with an external will meant an inward change of a permanent kind: the poet became the Muse's 'disciple', her 'priest', even – some poets claimed – her 'son'. He was thus enrolled in the Muses' service as a full-time professional poet, and as such he had to work at poetic techniques as well as waiting for the Muses' guidance and recording what they told him. The ancient poet did not have to choose between the fervour of inspiration and a laborious apprenticeship; both were necessary parts of his life after he joined the company of the Muses' followers. In both phases – the seizing of the idea and the working out of expression – he would need continual guidance from the nymph-like Muse who knew hidden truths.

Some variation of the pattern of dependence was possible, in that other goddesses might take the role of Muse for particular artists. Athena, in particular, could function like a Muse to craftsmen and sculptors and the makers of the Wooden Horse. In Roman usage her role was extended to include the guidance of poets. So Horace in the *Ars Poetica* says 'you must not write anything *invita Minerva*, without Minerva's consent', or – as Cicero explains the phrase – 'going against Nature'.[13] The suggestion is that one must write or carve without suppressing one's inclinations, and Minerva will look after the design of the work.

Minerva's affinity with the Muses throws clearer light on the description in the *Theogony* of the statesman whom the Muses have favoured with the gift of wisdom (*Theog.* 81-92). Solon (in a poem which begins by asking the Muses to give him prosperity and fame) speaks of 'the measure of wisdom which is the heart's desire' as something a man may come to know by gift of the Muses.[14] This is the poetic tradition followed by Horace when he claims to be set apart from common men by the ivy wreath, *doctarum praemia frontium*, 'prize for my learned brow' (*Od*. I. 1. xxix). The poet is marked out from other men as having a kind of knowledge that is holy and morally enlightening as well as accomplished.

If the Muse could impart to a poet detailed information on subjects he had not previously heard of, she was not merely drawing on his individual memory to revive awareness of things he had forgotten. Homer was believed to have learned from his Muse all kinds of practical knowledge as well as historical information, so that he could be consulted for guidance in almost any quandary. As Daughters of Memory the Muses could be conceived as having access to a limitless store of knowledge, all that had ever been known, remembered, or forgotten by any consciousness, human or divine. What had been experienced and stored for future recollection only in fragmented form might, through the agency of a Muse, be revived or re-presented for the apprehension and shaping into coherence which is the work of the poet's conscious mind. The Muses would thus be seen as continually extending the domain of reason and making life more intelligible as well as more beautiful.

No poet in the ancient world made his own experience as poet the subject of close scrutiny and literal formulation in the way that Wordsworth did when writing *The Prelude*. Roman lyric and elegy developed a manner that could be perceived as self-revelatory, but even when the expression of personal feeling can be taken as authentic, these poets do not attempt to communicate their experience as makers, or as channels for the Muse. Propertius' disclaimers of epic inspiration, in the first half of Book III, use all the traditional elements of Muse-imagery, including the dream of Ennius, much as a poet of the eighteenth century might use them. He allies himself also with Orpheus, since in returning to his poetry's 'own track' (*carminis nostri in orbem*, III. 2. 1) he can sway the hearts of the women who read him, just as Orpheus controlled wild beasts and running water. But none of this tells us anything about the genesis or growth of any of his poems. The most cogent expression of a personal encounter with the Muse, in Roman poetry, is perhaps the plainly written passage of autobiography in one of Ovid's latest poems:

> at mihi iam puero caelestia sacra placebant,
> inque suum furtim Musa trahebat opus.
> saepe pater dixit, 'studium quid inutile temptas?
> Maeonides nullas ipse reliquit opes.'
> motus eram dictis, totoque Helicone relicto,
> scribere conabar verba soluta modis.

> sponte sua numeros carmen veniebat ad aptos,
> et quod temptabam dicere, versus erat.

But when I was a boy my pleasure was in holy things of heaven and the Muse was secretly drawing me into her work. Often my father said, 'Why do you pursue this useless interest? Homer himself left no wealth.' I was moved by his words, and turning my back on all Helicon I started to try writing in language free from metre. Of its own accord a poem would come, to a fitting rhythm, and what I was trying to say became a line of verse.

(Tristia, IV. 10. 19-26)

This unadorned Muse directs Ovid with complete authority, and may direct us to take some of his statements about inspiration in other poems with more seriousness than has often been accorded to his affable charm.[15]

Coming to poetry at the end of the Greco-Roman tradition of love elegy, and at a time when narrative and didactic poetry had diversified and been enhanced in highly sophisticated ways, Ovid could have used the formulas of mythological inspiration much more mechanically, and more often, than he did. Certainly, most of his references to his Muse are, like those of Propertius, within the conventions of eighteenth-century wit. But his farewell to love elegy (*Amores*, III. 15) and to his *genialis Musa*, his 'Muse of gaiety', relates his poetic apprenticeship to the *mansurum opus*, the 'work that will last', to which he aspires with fervent simplicity of language.

The same fervour animates the longer poem (*Amores*, III. 1) which presents Ovid as subject of contention between the two Muse-like figures of Elegy and Tragedy. At first the choice seems weighted in favour of Tragedy (especially since the whole poem takes the form of a dialogue, dramatic in manner even though Tragedy has to condescend to speak in elegiac metre). The self-mocking humour of Elegy's speech sways the poet to plead for 'a very little time' for more love-poetry (and, the whole passage has implied, more love affairs). Even so – in the closing words of the poem – *a tergo grandius urguet opus*, 'at my back a loftier work is pressing upon me'; there is something active here that dwarfs the writer, just as *Musa trahebat*, 'the Muse was drawing, *pulling* me', made Ovid as a boy a passive instrument whose own will did not enter into the work. The Tragedy-Elegy dialogue is set in a woodland scene, with sacred fountain, cave, sweetly-plaintive birds, and Ovid wondering why the Muse impelled him to be there:

> quod mea, quaerebam, Musa moveret opus...

> what work, I asked, was my Muse setting in motion...

There seemed to be a *numen*, a divine force, in this spot; the experience has set Ovid in the company of Ennius and Hesiod. There is a *numen* wherever poets are, he says, in a passage of calm grandeur delicately inserted in the smoothly frivolous texture of the *Ars Amatoria*: girls should be kind to poets, he says, and not expect presents from them; their poetry is a gift from heaven, 'a god is within us':

> est deus in nobis, et sunt commercia caeli...
>
> (A.A. III. 519)

Similarly, the prayer in the opening lines of the *Metamorphoses*, where Ovid asks the gods to be spinners of his continuous thread of verse, from the beginning of the universe to his own time, must be taken as more than a literary formality; Ovid's sense of dependence on divine inspiration is more immediate and personal than anything expressed by other Roman lyric or elegiac poets, and among Greek poets its kinship (in spite of all generic differences) is with Pindar rather than Callimachus.

Pindar expresses with unique power the double awareness of his Muse, as an irresistible creative force outside himself and yet an interior impulsion, simultaneously part of himself and 'other'. He may invite the Muse to be present for a particular occasion, but the hymn can be sung only when she is pleased to begin: Pindar's task is to teach the choir the song delivered to him from the divine source (*Nem.* III, and many other odes). When the Muse is working in him, the creative impetus is compared to a gale, an eagle's flight, the onrush of a chariot; the poem itself to a weapon, an athlete's jump, a great hall whose entrance is set on golden pillars. These images might suggest that poems are seen as achievements, comparable to successes in many other human activities; but Pindar also speaks of poetry as a gift which the Muses bring forth from the poet's own mind. It is like wine received in a golden bowl from a rich man's hand to honour a young bridegroom; but it is richer and sweeter than wine, a divine drink drawn from the harvest of the poet's inner experience:

> So I too, sending flowing nectar, gift of the Muses,
> To men who win prizes – sweet fruit of the heart...
>
> (Ol. VII. 7-8)

To 'pick out' a song 'from the depth of the mind' (*Nem.* IV. 8), the poet needs the help of the Graces, who bestow the charm of poetic accomplishment, as well as the initial impulse from the Muses. What is valuable in past experience can, Pindar claims, be recovered and made immortal by the guidance of Memory and her Daughters:

> I pray to the Sky's daughter in her fine dress,
> To Memory and her children,
> To give me skill in my art.
> For blind are the hearts of men,
> Of all who without the maidens of Helicon
> Search out the deep path of wisdom.

(fr. Paean 7b, 15-20, tr. Bowra)

There is an immortality to be attained by poems that are truly 'the Muses' gift, sweet fruit of the heart', and it is not merely a matter of (comparatively) lasting renown for the winners of prizes or the heroes of battles long ago. Pindar is speaking of the poems themselves as 'immortal', as creations existing timelessly like light.[16]

William Blake also believed that the 'Giant forms' of his poetry might be immortal, and Pindar's imagery of light, fire, building, climbing, descending, and of natural things growing and rejoicing, is equally characteristic of those passages in the Prophetic Books which deal with the creation of works of art in every form. Blake, however, could not find guidance from 'the maidens of Helicon' in his search for deep paths and the fruit of the heart. Fatally emaciated, the Daughters of Memory whom Pindar and even Ovid had been able to follow had to be replaced by a totally new band of maidens:

> Daughters of Beulah! Muses who inspire the Poet's song...

(Opening line of Milton)

In the same decade when Blake was beginning to find imaginative forms that could embody his personal mythology, Coleridge also published a number of poems whose strange characters had a fabulous quality which baffled and shocked many readers. The Ancient Mariner might have seemed less alarming if he were called the Old Man of the Sea, and the Abyssinian maid of 'Kubla Khan' less weird if identified as a Muse. This 'damsel with a dulcimer', appearing to the poet in a vision, sings to him of the pleasure-dome built by the Khan beside the sacred river and the deep romantic chasm in Xanadu. If he could re-live the experience of hearing her music, Coleridge says, he would be able to re-build the sunny dome and caves of ice of which she sang. The stanza expressing this longing, 'could I revive within me...', follows the description of Xanadu, which most readers find breath-taking enough, but the poet suggests that if the damsel's song were fully recalled he would create a louder, longer music, bringing dome and caves so vividly before his hearers' eyes that they would be filled with numinous awe:

> And all should cry, Beware! Beware!
> His flashing eyes, his floating hair!
> Weave a circle round him thrice,
> And close your eyes with holy dread,
> For he on honey-dew hath fed,
> And drunk the milk of Paradise.[17]

Like Pindar's Muse, the damsel is able to reveal glorious realities not seen by those

> Who without the maidens of Helicon
> Search out the deep path of wisdom.

But (again like Pindar's Muse) she brings this revelation in a personal 'vision', as an inspiration rising from within rather than appearing from without.[18] Coleridge's theory of Imagination made this shaping power an inward one, although its force was not subject to the conscious will. He knew, with increasing frustration in the years that followed 'Kubla Khan', that the poet

> may not hope from outward forms to win
> The passion and the life, whose fountains are within.
>
> ('Dejection: an Ode', 1802)

The Abyssinian maid, however, did not reappear in any further visionary experience after the disruptive arrival of 'the person on business from Porlock'.[19]

Blake's Daughters of Beulah come from 'Realms of terror and mild moony lustre' (*Milton*), 'a soft Moony Universe, feminine, lovely,/Pure, mild, and Gentle, given in mercy to those who sleep' (*Vala*, 'Night the First'). In sleep they 'create spaces' in the dreams of men, so that they may be saved from eternal Death. The 'creating of space' allows the Spectre in every man ('insane and most/Deform'd') to be loved and tended, and to find its own form of life. When the boy and girl who represent fallen humanity are wandering desolate in despair, one of the Daughters of Beulah

> took a moment of Time
> And drew it out to seven thousand years with much
>   care and affliction
> And many tears, and in every year made windows into Eden.
> She also took an atom of space and open'd its centre
> Into Infinitude and ornamented it with wondrous art.

By securing the moment of time and the atom of space (the 'minute particulars' which Blake always insisted must be the stuff of art), the Daughter of Beulah enables the desolate children to survive the threat of annihilation; as Los (Imagination) and his female counterpart Enitharmon (Inspiration) they go on to build the City of Golgonooza, the city of

>   forms sublime,
> Such as the piteous spectres may assimilate themselves into...
>
> > (*Vala*, 'Night VII')

Moments from past experience are thus rescued from oblivion by the Daughters of Beulah, and become the fabric of poetry and all other arts.

The revelatory power which Blake found in particular moments and particular beings had a more specific theological character than Wordsworth's 'sense of something far more deeply interfused'. Blake asserted (in terms which seem to derive from Swedenborg) that 'there exist in that Eternal World the Permanent Realities of Every Thing which we see reflected in this Vegetable Glass of Nature', and these 'Permanent Realities' could, he believed, be embodied in verse that was inspired – or indeed 'dictated' – by the 'Eternals'.[20] Much more was needed than faithful recollection of past experience; Blake linked this creative recovery of the forgotten with the 'Innate Ideas' he believed to exist in every man, 'not abstracted or compounded from Nature, but...from Imagination'.

In the first paragraph of *Milton*, Blake invokes his Muses, the Daughters of Beulah, and invites them to deliver their message in a manner more intimate, more terrifying indeed, than any described by the ancient poets:

> Come into my hand,
> By your mild power descending down the Nerves of my right arm
> From out the portals of my Brain, where by your Ministry
> The Eternal Great Humanity Divine planted his Paradise
> And in it caused the Spectres of the Dead to take sweet form
> In likeness of himself.

The physical immediacy of this passage forces us to take literally the import of Blake's comment on this poem, 'I dare not pretend to be any other than the Secretary; the Authors are in Eternity.' Blake had no doubt that his poetry sprang from a divine source; he had observed himself at work as closely as Wordsworth did, and saw the same sequence, emotional experience – recollection – conscious direction and expression of revived emotion, bringing a sense of illumination and larger significance. The fantastic nature of Blake's poetry, contrasting so extremely with Wordsworth's fidelity to ordinary life – and with Pindar's glad acceptance of all that his own society offered in religious and mythological terms – obscures the deep affinity between these poets as they all seek to express their own creative experience.

What then is a poet? He is one who can consciously relate to supra-rational reality through a psychic function traditionally called 'the Muse'. This allows him to perceive the nature of things in a fullness not perceptible to the senses, and to make this awareness accessible to those who hear or read his work. This can cause the poet to be seen as a moral and practical authority as well as as a creator of revelatory forms. More generally, his work induces a sense of pleasure and excitement, and sometimes awe, as his motive force is felt to be some supernatural source of wisdom.

VII

The Naming of Creatures

CONSTANT apprehension of 'minute particulars' was affirmed as the task of poetry by Wordsworth and Blake; it was practised as the task of poetry by Sappho and Pindar. This act of apprehension is itself the subject of Rilke's ninth *Duino Elegy*, written in 1922, when he was already writing the first set of the *Sonnets to Orpheus*. The poem is filled with a celebratory fervour, revelling in the diversity of earthly things and the painful but ecstatic vocation of man, who alone of living creatures can perceive them as they are: each of them, in itself, in the *Hiersein*, the being Here and Now.

> Aber weil Hiersein viel ist, und weil uns scheinbar
> alles das Hiesige braucht, dieses Schwindende, das
> seltsam uns angeht. Uns, die Schwindensten. Einmal
> jedes, nur einmal. Einmal und nichtmehr. Und wir auch
> einmal. Nie wieder. Aber dieses
> einmal gewesen zu sein, wenn auch nur einmal:
> irdisch gewesen zu sein, scheint nicht widerrufbar.

> But because being here amounts to so much, because all
> this Here and Now, so fleeting, seems to require us and strangely
> concerns us. Us the most fleeting of all. Just once,
> everything, only for once. Once and no more. And we, too,
> once. And never again. But this
> having been once, though only once,
> having been once on earth – can it ever be cancelled?

(Duino Elegies, IX. 10-16, tr. Leishman and Spender)

What the Here and Now 'seems to require' is the act of *naming*, by which the single things of earth become living entities. The wanderer returning from the mountain slope, bringing back no tangible fragments of earth but only the names he has earned (*ein erworbenes Wort*), finds that these prove to be a 'saying' beyond the struggling consciousness that exists within the things he has learned to name. Rilke speaks many times in the *Sonnets to Orpheus*, either directly or by implication, of an inward need in material things for a response that only man can give. This is because only man has 'the tongue...the praising one': *die Zunge... die preisende.*

Praise was to become the central theme of the whole series of the *Sonnets*, and this ninth Elegy powerfully asserts its meaning for Rilke. Praise bestows a quickening upon the physical things of this world, a transformation which is also the assumption of true identity. In this new being, things become part of the poet's own inward life, living in his 'hands and eyes', so that he can bring them before the 'Angelic Orders' who are also continually present to him.

> Preise dem Engel die Welt, nicht die unsägliche, ihm
> kannst du nicht grosstun mit herrlich Erfühltem; im Weltall,
> wo er fühlender fühlt, bist du ein Neuling. Drum zeig
> ihm das Einfache, das, von Geschlecht zu Geschlechtern gestaltet,
> als ein Unsriges lebt neben der Hand und im Blick.
> Sag ihm die Dinge. Er wird staunender stehn; wie du standest
> bei dem Seiler in Rom, oder beim Töpfer am Nil.
> Zeig ihm, wie glücklich ein Ding sein kann, wie schuldlos und unser,
> wie selbst das klagende Leid rein zur Gestalt sich entschliebt,
> dient als ein Ding, oder stirbt in ein Ding –, und jenseits
> selig der Geige entgeht. Und diese, von Hingang
> lebenden Dinge verstehn, dab du sie rühmst; vergänglich,
> traun sie ein Rettendes uns, den Vergänglichsten, zu.

> Praise this world to the Angel, not the untellable: you
> can't impress him with the splendour you've felt; in the cosmos
> where he more feelingly feels you're only a tyro. So show him
> some simple thing, remoulded by age after age,
> till it lives in our hands and eyes as a part of ourselves.
> Tell him things. He'll stand more astonished: as you did
> beside the roper in Rome or the potter in Egypt.
> Show him how happy a thing can be, how guileless and ours;
> how even the moaning of grief purely determines on form,
> serves as a thing, or dies into a thing, – to escape
> to a bliss beyond the fiddle. These things that live on departure
> understand when you praise them: fleeting, they look for
> rescue through something in us, the most fleeting of all.

(Duino Elegies, IX. 53-65, tr. Leishman and Spender)

Rilke's idea of the poet's task here is in sympathy with the purpose which Apollinaire defined for his 'Orphic Cubism': the artist, he said, must be 'endlessly renewing the appearance which clothes the world of nature in man's eyes'.[1] Through close analysis of the being of individual things, he

would become aware of their individual nature, and able to give them new
forms, verbal or visual, 'names' which others had failed to perceive. In this
way, the artist was able to find meaning and order in what might otherwise
seem a chaotic mass of particularities. Early Cubist paintings were dismissed
by many as such a chaos, since the forms discovered by these artists were far
from naturalistic; but they were always presented, with insistence, as structures discovered in things, not imposed. In the same way, Rilke claimed that
only the poet can interpret the colour and movement of the world, and hear
the earth singing 'what is imprinted in roots':

> Nun, wie das Grüne, das Blauen, heisse,
> durfen wir fragen...
> und was gedruckt steht in Wurzeln und langen
> schwierigen Stämmen: sie singts, sie singts!
>
> Now we may ask what the greens and the blues mean...
> and what is printed into roots and in long tough stems;
> it sings, it sings!

(Sonette an Orpheus, I. 21)

When Apollinaire spoke of the artist's task as *endless renewal* of appearances – a succession of transformations as each artist revealed forms of life
not apprehended before – he was making a deeply traditional statement
about the poet's or painter's relation to the world and also to spiritual
realities. The Renaissance Neoplatonists spoke of mutability as 'the secret
gate by which the universal invades the particular'. The poet or artist could
grasp the key to this gate, by apprehending the nature of particulars and so
allowing the universal to enter our world. Mutability was in itself a source of
delight (inexhaustible, it seemed, to those Renaissance men who loved Ovid),
and the poet's special gift was to respond to this amplitude and fluidity in the
natural world. Keats had called this awareness a 'negative capability', but
Apollinaire preferred to speak of the artist in more positive terms; he saw
the universe as demanding a response that only a human artist could make.
This, rather than the attraction of the Orpheus myth as story, was his reason
for the choice of name, 'Orphic', for his artistic movement.[2]

Apollinaire's view of poetry, and painting, as creating endlessly changing
forms to make the world of nature apprehensible to men, follows the direction taken by Mallarmé when he defined the poet's one duty as *l'explication
Orphique de la terre*, 'the *Orphic* explanation of the world'. But how could
Orpheus be seen by a nineteenth century French symbolist as the *explainer*
of the world? The use of the term *Orphique* in French poetry was not at all
new. Mallarmé and his circle were reacting against an anti-Romantic demand for a more abstract and impersonal kind of poetry. This call was raised

during the years 1866 to 1876 in the journal *Le Parnasse Contemporain*, by those who saw the model for such ideal poetry in the sonnets of Hérédia. The 'Parnassiens', as their chosen name suggests, claimed to be following the classical tradition of European poetry, insisting on objective themes and formal purity. In resisting this movement, the Symbolists did not seek to go back to Romanticism, but presented the classical tradition itself in wholly different terms.

Poetry, as the Symbolists sought to realise it, was something more esoteric and yet more universal than the practice of a traditional expertise, with the exercise of highly cultured taste. It demanded spiritual as well as verbal discipline, because the poet was called upon to act as a mage, a kind of priest, who could reveal relationships between the perceptible objects of ordinary life and the hidden realm of the spirit. It is in this sense that the Symbolists saw their work as 'Orphic', unlocking the mystery of creation. Orpheus himself had always been a familiar figure in French literature, and his mystical stature was at least as well known as the tale of his lost love; in the sixteenth century, du Bellay had written of *le grand prêtre de Thrace au long surpelis blanc*, 'the great Thracian priest in his long white surplice'. It was easy then for the French Symbolists in the latter half of the nineteenth century to find in Orpheus and the idea of 'Orphic' poetry the materials for a different kind of 'classical tradition'.

The Symbolists regarded personal experience as the necessary stuff of art. This experience, they believed, must capture some of the minutiae which made up the vast fluidity of life: fountain, gate, jug, olive tree – all these things in the Here and Now demanded to be named, as Rilke would name them fifty years later, and as Gerard Manley Hopkins was already naming dappled things and manscape in his own poetry of 'distinctiveness'.[3] In French literature, this intent awareness of natural creatures and inanimate objects, this seeking to draw out their true identity through poetic regard, had been expressed before the Symbolists time by Gérard de Nerval:

> ...Respecte dans la bête un esprit agissant;
> Chaque fleur est une âme a la Nature éclose;
> Un mystère d'amour dans le métal repose;
> 'Tout est sensible!' Et tout sur ton être est puissant...

> Souvent dans l'être obscur habite un Dieu caché;
> Et comme un oeil naissant couvert par ses paupières,
> Un pur esprit s'accroît sous l'écorce des pierres!

> ...Look carefully in an animal at a spirit alive;
> every flower is a soul opening out into nature;
> a mystery touching love is asleep inside metal.
> 'Everything is intelligent!' And everything moves you...

> Often a Holy Thing is living hidden in a dark creature;
> and like an eye which is born covered by its lids,
> a pure spirit is growing strong under the bark of stones!

('Vers Dorés', 1845, tr. Robert Bly)

'Astonishing! Everything is intelligent!' was an exclamation which Gérard de Nerval found attributed to Pythagoras. However, his source for the idea of poetry as an active agent, revealing and also transforming the world by recognition, came largely from or through Germany rather than directly from the Greeks. De Nerval translated Goethe's *Faust* into French, and he knew the poetry of Goethe's teacher, Herder, which Goethe described as 'Orphic song'. The scope of Herder's poetry was boundless; the sense of liberation, of authentic inspiration, which it could bring to German readers at the time is expressed in a letter written by the twenty-five-year-old Goethe in 1774:

> He has descended into the depths of his feeling, has stirred up from there all the holy might of simple Nature, and now brings it up and sends it over the wide earth in half-conscious, summer-lightning-lit, sometimes morning-friendly-smiling Orphic song.

The poem described in these terms was the *Alteste Urkunde des Menschengeschlechts*, 'The Most Ancient Record of the Human Race'. When Goethe called this poetry 'Orphic', he was following in the direction pointed by Herder himself. For Herder, the poetry of Orpheus (which he believed had actually survived, in the *Orphic Hymns*; he read them in the Latin version published in Germany in 1765) was nothing less than the *Urgesang alle Wesen*, 'the original song of all Being'.

Throughout his life Goethe returned repeatedly to the theme of the spiritual identities revealed in nature, and the effectual transformation of living beings, by the power of poetry. His early 'prose-poems' on nature were intended as examples of Orphic utterance, and he used the same term to describe his poem *Urworte*, written when he was seventy-one. This work, like Herder's, sought to rediscover the true pristine source of poetic inspiration, of which Goethe found traces in Plato as well as in the surviving *Orphic Hymns*. As late in his life as *Faust* Part II, Goethe was striking the same note (with Apollo rather than Orpheus as the singer whose voice can vivify a world, in the 'Arcadia' passage of Act III). At the same time, also in Germany, Novalis was writing of poetry's power to express cosmic truths; his mystical *Hymns to the Night* (1800) had taken the lyre as their metaphor for the spirit of man, awaiting the hand of the musician, the poet, to arouse the music that lay deep in the nature of the universe.

The Continental tradition concerning Orpheus in the nineteenth century, beginning with this cosmic poetry in Germany, entering French literature with de Nerval and inspiring the avant-garde developments of Mallarmé and Apollinaire, returned to German poetry and found its richest fruition in the work of Rilke. The Orpheus-figure in this context is very different from the doomed lover who captured the Victorian imagination in England. This Orpheus is one who holds a key, knows a secret; he is a master of transformations, able to know true identities behind all fleeting appearances. Yet poets in the Goethe-de Nerval tradition claimed that they followed an Orpheus as truly classical as the Virgilian singer who fruitlessly lamented his lost Eurydice.

Both Orpheus-figures are to be found in Ovid. As so often in the *Metamorphoses*, Ovid surprises the reader by stepping outside his charming and sympathetically related love story to a wider world in which he will show other things to be much more interesting. (This was probably as surprising for his contemporaries, who had read the *Amores* and *Heroides* before the *Metamorphoses* was published.) The Orpheus of Books X and XI is an accomplished courtier and a whole-hearted winning lover, but he is also the master of metamorphosis. After the loss of Eurydice, he sings to the assembled trees and animals of the death of the boy Hyacinthus, changed to a flower, and then of the savage Cerastae, who turned into a herd of bullocks; these are humans transformed to other forms of life which fit their natures. He goes on to tell of Pygmalion, and the change from stone to living humanity. This story was obviously developed by Ovid from sources which went back to Cypriot folk-lore as well as Hellenistic poetry; but the coming to life of the statue under the hand of the passionate lover who is also the sculptor was apparently Ovid's own invention.[4] The tale expresses with vivid directness the animating power of the artist who pursues his vocation; and this is why the animals and trees respond to Orpheus' endearing voice.

'A Fact is not a Truth until you love it,' said John Keats, who strangely enough did not use the figure of Orpheus (except in very rare and brief references)[5] in any of his poems on themes of classical mythology. Keats' belief in love as an animating force in nature and the human world was a personal one which he related to his own experience and to his unsystematic reading of the classics; he probably did not know the Neoplatonist treatises which took Orpheus as the voice of sacred mysteries revealing the meaning of love. Vico had spoken of love as *nodus perpetuus et copula mundi*, 'the everlasting knot, and union of the universe'. This he called the 'Orphic Theology', and quoted as if from Orpheus himself the saying that love 'is above the intellect'. This exaltation of love had been attributed to Orpheus by Proclus in the fifth century AD, in his commentary on Plato's *Timaeus*. Proclus had spoken of love as a power far above mere passion, a supreme mystery beyond seeing or understanding, which the Orphic initiate was privileged to know. This supreme love was taken by Ficino to be the secret which Orpheus ('both Love and a great demon') had to impart, which was indeed the life-giving principle of the universe. The bearer of this secret was the Orpheus whom the French and German poets of the nineteenth century sought to follow; nothing demarcates them more clearly than this from the English post-Romantic writers who, when they thought of Orpheus, saw him as human lover rather than mage.

This division between English and Continental traditions had not always existed. Bacon, in the Tudor age, had seen Orpheus as 'a man admirable and truly divine, who being master of all harmony subdued and drew all things after him'. Orpheus, for Bacon, was a discoverer, and the possessor of *knowledge*; he knew the life-giving principle which ordered the universe:

> And therefore it is not the pleasure of curiosity, nor the quiet of resolution, nor the raising of the spirit, nor victory of wit, nor faculty of speech, nor lucre of profession, nor ambition of honour or fame, nor inablement for business, that are the true ends of knowledge; some of these being more worthy than other, though all inferior and degenerate; but it is a restitution and reinvesting (in great part) of man to the sovereignty and power (for whensoever he shall be able to call the creatures by their true names, he shall again command them) which he had in his first state of creation.

> *Valerius Terminus*, 1

To know the true names of the creatures, it was necessary to love them – as God, in Christian theology, is declared to love them and name them. The idea of a divine language, in which all names would be the true names, is implicit in the story of the Tower of Babel; this true language was lost at the fall of the Tower, and men are now struggling to find once more the exactness and perfection of that lost tongue which expressed a knowledge of creation now reserved to God. In the lost language (as some science-fiction writers have imagined) men would be able to use the true names of things.[6] Such knowledge, if men could attain it, would restore the paradisal order before the Fall.

In Christian doctrine, Adam was the only man who had ever spoken this language, who used the names of creatures and things that they had in their true being. This must be so, since God had given him the task and privilege of naming the creatures when they were first created:

> And out of the ground the Lord God formed every beast of the field, and every fowl of the air; and brought them unto the man to see what he would call them; and whatsoever the man called every living creature, that was the name thereof.

> (Gen. 2: 19)

In Milton's account, Adam saw all beasts and birds approaching to receive their names from him, and in that moment of giving the name he 'understood their nature'. The scene in Eden then became sportive and (with the exception of the serpent) blissfully innocent:

> About them frisking played
> All beasts of the earth, since wild, and of all chase
> In wood or wilderness, forest or den.
> Sporting the lion ramped, and in his paw
> Dandled the kid; bears, tigers, ounces, pards,
> Gambolled before them; the unwieldy elephant,
> To make them mirth, used all his might, and wreathed
> His lithe proboscis; close the serpent sly,
> Insinuating, wove with Gordian twine
> His braided train, and of his fatal guile
> Gave proof unheeded. Others on the grass
> Couched, and, now filled with pasture, gazing sat,
> Or bedward ruminating;

> (*Paradise Lost,* IV. 340-52; cf. VIII. 338-54)

The liveliness of this picture is Orphean: Simonides in the sixth century BC, had spoken of birds and fish *leaping* to hear the lyre-player's song,[7] and Orpheus it was

> Whose golden touch could soften steel and stones,
> Make tigers tame, and huge leviathans
> Forsake unsounded deeps to *dance* on sands.

The speaker is the young lover whom Shakespeare chooses to call Proteus in *The Two Gentlemen of Verona* (III. 2). The dancing leviathans have the right touch of extravagant fantasy in this context. But authentically Orphean also is the stateliness of Blake's *Adam Naming the Beasts*, painted in 1810; the painting is more than half-filled by the head and shoulders of Adam, curly-haired, and serenely wide-eyed like a Buddha, looking out from the canvas, with his right hand pointing upwards and his left gently holding the head of the serpent. Behind him, animals of both homely and wild families move slowly across a wide landscape; beside him is an oak tree, bearing acorns, not apples.[8] Adam has no musical instrument; otherwise this painting might take its place beside the 'animal paradise' scenes which show Orpheus, or David, attended by animals both wild and tame, who listen peacefully, and move (if at all) with obedient composure.

The iconography of Orpheus surrounded by animals in an attitude of orderly responsiveness has already been seen in the catacomb frescoes of the

Good Shepherd, and in representations of David. It can be recognised also, though less frequently, in illustrations of Adam in the Garden of Eden. Kern cited an early Christian ivory which showed this assimilation of Orpheus to Adam with exceptional clearness.[9] The docility of the animals in these scenes recalls also the prophecy of Isaiah, proclaiming peace between all creatures in the Messianic age to come. Their leader is not described as a musician but 'a little child'; yet he is 'a rod out of the stem of Jesse', a reborn David. The Messiah is seen as leading (not dominating) the animals, who recognise his authority, as the sheep in Christ's parable recognise the voice of the Shepherd. The divinely chosen Saviour speaks, or sings, and all parts of the creation are able to respond.

The importance of the *voice* in this scene is not surprising in a biblical context. The Messiah, or the Singer-king, is representative of God in this structure, and throughout the Old Testament it is by the *Word* of God that the order of creation takes its shape. The utterances of Adam, or David, are re-enactments of the divine purpose that was once effected at the beginning of time.[10] In the same way Orpheus could be seen, by Christians familiar with pagan myth, as following the sacred pattern, and so acceptable as an Adam-icon as well as in the Good Shepherd role.

If the poet-musician is believed to draw a response from the creatures whose inward identity he has addressed, this is because he is himself responding to a need in their nature; the living relationship is what the divine will has originally purposed for them. This is why Pindar can hope to copy in his songs 'that siren-voice that silences the Zephyr's swift gusts ...' (fr. 84), and he can speak of the Singer himself as 'stirred up to song like a dolphin of the seas when the lively tune of flutes moves in the deep of the waveless sea' (fr. 140a). Flutes, breezes, leaping dolphins, siren voices; all are at home together in one surge of expressive energy. The gift of stirring natural life in this way was never supposed to be uniquely given to Orpheus. Virgil's sixth Eclogue recounts how Silenus – drunken as always, but filled with a deep and secret knowledge – sang to animals, trees, and shepherds the poem that told of the world's creation:

> simul incipit ipse.
> tum vero in numerum Faunosque ferasque videres
> ludere, tum rigidas motare cacumina quercus;
> nec tantum Phoebo gaudet Parnasia rupes,
> nec tantum Rhodope miratur et Ismarus Orphea.

At once (Silenus) himself begins. And then you might see Fauns and wild beasts playing to the rhythm, and stiff oak-trees nodding their tops; not so much does the rock of Parnassus rejoice in Phoebus, not so much do Rhodope and Ismarus wonder at Orpheus.

(*Ecl*. VI. 27-30)

Silenus and the 'old man of Ascra' are able to address trees or winds or wild beasts, just as princes (or goose-girls) can talk with animals in fairy-tales. In the Middle Ages it was usually saints who were credited with this power; St Francis and St Cuthbert are just two well-known examples, of many less widely renowned. In ancient Greece such tales were told almost exclusively of poets or prophets. Such was Melampus, who was favoured by Apollo with the gift of soothsaying, and also talked with vultures and other birds, and even with woodworms.[11]

This gift of tongues, bestowed upon seer or saint or poet, is not usually seen in legend as breaking into forbidden or totally new ground; although only the specially gifted man, among his contemporaries, can communicate with other creatures or things, there is a recurrent tradition that once-upon-a-time everyone was able to do so. Babrius' version of Aesop includes a prologue explaining that men and animals could exchange conversation in the Golden Age. Plato introduced a more sophisticated Golden Age myth into his *Politicus* (272), where the Statesman expounds the history of human society, from paradisal unity with all creation to the confusions of life as we all know it. In the age of Cronos, the Statesman says, men could talk with animals and so learn from every creature. This power we lost, when 'the helmsman of the universe dropped the tiller and withdrew'. The withdrawal was not, in Plato's version (or in Hesiod), the result of a momentous wrongdoing by man, comparable to Adam's first disobedience; but the loss of harmony between man and natural life is comparable in classical and biblical traditions (and in other cultures also). The restoration of such harmony, through the poet-prophet's gift of speech, is part of his special task among men, and is as holy as his power to hear the Music of the Spheres. It is significant that Rilke, whose later poetry refined and penetrated this theme so deeply in the expression of a poet's individual experience, first approached it in terms of a traditional narrative about St Francis:

> Und wenn er sang, so kehrte selbst das Gestern
> und das Vergessene zurück und Kam;
> und eine Stille wurde in den Nestern...
> denn ihn erkannten alle Dinge
> und hatten Fruchtbarkeit aus ihm.
>
> Und als er starb, so leicht wie ohne Namen,
> da war er ausgeteilt; sein Samen rann
> in Bächen, in den Baumen sang sein Samen
> und sah ihn ruhig aus den Blumen an.
> Er lag und sang...

> And when he sang, days past and things forgotten
> turned in their courses and their steps retraced;
> a stillness hushed the nest of every bird...
> for him all things did recognise
> and drew their fruitfulness from him.
>
> And when he died – lightly, as though no name
> he bore – he was dealt out; in many a rill
> his seed ran, in the trees rang out its theme,
> and from the flowers it viewed him calm and still.
> He lay and sang...

(*Book of Hours*, 1905, III. 33, tr. A.L. Peck)

The singing St Francis, dying and 'dealt out' through streams and trees, reappears later in Rilke as a divided, or doubled, icon: the singing Orpheus and the dying Eurydice, who in 'Orpheus, Eurydice, Hermes', two or three years later, was 'dealt out' (the same word, *ausgeteilt*, is used in both poems) among the roots and veins of the earth, while Orpheus led the way, with his

> delicate lyre
> which had grown into his left arm, like a slip
> of roses grafted on to an olive tree.

The poet-singer, and his female counterpart, are indissolubly one with the unending life of the physical world; animal life, as well as the planetary music.

The iconographic tradition of Orpheus being at one with the life of the physical creation is very ancient, and unbroken. Renaissance artists took this subject from classic models rather than from the medieval illustrations to Ovid and other tales of the troubadour-charmer.[12] They had classic models in abundance for this subject; over fifty versions in mosaic alone show Orpheus with animals, in the style known as 'Nilotic'; many others show him as a single singing figure, or playing before Pluto. The theme was fashionable with Italian and also English aristocrats of the sixteenth century who liked to follow these ancient types, with minor variations. The artists they employed were not always highly skilled, as we can see at Haddon Hall, Derbyshire, where a plaster relief – apparently by a local craftsman – shows Orpheus surrounded by rather too many animals (some very exotic) to fill the space available over a fireplace. The decorative possibilities of diverse animals and trees grouped about a central figure who fascinates them all could not fail to attract artists in every medium. These scenes – on plates, enamels, tapestries, miniatures, panelling, decorations for furniture and garden ornaments; no setting was untried – are found in profusion in the seventeenth and eighteenth centuries, and they become increasingly frivolous – though usually no less charming – as time goes on: in 1909 a Lady Llewellyn Smith commissioned an 'Orpheus tiara' from a London jeweller; he was to be shown subduing a lion and lioness by his music.[13]

However frivolous, such representations go back in direct line to the classic age of Greece, when a vase dating from as early as the sixth century BC was decorated with scenes depicting a musician with an animal audience. There may be continuity with a still more distant past. The throne room at Pylos had a fresco showing a lyre-player seated on a hillock, or a crag, dressed in a long robe and apparently watching a large bird that has risen up in flight before him. This fresco could not have been painted later than 1200 BC; if not Orpheus, the figure must be a musician of Orphean skill and probably of priestly status. The earliest identified Orpheus in visual art is a metope sculpture from the Sicyonian Treasury at Delphi, which dates from the mid-sixth century BC. This shows two musicians on board a ship, one of whom is named as Orpheus; the other figure has been thought to be Arion, and the ship the *Argo*. One of these identifications may well be correct, but not both. Orpheus as Argonaut is first mentioned in Pindar's fourth Pythian, but no other musician is mentioned there, or anywhere else, among the canonical list of Jason's companions. Orpheus' role on the *Argo* is that of guide: when the Argonauts have to pass the Sirens or the Clashing Rocks, his music will provide protection and subdue hostile forces, by alluring all natural and even supernatural beings to his purpose.

Arion is indeed linked with Orpheus, as other musicians and poets of legend are, as examples of an archetypal pattern showing the singer-poet in harmony, and as exemplar, with the world of nature. What Orpheus does, other musician-poets may also do, and the creatures of the world also, following him. He is seen therefore as a kind of moral teacher (and this is a more universal role than the particular didacticism of the later Orphic cults). He can give enlightened moral teaching because he has the power to understand the inner being of inanimate nature as well as the animals. This provides the pattern for other musician-teachers: Arion, Linus, Amphion. Arion follows the Orpheus-pattern not only in his power to influence sea-creatures, but also because his lyre was finally translated as a constellation.

Amphion, who was said to have received his lyre from Hermes, had the power to move stones by his music, and so was able to build the walls of Thebes, with no exertion, from the rocks of Mount Cithaeron. This story gives the musician-poet equality with gods, the great Olympians Apollo and Poseidon who built the walls of Troy: it is more awe-inspiring than the stories of men conversing with animals partly because it is less believable (dogs and dolphins *do* respond to human voices and to music, in common experience). Ovid does not make much of Amphion's feat (*Met.* VI. 178-9), but later ages took it more seriously. For the thinkers and artists of the Renaissance, and of modern times, it was a memorable demonstration of the unity of nature, proving all forms of being in the created universe to be embraced in the divine harmony. Tiepolo, in the eighteenth century, was not indulging mere frivolity when he painted his *Allegory of the Power of Eloquence* for the Palazzo Sandi in Venice. The four mythological scenes chosen to illustrate this power include the spectacular *Amphion Building Thebes*: an astonished lyre player stands on a rock, a high wind lifting his garments and also the stones which soar about him to take their places on the half-built fortress walls on the hillside. Eloquence, musical utterance inspired by divine afflatus, is conveyed as powerfully in this great painting as it is in all the icons of the musician surrounded by responsive beasts.

The poet Paul Valéry, in the first half of this century, was preoccupied with ideas of metamorphosis and took these animated stones as the theme of one of his sonnets; it is Orpheus who controls them here, not Amphion:

> Je compose en esprit, sous les myrtes, Orphée
> l'admirable! Le feu, des cirques purs descend;
> Il change le mont chauve en august trophée
> d'ou s'exhale d'un dieu l'acte retentissant.
>
> Si le dieu chante, il rompt le site tout-puissant;
> le soleil voit l'horreur du mouvement des pierres;
> une plainte inouie appelle éblouissants
> les hauts murs d'or harmonieux d'un sanctuaire.
>
> Il chante, assis au bord du ciel splendide, Orphée.
> Le roc marche, et trebuche; et chaque pierre fée
> se sent un poids nouveau qui vers l'azure délire;
>
> d'un Temple à demi-nu le soir baigne l'essor,
> et soi-même il s'assemble et s'ordonne dans l'or,
> A l'âme immense du grand hymne sur la lyre!
>
> I form him in my mind, under the myrtles, Orpheus
> The wonderful...Fire descends, and pure performance;
> He transforms the bald mountain to a solemn trophy,
> And from it breathes a god's reverberating act.
>
> If the god sings, he shatters the scene, all powerful.
> The sun sees the shudder of the moving rocks;
> A wailing never known summons resplendent
> The high walls of a sanctuary, gold harmonious.
>
> He sings, seated at the glorious sky's margin: Orpheus.
> The crag moves, and stumbles; each magical stone
> Feels its weight anew, soaring towards the blue;

The evening bathes a half-bared Temple's flight;
Of itself it gathers, assumes an order amid the gold,
To the boundless soul of the great hymn on the lyre.

(*Poésies*, published 1930)

Many of the individual poems in this 1930 collection of Valéry's were known much earlier to Rilke, and the ideas expressed here are in accord with Rilke's thinking in the prose fragment which Butler calls 'a rhapsody on loneliness':

> If there has ever been a creator anywhere (I speak of creators because they are the loneliest of all) who in days of unutterable concentration created the world of a work of art; can it be that the progress and distance of this life should be lost to us, because time has shattered the form of his work and we do not possess it? Does not, on the contrary, the most confident inner voice assure us that the wind that was present in the work as it grew had its effect beyond its own limits on flowers and beasts, on dew and rising mists and on the birth-throes of women? Who knows whether this picture, or that statue, or that lost poem was but the next and the nearest of many transformations which the power of the creator accomplished in its hour of ecstasy? The cells of far-away things ordered themselves differently perhaps under the compulsion of new rhythms. The cause of new species was given; and it is not impossible that we have been conditioned by the might of a lonely poet who lived hundreds of years ago, and of whom we know nothing...

The serious claim that 'the cells of far away things ordered themselves differently' exalts the poet as no Greek philosopher ever did; but it is this implication in the Orphic tradition that caused Clement of Alexandria to denounce Orpheus, Arion, and Amphion as idolaters. Claims such as these would set the poet on a level with God. For the Christian preacher, the idea of a musical enchantment directed to fauns and wild beasts might be suspect, but a power over trees and stones would certainly challenge the theocentric order. The Orphic theogony which survives in several versions (parts of which must appear quite bizarre to modern readers) presents a universe more fluid and more contradictory than anything in biblical tradition. The place of man in this vast and unending creative process was a passive and irresponsible one unless he could assume the role of the poet, the master of language, of rhythm, of harmony; here, in Orphean myth, was the secret of creative power, of the Music of the Spheres, and the cells of far-away things.

Shelley expressed this vision of the poet's dominion, as a lifegiving and ordering force, in a memorable passage in *Prometheus Unbound*:

Language is a perpetual Orphic song
Which rules with Daedal harmony a throng
Of thoughts and forms which else senseless and shapeless were.

The poet, the 'maker', does not create out of nothing, but he is the supreme craftsman who can bring forth forms of living beauty, because he knows and intimately understands the true nature of what he works with.[14]

It was because the poet was believed to know the world, with this inward knowledge granted to him by the Muse, that Orpheus and his successors were said to relate the history of creation, or of some part of it, in so many of their cosmogonic songs and hymns. The song of Orpheus, as Apollonius Rhodius presents it, provides an example more attractive to most modern readers than either Hesiod or the *Orphic Hymns*:

> He (Orpheus) sang how earth, heaven, and sea once were knit together in a single form, and how after deadly strife they were separated from one another; then how in the sky the stars, the moon, and the paths of the sun for ever keep their fixed place; and how mountains rose, and resounding streams, with their nymphs, and all creeping things, came into being. And he sang how at first Ophion and Eurynome, daughter of Ocean, held rule of snowy Olympus...
>
> (*Argonautica*, I. 496-504)

In this tale of the Argonauts, Orpheus has a unique knowledge of the world's nature and history, and it is his function to tell the heroes things which they could not know without listening to his poetry. It is also shown, in this poem, that the song of Orpheus itself has the power to bring order out of deadly strife, and is analagous to the story of creation, of which he sings. The moment chosen for this song is the point at which the Argonauts begin to quarrel and their voyage is threatened by impatience and bickering. The Orphean song brings quiet and piety into the hearts of the heroes, creating harmony from strife as well as describing such creation on the cosmic scale.

The 'knowledge' attributed to Orpheus might, in such scenes as this, be considered to demonstrate a kind of wise enlightenment rather than any esoteric or mystical learning; it is here that the didactic Orpheus of the Baconian tradition can be seen to originate. Bacon, delighted by the picture of the singer at one with all beings in the natural order, equates Orpheus with the spirit of Philosophy:

> The story of Orpheus, which though so well known has not been yet in all points perfectly well interpreted, seems meant for a rep-

resentation of universal Philosophy. For Orpheus himself – a man admirable and truly divine, who being master of all harmony sub-dued and drew all things after him by sweet and gentle measures – may pass by an easy metaphor for philosophy personified.

(*Of the Wisdom of the Ancients*, II, tr. Spedding)

Bacon was interested in physical and metaphysical speculation as well as ethics and social thought; other writers of the same period look on Orpheus, and on poets generally, as instructors of mankind in society. George Chapman, writing at the beginning of the seventeenth century, saw the special knowledge possessed by poets, and the value of poetry, as a civilising insight which had inspired men to rise from barbarism; the whole Orpheus myth, including both the control of natural forces and the rescue of Eurydice, is interpreted as an allegory of this educative function:

> So when ye hear the sweetest Muse's son
> With heavenly rapture of his music won
> Rocks, forests, floods and wind to leave their course
> In his attendance: it bewrays the force
> His wisdom had, to draw men grown so rude
> To civil love of art and fortitude,
> And not for teaching others insolence
> Had he his date-exceeding excellence
> With sovereign poets, but for use applied,
> And in his proper acts exemplified.
> And that in calming the infernal kind,
> To wit, the perturbations of his mind,
> And bringing his Eurydice from hell
> (Which justice signifies) is proved well.

(Chapman, *The Shadow of Night*)

This rationalising of the Orpheus myth had been applied as early as the first century BC, in Horace's *Ars Poetica*. Horace does not go so far as to explain the Eurydice story as a moral fable of psychological application, but he does relate the social code of civilised man (including the vegetarian precepts of the Orphics) to the tale of Orpheus charming the beasts:

> Silvestres homines sacer interpresque deorum
> caedibus et victu foedo deterruit Orpheus,
> *dictus ob hoc* lenire tigris rapidosque
> leones...

> Before men left the jungle, a holy prophet of heaven,
> Orpheus, made them abhor bloodshed and horrible food.

Hence he is said to have tamed rabid lions and tigers...

(Hor. *A.P.* 391-3)

Horace goes on to recall Amphion's building of Thebes by his music's power over stone; this also is seen as a demonstration of the *sapientia*, the wisdom, inherent in the art of poetry, by which men were first taught the principles of law, religious practice, and the conduct of war. So *vitae monstrata via est*, 'song showed the way through life'.

This idea of the poet as philosophic instructor of mankind is not incompatible with the older image of the healer of the soul, and it can easily be accepted as part of a theistic scheme of human history seen as a providentially guided progress. However, the 'miraculous' elements in the Orphean story may easily be explained away if Bacon's 'easy metaphor for Philosophy personified' is taken as pointer to Orpheus' true identity. We are left, in the seventeenth century, with the rationalising and finally the discarding of myth firmly carried out by Bishop Sprat:

> the first Masters of Knowledge amongst them, were as well Poets as Philosophers; for Orpheus, Linus, Musaeus, and Homer first softened Man's natural rudeness...

> When the fabulous Age was past, Philosophy took a little more courage; and ventured more to rely upon its own strength, without the Assistance of Poetry.

(Thomas Sprat, *History of the Royal Society of London*, 1665-6)[15]

After Milton (who was writing in Sprat's lifetime), English poets were no longer able to use Orphean language or attribute inward awareness of the natural world to poets, except as a conventional decorative item. Milton, in *Lycidas*, assumed the voice of an 'uncouth Swain', who sang '*to* th'Okes and rills'. The texture of this poem, in all its wide-ranging movements, is enriched by the close relation between the Swain (and Lycidas his fellow-shepherd, who is dead) and the growing things of woodland and pasture, the animals and rough satyrs, and the waters of river and sea. The whole poem comes to the Swain as an utterance from the

> Sisters of the sacred well
> That from beneath the seat of Jove doth spring.

The Muses, helpless as they are to save their 'lov'd Lycidas' from drowning, are a living reality, on which Milton's whole poem depends; we are far from the etiolated figures whose departure from poetic minds of his day was lamented by William Blake. It is a far cry, in terms of creative experience, from Milton's generation to Blake's; yet not much more than a century separated them, a century that saw profound changes in the attitudes of educated Europeans to the world of nature and to the arts, and most of all to the relation between the two. Elizabeth Sewell spoke of the Orphic, Shakespearian line in English poetry as seeming 'to go underground after Milton', not to reappear until Coleridge and Wordsworth.[16]

The 'dissociation of sensibility' which restricts and impoverishes much of eighteenth-century poetry is now a commonplace of English criticism.[17] This severance of discursive thought from feeling, and of rationality from imagination, affected not only the work of poets but also their readers' understanding of what poetic experience is and what poets are doing. We can see this effect at work in poems such as Gray's *The Progress of Poesy*. Gray has been seen as a precursor of the Romantics, in his personal response to landscape and to human relationships, and in his readiness, sometimes, to use flexible structures less formal than the traditional patterns of his time. *The Progress of Poesy* risks much by announcing itself as a 'Pindaric Ode'. Gray aims at 'rapture', and his swooping historical survey, from Helicon to Latium and then to Albion's 'sea-encircled coast', brings him to an encounter with

> Such forms as glitter in the Muse's ray,

enabling him to 'mount' in a poetic flight which may not compare with that of 'the Theban eagle', but will at least

> keep his distant way
> Beyond the limits of a vulgar fate.

This aspiration is not alien to Pindar, or to Horace, who both believed and felt themselves lifted securely above the vulgar by their poetic gift; what is alien to the Pindaric tradition, in Gray, is the fumbling and shying away from climax, from distinctness, from all 'minute particulars'. The final line of the ode takes the poet lamely along his path, neither here nor there:

> Beneath the Good how far – but far above the Great.

The poem includes passages of noble rhetoric and scene-painting:

> In climes beyond the solar road,
> Where shaggy forms o'er ice-built mountains roam...

but they remain pieces of stage equipment for the performance called up by the poet's lyre:

> antic Sports, and blue-eyed Pleasures,
> Frisking light in frolic measures.

Not that the poet is limited to frivolities; Gray is aware of the astonishing claims made for Orpheus and his followers, long ago:

> Man's feeble race what ills await,
> Labour, and Penury, the racks of Pain,
> Disease, and Sorrow's weeping train,
> And Death, sad refuge from the storms of fate!
> The fond complaint, my song, disprove,
> And justify the laws of Jove.
> Say, has he giv'n in vain the heavenly Muse?

The Miltonic echoes here do not serve to cover the devitalised nakedness of these personifications; the device has honourable ancestry, but there is no Horatian particularity in the realising of these abstractions. When Horace spoke of Anxiety it was in the vivid single line

> post equitem sedet atra Cura

> behind the horseman sits black Care.

> *(Odes* III, i. 40)

(and he does not go on to ruminate about the divine dispensation). Pindar can take a much less promising abstraction, Theia, identified in Hesiod's *Theogony* as daughter of Earth and Heaven, and source of light: this bodiless figure becomes in Pindar's fifth Isthmian the source of radiance in human perception of all bright things, gold, racing ships, and horses yoked to chariots.

'Minute particulars' can be apprehended by the poet within any set of conventions, but some are more favourable to this Orphean perception than others. In eighteenth-century England only the great poetic genius of Pope at his best was able to maintain this kind of awareness within the poetic usage and forms of the time. Blake had to call for a new kind of vision, a new relation with the seen and unseen world in which the poet lived. This new relation was a return to a very old one, and meant the restoration of a unity long lost, the unity which Wordsworth celebrated when he called for the young lambs to 'bound/as to the tabor's sound'. When he evokes the natural energy of the spring in this pastoral moment at the end of the 'Immortality Ode', Wordsworth is finding deep strength in the

primal sympathy
Which having been must ever be.

The poet's voice, he is saying, speaks as it always did; Orpheus' role does not change.

In the twentieth century the awareness of the inscape of all things, and of a living relation to them, lost and rediscovered, informs the poetry of Kathleen Raine:

Message from Home

Do you remember, when you were first a child,
Nothing in the world seemed strange to you?
You perceived, for the first time, shapes already familiar,
And seeing, you knew that you have always known
The lichen on the rock, fern leaves, the flowers of thyme,
As if the elements newly met in your body,
Caught up into the momentary vortex of your living
Still kept the knowledge of a former state,
In you retained recollection of cloud and ocean,
The branching tree, the dancing flame.

Now when nature's darkness seems strange to you,
And you walk, an alien, in the streets of cities,
Remember earth breathed you into her with the air,
      with the sun's rays,
Laid you in her waters asleep, to dream
With the brown trout among the milfoil roots,
From substance of star and ocean fashioned you,
At the same source conceived you
As sun and foliage, fish and stream...

Sleep at the tree's root, where the night is spun
Into the stuff of worlds, listen to the winds,
The tides, and the night's harmonies, and know
All that you knew before you began to forget,
Before you became estranged from your own being,
Before you had too long parted from those other
More simple children, who have stayed at home
In meadow and island and forest, in sea and river.
Earth sends a mother's love after her exiled son,
Entrusting her message to the light and the air,
The wind and waves that carry your ship, the rain that falls,
The birds that call to you, and all the shoals
That swim in the natal waters of her ocean.

What is a poet? He is one who is able to perceive the true individual nature of created things, and speak their true names. This power makes it possible for ordered relationships to arise between them, realising a harmony between living and even inanimate things which was always inherent in their being, but lost to human consciousness until the poet brings it to birth.

By responding to the poet's work, men can widen and deepen their own awareness of the created world and their own place in it, so that poetry becomes a kind of science and a guide to more enlightened ways of living. For this reason poets have been seen as educators and moral guides, who alone could tell the whole true history of the creation.

VIII

Furor Poeticus

WHEN Pindar described the home of the Hyperboreans, the 'People beyond the North', where men were said to enjoy a paradisal life free from sickness and old age, he imagined a golden world of continual dance and feasting:

> and the Muse is never absent from their ways.
>
> (*Pyth*. X. 37-8)

The company of the Muse meant happiness and security as well as the vision of truth. Those who received communications from this gracious divinity must, it was felt, know a joyful tranquillity – and Orpheus above all other men, since he was not only her most favoured disciple, but her son. In ancient Greece poets were often said to be descended from Orpheus: Homer, at a distance of ten generations, and other epic poets, collectively called Homeridae, sons of Homer. All true poets and musicians shared to some degree in the gifts of the Muses, and were thus seen as blessed with felicity as well as knowledge. The vision granted to them, with glimpses even of the cosmic order and its eternal beauty, was above all a joyful one: 'Happy is the man whom the Muses love' (*Theog.* 96-7).

This is why the singers in the *Odyssey* take such an honourable place in the society of the heroic age. In the massacre of Book XXII, Phemius, the 'blameless', is spared by Odysseus because he can appeal to respect as well as pity:

> I clasp your knees, Odysseus. Respect me, pity. Remorse will come upon you later, if you kill a singer; I am one who sings for gods and men. I am self-taught; a god has planted all kinds of song-paths in my mind.
>
> (*Od.* XXII. 344-8)

139

Odysseus' response to this appeal is all the more striking since he has just rejected a plea from Leodes the priest, who claimed he had done no wrong: Phemius does not take this ground at all, but simply calls on Odysseus to remember his special nature and status as singer. Similarly in *Odyssey* VIII, at the court of Alcinous, the bard Demodocus is greeted by Odysseus with respect and honour, although his song of Troy brings private grief to the disguised hero. Demodocus is an authentic voice of the Muse, who taught him the paths of song and gave him true knowledge of all that the Achaeans did and suffered. As Demodocus begins to sing, 'stirred by the god', the singer and his hearers are drawn together in a collective feeling of pleasure mingled with awe and a sense of fulfilment, which Odysseus describes as 'something most lovely' (IX. 11). Like David, the sweet singer of Israel, the bard has a song that is 'put into his mouth', a song that brings joy to all who hear it and gives pleasure to its divine originator also.[1]

Even though the poet's skill was always acknowledged to be a highly specialised craft, requiring long apprenticeship and disciplined work, emphasis has always been given, in European tradition, to the pleasure felt by poets as well as listeners, and their sense of a divine energy at work, in the exercise of the poetic métier. The hard discipline was, after all, a subordinate part in the making of a poet. Sidney expressed this conviction with vigour and grace:

> For Poesie must not be drawne by the eares, it must be gently led, or rather, it must lead. Which was partly the cause, that made the auncient-learned affirme, it was a divine gift, and no humaine skill; sith all other knowledges lie ready for any that hath strength of witte; a Poet no industrie can make, if his own Genius bee not carried unto it; and therefore is it an old Proverbe, *Orator fit, Poeta nascitur.*

> (*Apologie for Poetrie*, 1594)

Almost by definition, divine gifts are felt to be rare things; and however warmly appealing, the picture of the Greek or Anglo-Saxon warriors raptly attentive after the feast, as the bard sings in the firelight, is not seen as a thing of every day. Only in the golden world of the Hyperboreans is the Muse 'never absent'. In the life of the poet, the visitation of the Muse is an unpredictable experience. Although it might bestow special wisdom and happiness, it could also bring a sense of peculiar exaltation, in which fear and precariousness were mingled with enlightenment. To be so near to the gods meant a dissolution of boundaries on which the human sense of direction in life ordinarily depends.

The poet's nearness to the gods has generally been described as an experience of receptiveness for which the inbreathing, inspiration, of a lifegiving air has been the most constant of metaphors. But the image of the poet-musician as he undergoes this experience of inspiration is not a uniform one.

The source of inspiration, generally agreed to be beyond the poet's own consciousness, may be seen as beneficent and illuminating. This image accords with the Anima-figure of the guiding Muse, as we have already seen her in Homer, Pindar, and much English poetry in the classical tradition. Visited thus by the Muse, the poet needs to respond with a receptive concentration, leading him to find that he knows things he did not consciously know before. The Muse, once allowed to function in the poet's unconscious, has extended his power of recall and re-presented fragmented experience in such a way that the conscious mind can apprehend it and shape it into poetic form. How this happened, the poet himself is unlikely to know.

It is because of this secession from conscious control that Plato so often expresses distrust of poetic experience, as a dabbling in irrationality which can lead to disastrous self-delusion. In the *Ion* Plato satirises the figure of the vain and somewhat mercenary rhapsode who understands nothing of what he recites. The *Apology*, much more serious in tone but still allowing a touch of mockery, exposes the alleged pretensions of poets who say 'many fine things', as soothsayers do, by inspiration, without comprehension. At the same time they imagine themselves to be wiser than others in all sorts of matters quite outside the range of their poetry.[2] This is an obvious absurdity; but even on the themes of his own poetry, a poet is often found to understand not more but less than other people do. Poets cannot answer questions about their own work, and even in the ordinary affairs of life are often the least sensible or intelligent of men. Plato asserts that art has, in fact, nothing to do with making life more intelligible or extending the domain of reason. The state of mind in which people write poetry is often disorderly and fervid, with a kind of irrationality which is dangerous to society – even if it does come from the gods. This holy madness is inseparable from the true poetic experience, for it

> comes from the Muses. It takes hold upon a gentle and pure soul, arouses it and inspires it to songs and other poetry, and thus by adorning countless deeds of the ancients educates later generations. But he who without the divine madness comes to the door of the Muses, confident that he will be a good poet by art, meets with no success, and the poetry of the sane man vanishes into nothingness before that of the inspired madman.

> (Plato, *Phaedrus*, 245a)

This experience of creative activity quickening the poet's own powers of thought and verbal/musical skill has been closely observed, and given scrupulous expression, by many poets and composers speaking of their own work. Dylan Thomas described his own experience, in a memorable passage:

> I make one image – though 'make' is not the word; I let, perhaps, an image be 'made' emotionally in me and then apply to it what intellectual and critical forces I possess; let it breed another, let that image contradict the first; make of the third image, bred out of the other two together, a fourth contradictory image, and let them all, within my imposed forced limits, conflict...Out of the inevitable conflict of images – inevitable, because of the creative, recreative, destructive and contradictory nature of the motivating centre, the womb of war – I try to make that momentary peace which is a poem.[3]

The active tension here between the creative power that is beyond the poet's control ('let an image be 'made', 'let it breed', 'let them...conflict', 'the womb of war') and the willed operation of the poet's own mind ('apply...intellectual and critical forces', 'my imposed formal limits', 'I try to make...') is in the tradition already seen in Pindar, Ovid, and Wordsworth when they spoke of their poetry as their own and yet not their own. The creative impulse that begins the poet's work has in England often been called Imagination:

> And, as imagination bodies forth
> The forms of things unknown, the poet's pen
> Turns them to shapes, and gives to airy nothing
> A local habitation and a name.

> (Shakespeare, *A Midsummer Night's Dream*, V. 1)

These lines suggest the Orphean figure of the poet diligently transcribing what the Muse has uttered, and (as Plato had remarked) not knowing what he was talking about. Goethe would have agreed: 'They come and ask me what idea I meant to embody in *Faust*, as if I knew myself and could inform them.'[4] However, the speech put into the mouth of Theseus by Shakespeare, as his guests await a festive entertainment after the enchantments and follies of the woodland night, does not leave the listener with the picture of poet as secretary or craftsman. As his pen writes, his eye

> in a fine frenzy rolling
> Doth glance from heaven to earth, from earth to heaven.

Theseus classes the poet, with lover and lunatic, as one who sees things that are not there; but what he sees are images which, as Hippolyta reminds us, may grow to 'something of great constancy'. This 'fine frenzy' is the 'divine madness' described by Plato in the *Phaedrus,* the 'momentary and passing madness' which Schiller said must be found in all creators,[5] a form of insanity which had to be respected, as a mark of genius.

The idea of such mental instability as a divine gift to poets is very ancient; it occurs in Democritus, who in the fifth century BC spoke of poets as eccentric figures who composed 'in a state of possession, by holy inspiration'. Democritus' remarks about Homer suggest that this state would, in his view, admit the operation of the poet's conscious and craftsmanlike part in the making of a poem:

> Homer, receiving a share in divine nature, built by his art an order of all manner of words.
>
> (Democr. *fr*. 21)

The idea of inspiration which Democritus and Plato entertained was, as Penelope Murray has shown,[6] associated with a strong belief in the importance of craft, of conscious purpose, and of the exercise of memory, as well as with a sense of dependence on a non-human source of knowledge or perception. The 'divine madness' of the *Phaedrus* seems to mean an intensity of excitement in which the poet-artist feels himself in touch with an idea that is 'given' for him to work on, an idea which impels him to go on without knowing what the final result will be, although it does not deprive him of all contact with ordinary reality or of reasoning capacity. The work he must go on to do is hard and in most cases long; in Stephen Spender's words, 'Everything in poetry is work except inspiration.'[7]

This state has been well described by Rosamond Harding: inspiration, she suggests, can be compared to a hint acting on ideas within the mind when it is

> pent up to a certain tension either by accumulation of 'visions, colours, forms', or by facts and pondering over them in an unsuccessful attempt to solve a problem...Inspiration places the recipient for the time being into a phase of existence different from that of his everyday world, because...his own wishes and desires are overruled by his knowledge of natural sequences of events, colours, forms, rhythms, tones...He follows and *must* follow where the truth leads him.[8]

This intense awareness of 'natural sequences', which makes personal interests and the everyday world seem insignificant to the inspired artist, is comparable to the poet-musician's awareness of the Music of the Spheres. Another order of creation, not normally accessible to men, is being revealed by 'inspiration' in this sense, and such an experience might well take the poet beyond the borders normally defining human sanity.

Murray's examination of the earliest Greek accounts of inspiration suggests that this finely balanced and securely dignified view of the poet's experience and status was indeed the norm in early Greece. The poet was above all wise, but not in an intellectual sense: he was wise in that he understood a particular craft, and was alert to communications from the divine world. Whether he lived on the borders of irrationality or not, he was a happy and enviable man, living close to the Muses, the bringers of joy.

This delightful poet-icon is quite distant from the 'fine frenzy' of Shakespeare, a phrase which seems to have crept into Theseus' genial speech from some source alien to the mischievous sweetness of the *Dream*'s closing harmonies (unless we take the view of some modern producers who think we are meant to experience panic as the primary response to this play). 'Fine frenzy' suggests a loss of identity in wild and glorious revelation, an experience that obliterates the human in a moment that is all terror. D.H. Lawrence knew this: 'I always feel as though I stood naked for the fire of Almighty God to pass through me.'[9]

For Lawrence, the creative experience was, at its essential moment, an agony of self-annihilation. What he describes can more readily be drawn from Old Testament sources than from classical ones:

> Whatsoever I command thee thou shalt speak...Then the Lord put forth his hand, and touched my mouth; and the Lord said unto me, Behold I have put my words into thy mouth...
>
> (Jer. 1:7-9)

> And behold, the bush burned with fire, and the bush was not consumed...and God called to him out of the midst of the bush, and said, Moses, Moses...And Moses said unto the Lord, O Lord, I am not eloquent, neither heretofore, nor since thou hast spoken unto thy servant...And the Lord said, Who hath made man's mouth? or who maketh a man dumb, or deaf, or seeing, or blind? is it not I the Lord? Now therefore go, and I will be with thy mouth, and teach thee what thou shalt say.
>
> (Exod. 3:2, 4; 4:10-12)

> Then flew one of the seraphim unto me, having a live coal in his hand, which he had taken with the tongs from off the altar: and he touched my mouth with it...Then I said, Here am I: send me.
>
> (Isa. 6:6-8)

The Hebrew prophets, overwhelmed by a divine visitation which allowed no question and no rational consideration on their side, went on to utter messages to their people in poetry generally judged sublime in their own and later generations (even when known only in translation). They may very well have exhibited symptoms of insanity, in ordinary terms, as many poets have done in later ages, from the Roman Lucretius to the English Christopher Smart.

In the Greco-Roman world, this kind of naked encounter with divinity was the unenvied lot of prophets – more often, prophetesses – who were chosen as vehicles for a possessing spirit, not a Muse but a god in full annihilating power, Apollo or Dionysus or Pan. We have seen that in the earliest representations of the Muses the group of figures was not individualised at all; they were attendants of Apollo, one of whose titles was Musagetes, 'leader of the Muses'. The Homeric Hymn to Artemis speaks of the Dance of the Muses and Graces as taking place not on Mount Helicon but at Delphi. Apollo is, of course, the presiding god of music and poetry and oracular truth; but he is also the giver of pestilence and lunacy. So great is the charge of power with which he may descend upon men or women that the contact with him is felt like a blast of lightning. The most famous accounts of direct possession by Apollo are those of Aeschylus and Virgil: the frenzy of Cassandra in *Agamemnon*, when she struggles against the divine force and screams incoherently before uttering her prophecy of doom, and the description of the Sibyl of Cumae in *Aeneid* VI.

The visionary experience of Cassandra follows and develops that of Theoclymenus, the 'godlike', who speaks to the laughing suitors in Odysseus' hall of blood-dripping walls and 'the sun perished out of heaven' (*Od.* XX. 350-8). Cassandra is seen in agony, looking 'like a wild creature newly trapped', cut off from communication not (as the Chorus at first think) because she cannot speak Greek, but because the god's possession of her impels her to wail insanely in a 'song that is no song' (1137). The verses in which Cassandra sings of coming slaughter are dochmiacs, a metre which tends to produce rapid staccato effects, and an unusual metre for an actor (as distinct from a Chorus) in tragedy. When Aeschylus calls her song 'no song', he is not suggesting any technical defect in this poetry.[10] Cassandra's prophecy is uttered in stanzas (after her first unintelligible cries and the repeated name of Apollo) in which a pattern is sustained in the metre and diction while the imagery changes and the emotions of fear, grief, and revulsion shift and also deepen continually. What makes her song 'no song' is its lack of rationality; the tones are shrill (1151) and terrifying, piercing the hearers' hearts with an irresistible sense of their divine source:

You are one frenzied in mind, possessed by God

(1135)

Whence do you have this meaningless onrush of agony, brought by God?

(1149)

And what spirit of evil will, swooping down upon you, heavy from above, sets you to sing deathly laments of suffering?

(1174-5)

In the same way, Virgil's Sibyl is overwhelmed by the onset of Apollo's unmediated power. She speaks in oracular poetry, which is full of paradox and pungent phrases suggesting vast menace and a faint hope.

> Excisum Euboicae latus ingens rupis in antrum,
> quo lati ducunt aditus centum, ostia centum,
> unde ruunt totidem voces, responsa Sibyllae.
> ventum erat ad limen, cum virgo 'poscere fata
> tempus' ait; 'deus ecce deus!' cui talia fanti
> ante fores subito non vultus, non color unus.
> non comptae mansere comae; sed pectus anhelum,
> et rabie fera corda tument, maiorque videri
> nec mortale sonans, adflata est numine quando
> iam propiore dei. 'cessas in vota precesque,
> Tros' ait 'Aenea? cessas? neque enim ante dehiscent
> attonitae magna ora domus.' et talia fata
> conticuit. gelidus Teucris per dura cucurrit
> ossa tremor, funditque preces rex pectore ab imo:
> Phoebe, gravis Troiae semper miserate labores,...
>
> At Phoebi nondum patiens immanis in antro
> bacchatur vates, magnum si pectore possit
> excussisse deum; tanto magis ille fatigat
> os rabidum, fera corda domans, fingitque premendo.
> ostia iamque domus patuere ingentia centum
> sponte sua vatisque ferunt responsa per auras:
> 'o tandem magnis pelagi defuncte periclis
> (sed terrae graviora manent),...
>
> Talibus ex adyto dictis Cumaea Sibylla
> horrendas canit ambages antroque remugit,
> obscuris vera involvens: ea frena furenti
> concutit et stimulos sub pectore vertit Apollo.
> ut primum cessit furor et rabida ora quierunt,
> incipit Aeneas heros:...

A spacious cave, within its farmost part,
Was hew'd and fashion'd by laborious art
Thro' the hill's hollow sides: before the place,
A hundred doors a hundred entries grace;
As many voices issue, and the sound
Of Sibyl's words as many times rebound.
Now to the mouth they come. Aloud she cries:
'This is the time; enquire your destinies.
He comes; behold the god!' Thus while she said,
(And shiv'ring at the sacred entry stay'd,)
Her color chang'd; her face was not the same,
And hollow groans from her deep spirit came.
Her hair stood up; convulsive rage possess'd
Her trembling limbs, and heav'd her lab'ring breast.
Greater than humankind she seem'd to look,
And with an accent more than mortal spoke.
Her staring eyes with sparkling fury roll;
When all the god came rushing on her soul.
Swiftly she turn'd, and, foaming as she spoke:
'Why this delay?' she cried – 'the pow'rs invoke!
Thy pray'rs alone can open this abode;
Else vain are my demands, and dumb the god.'
She said no more. The trembling Trojans hear,
O'erspread with a damp sweat and holy fear.
The prince himself, with awful dread possess'd,
His vows to great Apollo thus address'd:
'Indulgent god, propitious pow'r to Troy,...'

Struggling in vain, impatient of her load,
And lab'ring underneath the pond'rous god,
The more she strove to shake him from her breast
With more and far superior force he press'd;
Commands his entrance, and, without control,
Usurps her organs and inspires her soul.
Now, with a furious blast, the hundred doors
Ope of themselves; a rushing whirlwind roars
Within the cave, and Sibyl's voice restores:
'Escap'd the dangers of the wat'ry reign,
Yet more and greater ills by land remain....'

Thus, from the dark recess, the Sibyl spoke,
And the resisting air the thunder broke;
The cave rebellow'd, and the temple shook.
Th'ambiguous god, who rul'd her lab'ring breast,
In these mysterious words his mind express'd;
Some truths reveal'd, in terms involv'd the rest.

> At length her fury fell, her foaming ceas'd,
> And, ebbing in her soul, the god decreas'd.
> Then, thus the chief...

In spite of the expansion and occasional decoration which Dryden allows himself when the Latin is over-terse or plain, to a late seventeenth-century taste, his version of this passage may well suggest the numinous and majestic beauty of the original more richly than any modern translator has been able to do. Virgil does not call his Apollo either 'pond'rous' or 'ambiguous', but the sense of these adjectives is there in the picture of the powerful rider breaking in a foaming horse and then uttering riddles through the lips of the possessed Sibyl. Dryden makes the limited pattern of the couplet a strong underpinning for the wild movements and surges of feeling in the struggle between Apollo and his mouthpiece:

> Her staring eyes with sparkling fury roll;
> When all the god came rushing on her soul.

Like Cassandra, the Sibyl speaks of blood and conflict as immediately visible to her, vivid but unexplained. The experience of direct contact with Apollo does not lead to her death, as it did for Cassandra, but it does give her the power to guide Aeneas into the world of the dead, where she remains a sombre figure, who has been instructed by Hecate and can strike awe into the immortal Charon as well as the restless spirits of men such as Palinurus. The authenticity of the poetic utterance that comes from Apollo in this way is absolute, as is the agony of the direct encounter with the divine source of the poet-artist's inspiration. No one would seek this for himself and (however it may hold the attention) no one would hear such song with pleasure.

The experience of Cassandra, and the Sibyl, (or, for that matter, of Lucretius), was clearly incommensurate with the happy sense of divine favour and the easy flow of poetic expression which Hesiod, or Ovid, believed to be the results of encountering the Muses. A Muse-encounter must be preferable; yet accounts like those of Aeschylus and Virgil were written with so much power, and in works so central to the educational tradition of ancient times, that it is not surprising to find Latin poets in the Imperial centuries asserting their own madness (bestowed by Apollo) with an air of pleasure, as a guarantee of poetic talent. The habit of claiming divine aggressiveness directed against the poet himself was thoroughly traditional. Virgil himself had claimed (in the passage from the *Georgics*, already quoted on pages 109-10, where he prays for understanding of all earth sciences, the 'mysteries of the universe') to be *ingenti percussus amore*, 'smitten with a huge passion' for the Muses whose adoring servant he was. Claudian, in the fifth century AD,

introduces his thoroughly rational account of the rape of Proserpina with an
account of still wilder possession:

> gressus removete profani.
> iam furor humanos nostro de pectore sensus
> expulit et totum spirant praecordia Phoebum;
> iam mihi cernuntur trepidis delubra moveri
> sedibus...

> Leave me alone, unless you understand these things. The divine
> madness has expelled all human thoughts from my breast: I am filled
> with the breath of Phoebus who has become my spirit and now I can
> see the holy place swaying...

> *(de raptu Proserpinae*, I. 4-8, tr. Isbell)

In later ages of strongly classical literary tradition, the idea of such
inspired lunacy became a commonplace. So Dryden remarked of an earlier
poet whom he admired (it was Marlowe):

> For that fine madness still he did retain
> Which rightly should possess a poet's brain.

> (*To Henry Reynolds, Of Poets and Poetry*)

There is no sense of disquiet in Dryden's account of this poetic frenzy, which
suggests none of the intensity and dread of which he was aware when he
translated Virgil. The difference between the searing encounter with naked
divinity, when Apollo seized the consciousness and the poet was left 'mouth,
no more',[11] and the docile attendance on the Muse who would lead, inspire,
delight her follower so that he could sing with conscious proficiency – this
difference, it seems, had become lost to Dryden's regard. Restoration literature could admit the dramatist 'Mad Nat Lee' as providing glorious
ravings for the stage, and such forms of madness continued, in the eighteenth
century, to be licensed as fitting for the inspired poet; but now there was no
sense of terror in this madness. The absence of any real threat to sanity in
the procedures of eighteenth-century poetry was precisely a reason for
Blake's revolt against those roving Muses who had left poetry so languid and
forced. The Muses of his lifetime were not, it seemed, even able to mediate
between Apollo and the human disciple; the life-giving contact was lost, and
the poet must often push aside the Muse-figures entirely and turn to the
divine source of the creative power itself. This had always been seen as a
masculine power, quickening or destroying, not nurturing: Zeus, in so far as
he was father of the Muses; Apollo, still more alarming; Dionysus; perhaps
most terrifying of all, the animal divinity of Pan – to meet any of these gods
face to face might be more than a human being could endure; it might mean

madness, perhaps death. Rilke's 'Angels' brought him to this pitch of terror, which makes the starting-point of his *Duino Elegies*:

> Wer, wenn ich schriee, hörte mich denn aus der Engel
> Ordnungen? und gesetzt selbst, es nähme
> einer mich plötzlich ans Herz: ich verginge von seinem
> stärkeren Dasein...
> Ein jeder Engel ist schrecklich.

> Who, if I cried out, would hear me among the angels'
> hierarchies? and even if one of them pressed me
> suddenly against his heart: I would be consumed
> in that overwhelming existence...
> Every angel is terrifying.[12]

Even at that cost, Blake proclaimed, the artist must follow his Genius ('which by the Ancients was call'd an Angel and Spirit and Demon'[13] and must disregard the Muses until such time as 'the Daughters of Memory shall become the Daughters of Inspiration'.[14] His fervour in this choice is like Milton's, when he rejected the classic Nine and called on the Holy Spirit, God Himself, to inspire the awesome work of recounting 'man's first disobedience...and all our woe'. Although Milton calls on the 'Heavenly Muse' at the opening of *Paradise Lost* I, and on 'Urania' at the beginning of Book VII, this eternal voice is carefully distinguished from the classic Muse who could not even protect Orpheus her son when he was attacked by the Maenads of Thrace. Milton's Muse was pre-existent and is ever-present; she may or may not be called Urania:

> The meaning, not the Name I call...
> For thou art Heav'nlie, shee (the Muse) an empty dream
>
> (*Paradise Lost,* VII. 5, 39)

Milton believed, as Blake did, that true inspiration must come from God, with pain, as it came to Isaiah; and only so, he insisted, could he create

> something so written to after-times, as they will not willingly let die...nor to be obtained from the invocation of dame memory and her siren daughters; but by devout prayer to that eternal Spirit, who can enrich with all utterance and knowledge, and sends out his seraphim with the hallowed fire of his altar to touch and purify the lips of whom he pleases.
>
> (*Reason of Church Government,* 1641)

For the sake of such enriching knowledge, Milton was willing to be consumed by the divine fire. He was not 'deliberately devising' his poem to act as a kind of lightning-conductor, as Thomas Bodkin suggested a painter might devise a picture 'to divert the shock of overwhelming perception'.[15] Without the archetypal Anima-figure of the mediating Muse, Milton knew he might well be destroyed by the divine energy, as he knew Orpheus himself had been destroyed when he met 'the rout that made the hideous roar'. As long as Orpheus was protected by the Muse, his mother, and guided by Eurydice, his wife, his inspiration was not destructive to him: his song could bring healing and spiritual enlightenment as well as pleasure to all; creativity shaped and developed the poet's intellectual powers so that he could assume the role of social and spiritual leader. Yet this might not be enough, as Milton realised when he called on Urania, to make him a pure channel for the unthought poetic truth that he was willing to receive directly from God. Some consequences of this brave request can be seen in Milton's latest work, especially in the more flexible verse and bold paradoxes of *Samson Agonistes*.

When Gerard Manley Hopkins endured a period of painful aridity, he prayed to God, as William Blake did through his twenty dark years.[16] This was the God 'mastering me', the 'Lord of life', the Holy Ghost, or (when he chose to write in more classical terms) 'Sweet fire the sire of Muse', from whom he sought 'the one rapture of an inspiration'. Hopkins, like Milton, chose to submit himself to the terror of the unmediated divine energy rather than look for a lost Anima-figure who might take the protecting role of Muse.

In the Orpheus myth – whatever its variant episodes at different periods and in different places – the poet's power to order the world of nature, to communicate with creatures of all kinds, and to open the ears of men to the Music of the Spheres, depends primarily on his relationship with the sustaining Muse. Orpheus' loss of Eurydice means that he also loses this power. This is not because Eurydice *is* the Muse, although some late versions begin to treat her as if she were: it is because Orpheus becomes so preoccupied with the search for the lost Eurydice (his Anima-counterpart rather than his sustaining mother) that he can no longer interpret nature and unite the world with the everlasting cosmic order. His songs, after Eurydice's death, are described as endless laments and love-poems of intense but always personal beauty. The journey to Hades in pursuit of Eurydice cannot leave him unchanged. He becomes solitary, strange and alarming to his fellow- men, and is no longer 'the man whom the Muses love', as Hesiod called him. For this new poet-figure,[17] the recovery of Adam's gift, the knowing of true names and the awareness of divine energy in the world, is an experience of anguished struggle and terror.

What is a poet? He is a man who experiences unusual mental states which may sometimes make him appear eccentric or frenzied, as if he is losing touch with what is ordinarily called sanity. His work is often composed in the course of such experiences, or immediately after them, and may not be comprehensible even to himself. Poetry that originates in states which appear to resemble ecstatic possession often seems to carry a kind of authenticity which makes it both illuminating and disturbing. Yet those artists who illuminate and disturb most profoundly are often destroyed by the divine creative energy.

This destructive poetic force represents a kind of inspiration distinct from the traditionally Orphean, which allied music and poetry with healing and teaching functions, allowing Orpheus to assume an enlightening role as social and spiritual leader. Any attempt to reconcile these conflicting images of creativity by dependence on the gentler Muse-archetype may be seen as evasive, leading only to false or superficial artistic expression. The true poet must be willing to step into insanity, or – in Lawrence's terms – stand naked before the fire of Almighty God.

IX

Poets' Sinews

THE anguish and terror of Orpheus' encounter with divine powers led, in all versions of the myth, to death in a particularly agonising form. The story of his dismemberment at the hands of a group of frenzied women is known from sources much earlier than those which include the loss of Eurydice, or any association of music-making with pain. Suffering, for the poet-musician, seems at first to have come only with death, after a life of joyful inspiration.

When Theseus in *A Midsummer Night's Dream* reads the list of possible entertainments for his wedding party, he rejects 'the riot of the tipsy Bacchanals/Tearing the Thracian singer in their rage' as an 'old device' (along with 'the battle with the Centaurs' and 'the thrice-three Muses mourning for the death/Of Learning'). The story will have been familiar to Shakespeare and his audience from the version in Ovid's *Metamorphoses*, (source also for the 'fine tragedy' of Pyramus and Thisbe, chosen by Theseus), which tells the story of Orpheus' death at some length. The women are described as frenzied creatures dressed in animal skins, who suddenly appear on the crest of a hill and attack Orpheus while he is singing to the woodlands, rocks, birds, and wild beasts. There is no provocation from Orpheus, but one of the women cries *en hic est nostri contemptor*, 'Look, here is the man who despises us!' (*Met.* XI. 7). At first, weapons and stones thrown at Orpheus fail to strike him, because they respond to his song and so fall harmlessly; but as the cries of the women and the wild sound of Phrygian flutes and tambourines drown his music, he is overpowered and finally torn to pieces, together with the birds and animals who were listening motionless to his last notes.

Ovid's Thracian women do not say how Orpheus has shown his scorn for them, or why. Their 'Bacchic howls' and their style of dress might suggest that he has offended against their worship of Dionysus; indeed, this is the most frequently suggested explanation for the attack. The only alternative explanation, found in the work of some later, less well-known writers such as Phanocles, was that the women resented Orpheus' preference for homosexual love after the death of Eurydice.[1] The tale mentioned by Pausanias (IX. 30), suggesting that the women resented Orpheus' taking away their husbands, reduces this motive to personal jealousy. Ovid records Orpheus' homoerotism, but not in the context of the Maenads' attack.

At the moment when the first weapon is thrown, Ovid calls Orpheus 'prophet of Apollo' (*vates Apollineus*, XI. 8). Other versions of the death-story often emphasise the antagonism between Apollo and Dionysus, and even make Dionysus directly responsible for impelling the Bacchants to destroy Orpheus.[2] Ovid, however, ends the episode in a somewhat surprising way: Bacchus (here called Lyaeus, 'the Liberator') regards the killing of Orpheus as a crime which he will avenge, and causes the Thracian women to be metamorphosed as trees; rooted to the spot where each had been pursuing Orpheus, they become gnarled and immovable oaks. Meanwhile, Bacchus departs from Thrace for Lydia, where he calls upon the mountain Tmolus and his swaying forests to judge between the merits of Pan's country piping and the majestic lyre-playing of Apollo.

To see the traditionally grave and pacific Orpheus as priest of Apollo might seem to be more appropriate than casting him in the role of Bacchic celebrant. Yet in ancient times the 'mysteries' which Orpheus is said to have founded seem to have been Dionysian as often as strictly Orphic.[3] The names of Orpheus and Bacchus are linked in legend – as well as in ritual – by the author of the tragedy *Rhesus*, for example, where the dead son of the Muse is described as Orpheus' friend and also as prophet of Bacchus (*Rhes*. 966, 972). Some aspects of Dionysus would link Orpheus to him much more intimately than he was linked to Apollo: the origin of Dionysus' religion was usually said to be in Thrace (though Euripides places it in Phrygia); he was a god of woodland and of animal life, for whom panthers would draw a chariot, and a ship's mast put forth vine leaves; his poetry was dithyramb and drama, performed by groups in active participation; the incomparable choruses of Euripides' *Bacchae* call up a riot of music and dance, 'the whole land shall dance', in the worship on the mountains – so far, the Dionysian inspiration seems close to the Orphean. The difference, indeed total divergence, comes with the frenzied eating of raw flesh, torn from live animals by the Bacchic worshippers. The action of Euripides' play leads inexorably to the killing and dismembering of Pentheus, scorner of Dionysus, the human victim whom the Bacchants in their ecstasy see as a mountain lion.

Dismemberment of victims in the worship of Dionysus was not practised at Athens, but this scene in the *Bacchae* cannot be seen simply as an imaginative climax for Euripides' drama. Vase-paintings of Dionysus and the dancing Maenads are numerous, some of them dating from as early as the sixth century BC, and the death of Pentheus was frequently depicted on vases dating earlier than Euripides.[4] This was the invariable ending of the Theban story. But the *sparagmos* (tearing to pieces) practised by Dionysus' worshippers was not merely legendary. Its practice is attested in cult regulations which survive from 276 BC at Miletus, and in Plutarch's account of Themistocles' sacrifice of three Persian youths to Dionysus *Omestes* ('raw flesh-eater').[5] In Dionysiac ritual the victim was usually a bull, often seen as an epiphany of Dionysus himself. The famous hymn of the women of Elis, quoted by Plutarch,[6] identifies the bull with Dionysus, and speaks of animal and god in words of cherishing love. But according to Pausanias and others,[7] the rending of Dionysus himself was an accepted part of his myth, and had been ascribed to the evil deeds of the Titans in the pre-Olympian age. References to the killing of the infant Dionysus by Titans are numerous in Orphic literature,[8] although these seem to be imaginative elaborations of philosophic intention, and of much later date. But the tearing of the god was ancient, the eating of the bull's raw flesh being a symbol of participation in the life of the god himself, giver of 'all that is moist in nature', as Plutarch says: 'that is, not only wine, but the life-blood of animals, the male semen which fertilises the female, the juicy sap of plants'.[9]

By this act of union with the god, the worshipper became *entheos*, filled with divinity, and (at any rate among the Thracians)[10] could attain immortality. It can hardly be supposed that the Dionysian *teletae*, whose introduction into Greece was so often associated with Orpheus, were totally different in aim and practice from these older cultic celebrations which included ecstatic dancing and *sparagmos*. Dionysus, the dismembered god, was associated with others who suffered similarly, such as the Cretan Zagreus, and Linus the supposed 'flax-spirit' who was sometimes conflated with the brother, or teacher, of Orpheus.[11] The link between Orphic and Dionysiac mysteries consisted in this commemoration of earlier *sparagmos*-rites as well as in the pursuit of ecstatic devotion; this is made clear when Proclus describes Orpheus as 'principal in the Dionysiac rites', who therefore suffered the same fate, dismemberment, as that suffered by the god himself.[12]

Nevertheless, it is hostility to Dionysus which, in Euripides' *Bacchae*, brings Pentheus to share in this form of death. The *sparagmos* which is climax to the play shows not the god, or an animal substitute, as victim, but a deluded human who wants to oppose Dionysus, one who has been involuntarily drawn into the victim-role by a horrifying kind of possession. Dodds pointed out that this narrative structure had appeared before Euripides, in a number of variants: the stories of Lycurgus, Boutes, and the daughters of Minyas are only three examples of narratives which relate how madness and violent death came upon those who tried to resist the authority of the invasive god. Death by *sparagmos* was then accepted as a foreseeable end for creatures representing Dionysus – and also for those humans who resisted him.

That Orpheus should be torn in pieces in this way, therefore, indicates nothing of his real relation to Dionysus, except a significant closeness, of fellowship or antagonism. The fragments that remain from Aeschylus' play the *Bassarids* introduce Orpheus as victim of *sparagmos*, destroyed because he rejected the religion of Dionysus in favour of Apollo. The Bacchants' attack takes place at dawn, while Orpheus is making his daily climb up the slopes of Mount Pangaeus to worship Helios-Apollo. The *Bassarids* was the second play of a trilogy whose main theme was the destruction of Lycurgus, for similar reasons. The fragments are brief, but include lines of great intensity describing the Dionysian ecstasy which leads to Orpheus' dismemberment.

Even though all accounts of Orpheus' poetic voice and of the response it drew from all hearers suggest the happiness of a serene and ordered beauty, a kind that might seem Apollonian rather than Dionysiac, the story of his death subjects him completely to the orgiastic music of the 'Thracian god'. Euripides' *Bacchae*, in the one passage that refers to Orpheus, suggests the ambiguity of his poetic gift and his communication with the natural world, by bringing Dionysus to what were *perhaps* the 'thick-wooded coverts of Olympus, where Orpheus once played on the lyre and gathered trees and beasts by his music'. Is Dionysus approaching near to Orpheus' haunts, or not? At this point in the play, Dionysus is invoked as a kindly and cherishing power (556), leading his followers over the mountains as Orpheus led trees and animals. The Chorus sings of Dionysus as *perhaps* on Nysa (the place of Lycurgus' resistance to him), *perhaps* on Parnassus (ruled by Apollo), *perhaps* on Olympus, but soon to come to Pieria, home of the Muses. At the end of this choric epode, the voice of Dionysus himself is heard calling triumphantly from Pentheus' palace, where the god has shaken the building apart in an earth tremor. Fire blazes up on his mother's tomb, and Pentheus the king – her nephew – rushes out, enraged and demented, soon to fall victim to the frenzied women who will tear him to pieces in hallucination. The Chorus' references to Nysa and Olympus, and to Orpheus as leader of trees and beasts, have served to blur these separate sceptic-victims of Dionysus into one identity, and to merge all of them with the figure of the god himself.

At the end of the *Bassarids,* according to Eratosthenes,[13] the fragments of Orpheus' body were reassembled (a pattern followed by Euripides in his *Hippolytus*, where the so-called Orphic, the ascetic prince, has similarly been dismembered as a result of his pride). The Muses are said to have lamented over Orpheus' body, and buried it at Leibethra. A reconciliation between Dionysus and Apollo has been conjectured[14] as a possible ending of the trilogy, as Athena and the Eumenides were reconciled at the end of the *Oresteia*.

Whether the Greek dramatist showed this symbolic reconciliation or not, Renaissance thinkers were not willing to leave uncertainties. Pico della Mirandola believed that Apollo and Dionysus could not remain totally apart. He asserted[15] that those who have been inspired by Apollo must undergo dismemberment before they can communicate to men in general the profound truths revealed to them during ecstasy. If Pico's intuition led him aright, the *sparagmos* would not indicate whether the fragmented human had been a follower or an enemy of Dionysus, but it would show whether his poetic gift was a genuine one, sanctioned by Apollo. According to this view, Orpheus' continuing power of song after death – in the oracle that spoke through his head at Lesbos – was surely a gift of Apollo, but also the fruit of his death-agony at the hands of Dionysus' worshippers.

The only alternative form of death in any Orpheus-story survives in Pausanias (IX. 30). This relates that Orpheus was killed by a thunderbolt because he had revealed divine secrets to men. This seems to be a literary invention of later date.[16] Even so, it retains an important aspect of the older story's structure: the exposure of the musician (who made his song a universal beneficent gift) to unmediated divine energy that would destroy even as it created.

Ovid relates that after the Bacchants' frenzy had silenced and dismembered Orpheus, the Muses mourned over his body, though they could not recover the head. This was carried by the waves of the sea to Lesbos, which thus became the home of lyric poetry and of a much venerated oracle. In succeeding centuries, the Lesbian lyricists' usual channel of inspiration was the Muse Erato (or Euterpe), but for the prophetic head no Muse was needed, or able, to assist; her inspiration was now lost to Orpheus for ever.

The helplessness of the Muses was a common theme for later poets who described Orpheus' agony. When Milton introduces Orpheus into his *Lycidas*, it is to compare the nymphs of the Irish Sea (who did not save Edward King) with the impotence of Calliope herself:

> Had ye been there: for what could that have done?
> What could the Muse herself that Orpheus bore,
> The Muse herself, for her inchanting Son
> Whom Universal Nature did lament,
> When by the rout that made the hideous roar,
> His goary visage down the stream was sent,
> Down the swift Hebrus to the Lesbian Shore?

> (*Lycidas*, 57-63)

This impotence is again recalled in *Paradise Lost*, when Milton insists that he needs a truly heavenly Muse, his 'Urania', who is not the astronomical Urania of the classic Nine but a truly divine power, the voice of the Holy

Spirit. This true Muse will not, Milton says, be an 'empty Dreame', like Calliope who could not defend her son. Urania is confidently invoked, to

> drive far off the barbarous dissonance
> Of Bacchus and his revellers, the Race
> Of that Wilde Rout that tore the Thracian Bard
> In Rhodope, where Woods and Rocks had Eares
> To rapture, till the savage clamor drownd
> Both Harp and Voice...

(Paradise Lost VII. 32-7)

It would seem that Milton derives this *topos* from the plaintive elegiacs of Antipater of Sidon, written in the second century BC:

> No more, Orpheus, shall you lead charmed oaks,
> no more rocks, or herds of beasts ranging at will.
> No more shall you lull the roar of winds, nor
> hail, nor the drifting snow, nor clashing sea.
> For you have perished. And you the daughters of
> Memory mourned, and your mother above all, Calliope.
> Why do we lament for mortal sons, since even
> gods have no power to hold off death from their children?

(Anth. Pal. VII. 8)

The Muses could not prevent Orpheus' death, and they could not silence the 'barbarous dissonance' of the Bacchants. Nor could they retain any relationship with Orpheus' head, inspired as it was to utter prophetic poetry that was not of their giving. The inspiration which Orpheus received in this mutilated, immortalised form was (like that attributed to mantic heads in Celtic tradition) unmediated and always full of pain.

The Roman poets make Orpheus' head sing endless laments for Eurydice on its journey to Lesbos, but they have nothing to say of its oracular powers.[17] In later Greek writers, however, the poetic pronouncements of the head are of much wider range. Some, like the well-known story in Philostratus,[18] offer the rather cruel witticisms traditional in oracular replies to the powerful: Cyrus the Great was told 'my fate, Cyrus, you (will also meet)' – meaning not, as Cyrus supposed, glory throughout the Greek world, but decapitation by the Queen of the Massagetae. Other tales suggest more of the old Orphean music. The head was said to inspire young poets by direct teaching or even dictation, as is frequently shown on vases, when a young man listens intently as he writes, in the attitude of Blake as 'secretary...the Authors are in eternity'. Poetry which came to the ears of the young amanuensis in this way had the oracular characteristics of obscurity and intensity, bringing to all who listened its own assurance of an authentically divine source. The unquestioned renown of the oracle made Orpheus' head a fitting symbol (for Renaissance writers such as Boccaccio,[19] as well as those of ancient times) for the true poet's undying fame.

Philostratus relates[20] that the authority of the oracle at Lesbos became so great that the Apolline oracles of Delphi and Claros were almost abandoned. Finally, Apollo became jealous of its influence and commanded it to be silent. Neither Dionysus nor the Muses was said to have intervened. There seems to be no other version of how the prophecies ceased.

The final fate of the lyre, according to a story included in the *Catasterismoi* attributed to Eratosthenes, was to ascend into the heavens as a constellation known as the 'Lyre of Orpheus'. Some said that this was identical with the Pleiades, whose seven stars conveniently corresponded with the seven strings of the lyre. This story would seem to be no older than the second century BC at the earliest, and relates rather to the strength of astrological beliefs already seen in Orphic iconography than to any element in true Orphean myth.

When Phanocles, in the third century BC, elaborated the theme of Orpheus' homosexual loves, he went on to tell what happened to the head, in terms that are romanticised rather than oracular:

> they cut off his head with their bronze swords, and fastening it to his lyre with a nail they threw it at once into the Thracian sea... and the head and lyre together were washed to the blue-green shore. And the sea put the head and lyre, still together, ashore at the sacred city of Lesbos. The sound of the clear-toned lyre reached both to the sea and the islands, and to the shore where the rivers flow into the sea, and there on the shore men buried the clear-toned head of Orpheus, and put into the tomb the clear-toned lyre as well, which had prevailed over both the dead rocks and the bitter waters of Phorcus. After this, the island had both songs and the lovely art of harping, and of all islands it is the most tuneful.

> (*Collectanea*, p. 107, 23-8)

The nailing of the head to the lyre may be an invention of Phanocles, but the suggestion that they must stay together if music is to be made in the future carries conviction, as inherent in other versions of what happened in Lesbos. Lucian relates[21] that the lyre was dedicated to Apollo, and the head buried 'where the Baccheion now stands'; so all ended in reconciliation, allowing the oracle to deliver its verses. Although Orpheus could no longer perform on the lyre, the instrument had to be there, or the head could not prophesy;

and no one else could prophesy either, even using the lyre, as a story in Lucian illustrates. He describes how the head floated to Lesbos with the lyre, singing a *threnos* for Orpheus (not for Eurydice), and was finally buried, and the lyre hung in Apollo's temple. The son of the tyrant Pittacus, Lucian continues, heard how the lyre had charmed animals and plants and stones, so he bribed Apollo's priest to bring it to him and put another in its place. Thinking it might be unsafe to play this instrument in the city by day, he went to the suburbs at night with the lyre under his cloak, and then jangled the strings, imagining he would be able to enchant everyone and even become immortal. But dogs gathered around and tore him to pieces – his one point of resemblance to Orpheus, as it proved. Obviously, it was not the lyre that had the power to charm, but the skill and the voice of Orpheus, 'the only distinctive gifts that he had from his mother, while the lyre was just a piece of property' (*On the Ignorant Book-Collector*, II).

This story may possibly have been in the mind of Jean Cocteau when he showed his Orphée (not yet dismembered, but deeply disturbed by the death of the young poet Cégeste who is a kind of *alter ego* for him) receiving scraps of poetry through a car radio which no other human character can hear. These fragments are incomprehensible to Orphée and to the audience. (Sometimes they are lines from Apollinaire, such as the enigmatic 'l'oiseau chante avec ses doigts': 'the bird sings with its fingers'.)

Cocteau devised many variations on this theme, from *Le Sang d'un Poète* in 1931 to *Le Testament d'Orphée* in 1960. In all of them the death of Orphée is the end to which all action and experience moves; it is more than dramatic climax, it represents the moment of release for a creative force. Death appears (in the version most widely known, the film of 1949) as a Princess of erotic power, who allures Orphée and is only unwillingly compelled by still greater authorities to let him go, after his entry into the world of the dead. Orphée has been assailed by hysterical women (as Cégeste also was crushed to death in a crowd) and this experience, as well as the death of his Eurydice, is as necessary to his poetry as the strange alarming voice that he hears when he is alone and switches on the radio in his car. This pattern is not uniform in all the Cocteau versions: in *Le Testament*, the poet is not killed by frenzied women but by Minerva. Nevertheless, death and disintegration remain his ineluctable lot, without which his poetry cannot come into being.

Post-Cocteau, the Orphean narrator of Hoban's *The Medusa Frequency* receives messages in the form of letters on a computer screen. These may be poems, or sentences in a dialogue, or sometimes letters like NNVSNU TSRUNGH, which give the modern Orpheus an awareness of 'the numinosities and nexialities that were the frail but constant web of the universe', a shimmering order realised through a comic-strip story on the back of cereal packets. The computer messages and the foreign songs heard on his short-wave radio at night are not in themselves powerful enough to release Herman

Orff's poetic voice. A junk-mail offer from Hermes Soundways prompts him to undergo the charges from thirty-six electrodes harnessed to his head; the terror and the spectacular beauty of the book begins from this point, and Herman Orff does indeed 'get to those places in your head that you can't get to on your own'. Until he finds the head of Orpheus, slimy in the Thames-side mud, he is dumb and stagnant in a futile eight-year struggle to begin a third novel, after two that were failures. The complicated adventures which follow this encounter bring him eventually into hospital, after an attack of angina; there, at three o'clock one morning, he looks out from a balcony and the figure of Orpheus comes into his mind, imagined as athlete, running along a dark road of Fulham or Thrace, 'the dim white of the road that runs behind the eyes to otherwhere...I'd never thought of the body before, only the head'.[22]

Russell Hoban's earlier novel, *Kleinzeit*, also follows a frustrated writer, this time of commercial scripts, through a series of experiences which take place at shifting levels of realism. Kleinzeit travels about London, and about his mind, conversing with doctors, with passers-by, with God and Thucydides and the small black figure of Death. Images of hospital and of the London Underground appear, as in *The Medusa Frequency*, and Kleinzeit has to listen to the story of Orpheus' head, although he never sees it. The function served by Cocteau's car radio and by Orff's computer screen is here fulfilled by sheets of yellow paper which appear in unpredictable places and demand (sometimes verbally) that those who find them shall write on them. For some, the imperious sheets of paper are not yellow but ruled foolscap, or Rizla cigarette papers; for each, the kind of paper that comes is 'universal'. Writing on this paper, Kleinzeit discovers, is an act requiring heroic courage, a quick and confident courage like the restless daring of Thucydides' Athenians:

> 'In a word' [Kleinzeit reads] 'they are by nature incapable of either living a quiet life themselves or allowing anyone else to do so.'
> Right, said Kleinzeit. Enough. He opened the door of the yellow paper's cage, and it sprang upon him. Over and over they rolled together, bloody and roaring. Doesn't matter what the title is to start with, he said, anything will do. HERO, I'll call it. Chapter I. He wrote the first line while the yellow paper clawed his guts, the pain was blinding. It'll kill me, said Kleinzeit, there's no surviving this. He wrote the second line, the third, completed the first paragraph. The roaring and the blood stopped, the yellow paper rubbed purring against his leg, the first paragraph danced and sang, leaped and played on the green grass in the dawn.

This apparent success in subjugating the artistic medium takes place about half-way through the novel, and Kleinzeit is only half-way to discovering his true relation to the creative power which Hoban calls 'Word'. As the yellow paper weeps in longing for the return of its human lover, Word itself descends in 'enormity' and 'awful tremendousness', shooting its seed on to the paper in a cosmic flash, faster than light. Kleinzeit had 'wanted to do it all at once', with his act of Athenian heroism, but

> Nobody does it all himself, said Word. Nobody does it unless I have shot my seed as well...,
> From time to time, as I said, I see to it that one wiggles through. Kleinzeit? said the yellow paper.
> I don't know what his name is, said Word, and I don't care. Whoever it is that writes on you, let him get on with it...
> The machine, whether typewriter or Japanese pen, is from the god. Where else could it be from.

The acceptance of Word's supremacy, and the abandonment of all heroic claims, is the final demand made upon Kleinzeit before Death's black shape is willing to let him alone, to find what is on the yellow paper and let it be, a fat black circle of Japanese calligraphy. This sweep of perfect form is explicitly related to Milton's lines calling for

> soft Lydian aires
> Married to immortal verse
> Such as the meeting soul may pierce...
> Untwisting all the chains that ty
> The hidden soul of harmony.
> That Orpheus self may heave his head
> From golden slumber...

('L'Allegro', 135-146)

In this passage Milton evokes Orpheus as a listening, not a performing figure. The music that unchains the hidden soul of harmony is a pre-existent cosmic reality, like the calligraphic circle, or the planetary relations that produced the Music of the Spheres; because Orpheus, Orphée, Orff, is able to hear this music, he may also be able to transpose what he has heard into new keys, new poetic forms, even new advertising slogans.

One of the positive values asserted in modern recastings of classic myth is the overriding of hierarchic cultural boundaries, so that Harrison's satyrs can perform a clog-dance and Cocteau's underworld be reached through mirrors that wrinkle and melt in trick photography. This is not merely 'Shakespeare in modern dress'. The author (or composer – the same kind of new patterning is found in Birtwistle's recent opera, *The Mask of Orpheus*)[23] is identifying Word at work in cultural currencies of the modern world which artistic tradition might seem unable, or unwilling, to recognise. The versions of the Orpheus story which have shown this authentic, creative power in the

use of modern media or imagery have invariably paid particular attention to
the agony of Orpheus' dismemberment, as an essential part of the myth.
Indeed, this could almost be taken as a distinguishing mark to set them apart
from such etiolated Orpheus-versions as those of William Morris and Jean
Anouilh.[24]

The need for head and lyre to remain together if music is to arise from
the poet-musician's agony is beautifully expressed in Rilke's sonnet 'Wie
ergreift uns' (*Son. an O.*, II. 26). Here Rilke's attention is caught by a bird's
cry and then by the more intense crying of children, which, he says, sends us
chasing 'like kites broken loose', unable to catch meaning or even the
laughter that fringes our awareness: only the 'singing god' can order our
perception so that crying children and birds may become a stream on which
head and lyre may move together:

> Ordne die Schreier,
> singender Gott! dass sne rauschend erwachen,
> tragend als Stromung das Haupt und die Leier.

> Arrange these criers,
> singing god! that they waken and thunder together,
> a current to carry the head and the lyre.

(tr. Young)

Lyre and head both remained unbroken by the onslaught of the Maenads, as
Rilke asserted in another sonnet (I. 26). This is why the 'building song'
continued to sound even through the destruction and frenzy of Orpheus'
death, and so the music passed into the natural world, where it lingers still,
as an 'everlasting trace' of the lost god. Only through this agony are we able
to listen to the faint remaining sound, and to become 'mouth' for nature:

> O du verlorener Gott! du unendliche Spur!
> Nur weil dich reissend zuletzt die Feindschaft
> Sind wir die Horenden jetzt und ein Mund der Natur verteilte

> O you lost god! You never-ending clue!
> Only since hatred at last parceled you
> among us, are we hearers and a mouth for nature.

(tr. MacIntyre)

When Shakespeare made his young Proteus declare that 'Orpheus' lute
was strung with poets' sinews',[25] he was arguing that the most exquisite and
poignant love poetry will be written by one who is himself suffering the pains
of unfulfilled passion. The story of the lyre's making by the killing of tortoise

and cattle is thus re-shaped to become much more human in emphasis: the poet's own anguish and mutilation (rather than the death of an animal) contribute to the making of the instrument.

The theory that personal suffering was a prerequisite for the composition of great poetry or music seemed to find confirmation in the lives and early deaths of many poets and artists of the Romantic era: Keats, Shelley, Byron, Chopin, de Musset, to name but a few. The preoccupation of the young Berlioz with the death of Orpheus was also entirely in keeping with this image of the doomed artist (his brilliantly 'unplayable' cantata *La mort d'Orphée* was written when he was twenty-three, as an entry for the 1827 Prix de Rome). This Romantic vocation of personal torment was not the same fate as the *furor poeticus* (eccentricity or insanity), though in some cases, such as Schumann and Hölderlin,[26] the 'divine madness' did come upon the gifted young victim. The Romantic figure is a long way from any ancient image of the artist (though Catullus and Propertius have sometimes been seen in this light). Yet among the Romantics of France and Germany in the early nineteenth century, Orpheus was exalted as an archetypal figure for the artist's consciousness; what made him so was the *sparagmos* on the banks of the Thracian Hebrus and the wailing of the severed head bound to the lyre.

What is a poet? He is one who must suffer disintegration before he can reveal beauty and truth. Without this personal dismemberment his work cannot attain the oracular authority of true poetry. The voice of the poet who has undergone death and dismemberment may indeed become oracular, uttering prophetic truths that are timeless and universal.

X

The Lost Bride

IN both his Orpheus novels, Russell Hoban's unheroic Orpheus-figure eventually overcomes his writer's block and commences writing, in an idiom which is both fantastic and mundane. The bizarre adventures are over, the reader must suppose. However, for Kleinzeit and Orff alike there remains a feminine presence, a lover who has been elusive throughout the story but is now found; moreover, once found she will never be lost. A wry kind of domestic stability asserts itself at the end of *Kleinzeit*, while on the last page of *The Medusa Frequency* reassurance is communicated to both Orff and the reader by the changed icon of the 'Vermeer girl' whom he has pursued since the beginning: looking at the print on his wall, or the postcard stuck on the edge of his computer screen, he sees her as Medusa, crowned with snakes, 'flickering and friendly, trusting me with the idea of her'.

Because Orff and Kleinzeit have both so clearly taken on the Orphean identity, the reader cannot fail to see these female figures in the two novels as realisations of Eurydice. In both books the relation won at the end suggests not only security, but also animation and excitement; each of these women is alive, and makes her lover more alive. But these are not simply new versions of the happy-ending Orphean story, so popular from the Middle Ages onwards (and indeed since the Hellenistic novel, though the story of Orpheus and Eurydice was not cast after this pattern at that time).

The structural features of the medieval *Sir Orfeo* are clear in many later stories, poems, and then romantic novels: bride snatched away by serpent's bite or equivalent evil force, but restored by devoted love, to share a life of happiness with husband who faced danger of death and often supernatural menace for her sake; the husband is traditionally a knight, though he may be a minstrel; he sometimes has magical powers. In more recent literature, his distinction may appear in settings ostensibly more everyday, as with John Ridd, the Somerset 'clodhopper' of great physical strength who wrested Lorna Doone from the robbers' glen and from the villain who shot her at the altar. The life shared by the lovers after the bride's rescue is usually uneventful, and the woman rarely shows any personal qualities. (Lorna Doone has more individuality than most such heroines.) Hoban develops both persons and incident much more fully than the traditional retellings.

Ancient versions of the Orpheus myth say nothing of Eurydice's life with Orpheus after her return (if she did return) or of her earlier life without him. She is generally described as a nymph: not quite divine, or quite human, a minor goddess, perhaps a water-spirit; the word also means a bride. Her name, meaning 'wide justice', is awe-inspiring rather than attractive, and is perhaps a surprising one for a nymph. She was certainly not related to the numerous Eurydices named in royal families, such as those of Tros and Pelops. (We may remember that the earliest recorded name for Orpheus' wife was a different one, Agriope, 'wild face'.) Soon after her marriage (some versions even implied that it happened on the same day), she was attacked by a snake, as she ran along a river-bank. The pursuit by Aristaeus is not mentioned by Greek writers.

The familiar tradition of Orpheus' overmastering love for his wife encouraged the supposition that she must have inspired his poetry and music, as if she were a Muse. There is no ancient warrant for describing Eurydice in these terms; indeed, Eurydice is never included in any description or representation of the singing Orpheus, except in the story of her death. At that point, all agree, his song turned to lament. Until then, he was charming animals, setting landscape in its right order, naming the elements of the universe. But in no version does Eurydice sit beside him, follow him, or even listen. Until she dies, she might as well not exist for Orpheus at all. What matters, for the myth, is her death and his search for her.

The identification of Eurydice as a Muse-figure, however, is not wholly unjustified. The music made in Hades is Orpheus' supreme work. However potent and glorious his song had been on earth, the raising of the dead must surpass all that had been done before. To lead his wife back to the upper world – and, as Orphic tradition claimed, to bring his initiates to eternal life – his music must have been inspired by a truly divine power. This inspiration came to him only because he had faced the dreadful journey to the world of the dead.

This journey, briefly evoked by many Greek authors, is most fully described in Virgil's Orpheus narrative, which together with his account of Aeneas' *katabasis* became the master-source of all such *topoi* in European literature:

> Taenarias etiam fauces, alta ostia Ditis,
> et caligantem nigra formidine lucum
> ingressus Manesque adiit regemque tremendum
> nesciaque humanis precibus mansuescere corda.
> at cantu commotae Erebi de sedibus imis

umbrae ibant tenues simulacraque luce carentum,
quam multa in foliis avium se milia condunt,
vesper ubi aut hibernus agit de montibus imber,
matres atque viri defunctaque corpora vita
magnanimum heroum, pueri innuptaeque puellae,
inpositique rogis iuvenes ante ora parentum;
quos circum limus niger et deformis harundo
Cocyti tardaque palus inamabilis unda
adligat et noviens Styx interfusa coercet.

He entered Taenarus, the cavernous gate of Dis,
And found his way through the black and fearful maze
To face the King of the Dead in his ghostly kingdom
Where all prayers fail and hearts are dead as stones.
He gathered an audience of shadows to hear his song
And made them feel again. From the crannies of Erebus
They flocked about him like birds that hide in the leaves
When dusk or breaking weather drives them from the hills –
Grown men and women, the strengthless forms of heroes
Drained of their brimming life, young boys and girls,
Young men set on the pyre while their parents watched –
Imprisoned beyond black mud and jagged reeds
And stagnant water, the clogged stream of Cocytus,
Wound in hateful coils by the ninefold Styx.

(*Geo.* IV. 467-80, tr. Wells)

'The black and fearful *maze*' might be questioned as a translation for Virgil's *caligantem nigra formidine lucum*, 'a grove darkening with black terror', but *caligare* is principally used of fog and dark vapour, suggesting loss of direction as in a maze, and the labyrinth is well known at the approach to tombs or in *katabasis*-legends (including that of Aeneas). The Virgilian sense of human helplessness in this lifeless world is well expressed in this translation.[1] Specific details of Hades' landscape were drawn from Greek sources; Virgil uses the traditional darkness, dampness, and immobility in his bird-simile, transposed from Homer, as well as in the description itself.[2] The region is enclosed by ninefold Styx, the black river which is crossed in Charon's boat; before that, Aeneas, or Orpheus, must approach the dark waters of Avernus.

The elements of the Hoban narratives are deeply Virgilian. It is after this pattern that Herman Orff must go by overnight boat (not by plane) to Amsterdam in search of the Vermeer girl, while in Kleinzeit's hospital the Sister on night-duty (who is his Eurydice) sits 'glowing in the lamplit binnacle of her office, watching the black bow cleave the white wave'. (This hospital, it seems, does not usually discharge patients before they are dead.)

If the dead Eurydice is able to inspire her lover to create music that can draw her out of the lifeless realm and into the light, she is evidently not dead at all in any ordinary sense. This is not a passion that destroys, as La Belle Dame Sans Merci destroyed her pale warriors. Life springs up from the region where Eurydice lives among the dead.

We have seen that in the Middle Ages, and sometimes later, the figure of Eurydice was often identified with the lost and fallen Eve. The image of the first woman, expelled from Eden to bear her children in pain, seems at first sight very remote from Eurydice, but it may still invite us to respond to some aspects of the myth which have often been unregarded or unvalued.

The death of Eurydice by the bite of a serpent is the most obvious link with the fall of Eve. Boethius' version[3] shows very clearly how the ambiguity of Eve's moral nature in turn casts ambiguities over the Orpheus story. The medieval Eurydice might stand for virtue or vice, according to the moral preoccupations of the writer or artist. Eve could be seen as the source of all human sin as well as of sorrow, since she gave consent to the serpent and then persuaded Adam to share her guilt, so that he was condemned with her to enter into the realm of Death. When Adam fixed his eyes on her instead of on his heavenly mentor, he became a fallen sinner who could recover his status as child of God only by an act of divine grace. Many medieval theologians and preachers did not appear to believe that Eve could ever recover such prelapsarian status at all. For those who held this view of women it was clearly better that Eurydice should not be allowed to return from Hades; better for Orpheus, and for the music he could go on to create to the glory of God.

The artist or poet of the Middle Ages did not recognise any relation which he needed to maintain, or re-establish, with a female Muse-figure. The medieval writer of sacred poetry (like the sculptors or painters working on the great cathedrals of Europe) could pray for inspiration from the Holy Spirit. The work of the secular poet was clearly distinguished from the sacred: the code of courtly love which he often adopted would make him the follower of a human (perhaps quite imaginary) female who was quite detached from questions of sin and redemption. This tradition of love poetry cast the poet in the part of devoted servant of a woman who inspired him, though she could never become his bride. But in narratives such as *Sir Orfeo*, and many secular stories, the serpent and the rescue-theme remained. Orpheus, seeking to rescue his bride from Hades – the prefiguration of the Christ who harrowed hell and brought up Eve – could also become the knight in quest of a captive princess. The serpent reappeared as the familiar dragon of fairy tale, to be slain – or in a few cases tamed[4] – in order to free the distressed maiden; and she, in stories of this type, is usually seen as wholly virtuous. The happy ending of the *Sir Orfeo*-type story leaves the freed princess sharing the hero's kingdom, and the dragon dead after a fearsome struggle.

The classical forerunner here was the story of Perseus and Andromeda, known in later times, as so many ancient stories were, from the *Metamorphoses* of Ovid; ancient tragedies on the theme are lost. Affinities with the Eurydice story are very obvious. Andromeda was condemned to be the victim of a sea-monster (it is not clear whether to be devoured, raped, or otherwise maltreated) because her mother had proclaimed her more beautiful than the Nereids. Perseus, with Hermes' winged sandals on his feet, arrived from the far west, where he had killed the Gorgon Medusa. Her snaky head, which became Perseus' most powerful weapon against human enemies and against the giant Atlas, was not lifted up on this occasion to overcome the sea-monster. Instead, the predator was pierced by the hero's sword ('up to its crooked hilt', says Ovid), and then repeatedly run through as Perseus clung to a rock amid surging waves (*Met.* IV. 711- 39). The story ended – predictably – with the marriage of Andromeda and Perseus (who took her 'without a dowry').

Perseus' killing of the sea-monster follows the pattern of Heracles' dragon-conflicts, when he overcame the hundred-headed Hydra (his second Labour) and the guardian of the Hesperidean golden apples (his eleventh or twelfth). These exploits had been foreshadowed by Heracles' strangling of serpents when he was an infant. Perseus and Orpheus are both linked with the Hesperides story by Apollonius Rhodius, who not only makes Perseus visit that region, as was customary, but also the Argonauts, who arrive on the day after the fight, to see the dragon lying dead. Orpheus takes his usual role as intermediary for the Argonauts when they need divine guidance, and the nymphs, transformed to trees, point out a spring of fresh water which has gushed from a rock that was struck by Heracles' foot. The heroes are saved from desperate thirst by this intervention, and (after further adventures with a poisonous snake and the sea-god Triton, which are embellished or perhaps wholly invented by this almost rococo writer) they secure safe departure from Africa after Orpheus has directed them to propitiate the gods (Ap. Rhod. IV. 1393-1561).

The links between Perseus and Heracles, Heracles and Orpheus, which are made by Apollonius, are not taken up by Ovid, who (perhaps prudently) avoids the Twelve Labours in his plan of the *Metamorphoses*. He does, however, refer twice to the birth of the winged horse Pegasus from the blood which dripped from the Gorgon's severed head (the source, as Apollonius also notes, of all the snakes in Libya) causing the Hippocrene fountain to spring from Pegasus' hoof on Helicon, home of the Muses (*Met.* IV. 785-6;

V. 256-266). This story forms the link between the long passage dealing with Perseus and the tales told by the Muses to Minerva. These also relate attacks upon maidens (Proserpina, Arethusa) which take them beneath the earth and in each case lead to a life-giving transformation. Both Proserpina and Arethusa are finally reconciled with the attacker, who is not destroyed but revealed as benevolent rather than predatory in his love. The happy ending here, when the dragon is not only tamed but rediscovered, exemplifies the pattern of *Beauty and the Beast* rather than of the medieval dragon-slaying tales such as *Guy and Felice*.

The most awe-inspiring of all such conflicts is the battle of Michael the Archangel against the Devil in dragon form. This dragon has traditionally been related – in biblical commentary and in theology, as well as in iconography – to the serpent that tempted Eve. In all the narratives we have mentioned, the overcoming of the dragon is necessary before a better order can be established: the rightful king must rule, the rightful owner must possess the treasure, the rightful groom must win the bride. Again, the biblical example is the most majestic as well as the most fully realised: the Dragon of the Apocalypse threatens the Woman 'arrayed with the sun, and the moon under her feet, and upon her head a crown of twelve stars', Michael and his angels cast down 'the great dragon, the old serpent', and on earth he continues his persecution of the Woman and all her offspring (Rev. 12). This passage clearly relates to the prophecy made to the serpent cast out of Eden with Eve: 'I will put enmity between thee and the Woman, and between thy seed and her seed' (Gen. 3:15). As the Second Eve, the Woman of the Apocalypse has been recognised as Mary, who was believed to give birth as a virgin and without pain, thus reversing the condemnation laid upon the first mother.[6] Mary's son is revealed as rightful ruler of the world, and she has escaped all injury from the Dragon, whether its attack was seen as violently destructive or sexually aggressive.

The phallic nature of the assault by serpent or dragon or sea-monster has always been evident enough. Though commentators on the Genesis narrative might not choose to make this explicit, it has been implied in a moralistic spirit by countless Christian preachers who have gone on to assume the presence of evil in all forms of sexual contact.[7] The promise made by the serpent, and fulfilled by what follows, is a promise of knowledge, to include good as well as evil. This knowledge does relate to sexual awareness, but does not end there. It forces Eve into the realm of Death, and Adam has to go with her, facing a life of unending struggle if he is to maintain relationship with her at all, or any hope of a restored relationship with God.

In the Eurydice story, the attacker was always a snake, and this was further identified as a phallic threat when the figure of Aristaeus was introduced into the story as pursuer. Russell Hoban takes the imaginative leap of allowing

Eurydice's snake to take the huge oceanic identity of the Kraken of Norwegian legend, imagined by Tennyson 'in the abysmal sea', where

> Unnumber'd and enormous polypi
> Winnow with giant arms the slumbering green.

On Herman Orff's monitor screen, the words of Eurydice imprint themselves:

> Always in the dream are
> the sea and the dream of the sea.
> In the dream I am the fishergirl in
> the twining embrace of the giant squid,
> its dark eyes are on me as
> it penetrates and inseminates me.

The image in this poem implies that the snake must possess Eurydice sexually if the myth is to be enacted at all. The offspring of this union is 'the Kraken in its terror, at the bottom of the sea'. In the classic story the snake does not do this; Eurydice's only sexual partner is Orpheus, and no offspring is ever mentioned. The serpent's gift to her is her death, which makes her a life-giving force for Orpheus as poet.

If the classic myth omits sexual possession of Eurydice, it is also true that it never includes the killing of the serpent. For Orpheus, the one Greek hero who never killed at any time, such action would be impossible. His power to tame wild beasts would suggest a parallel with Jason, who put the guardian dragon to sleep in order to to gain the Golden Fleece, rather than killing it as Heracles and Perseus are said to have done. But we have to recognise that these are variants of the same pattern: Jason overcomes the monster as surely as Heracles does, to gain the golden prize and marry the princess. Similarly, Orpheus lulls the raging Cerberus to sleep, and overcomes all threatening and monstrous forms that rise before him on his path to Hades. The serpent that bit Eurydice is never mentioned among these menacing presences; after the bite, it disappears from the story. None the less, the journey to Hades must be seen as an enactment of heroic struggle, analogous to Perseus' battle with the sea-monster or St Michael's with the dragon. By this struggle Orpheus asserts his claim to the role of husband and guardian of the treasure. What he secures by his heroic quest is never seen as golden fruit or fleece, or any other material prize, but as a secret spiritual gift comparable to the knowledge of good and evil, which in Genesis was said to make men as gods (Gen. 3:5, 22).

———— ◇ ————

In Robert Henryson's fifteenth-century version of Eurydice's story, a special part is played by Proserpine, 'the goddess infernall'. It is she who summons Eurydice to the world of the dead (when she falls 'in a deidly swoun' at the bite of the serpent) and she who decides that Orpheus may lead his wife back to earth; but

> sen I her hither brocht,
> We sall nocht pairt without conditioun.

Proserpina/Persephone herself had entered Hades as a victim of a sexual attack by Pluto; and like Eurydice she did return to earth, but not 'without conditioun'. As the daughter of Demeter/Ceres, she arose from the earth each year in spring, returning in the autumn to resume her rule as queen of the dead. The act which destroyed her virginity and her life as human maiden (Kore) also made her immortal, royal, and the source of endlessly renewed life for the world.

Henryson was not the first to make an association between Eurydice and Persephone. 'The Mysteries' which Orpheus was said to have instituted in Greece would most naturally be taken to include those of Eleusis, the rites of initiation in the worship of Demeter and her daughter.[8] The link between Orpheus and Persephone was asserted in visual terms by Polygnotus, according to the description given by Pausanias of his painting at Delphi: Orpheus was shown touching a willow tree in a grove sacred to Persephone, the place where he received his gift of mystic knowledge.

In celebrating Persephone's annual descent and return, her worshipper was always enacting the pattern that Eurydice had enacted, and receiving union with the goddess just as she had done. To identify Eurydice with Persephone, as another manifestation of the chthonic goddess whose life-giving power arose eternally from the world of the dead, was not an intellectualised interpretation of the myth but an intuitive understanding that could not be argued away, even if any writer had tried to do so.[9]

If Eurydice is seen as a chthonic goddess, sought in the underworld because that is her true home, her return to earth for a limited period only, and under immutable conditions, is entirely appropriate. The particular 'condition' applied to Eurydice's release also makes sense – in terms of the myth's association with other stories. It was well understood in the Greek world at all periods that gods of the nether world should be approached only with averted face (and with torches inverted, as is shown on many sculptured reliefs in funereal contexts). The tabu imposed on Orpheus, that he should not look upon his wife in Hades, needs no explanation beyond this. Its power is reinforced, however, if we remember the links between Eurydice and the snaky-headed Medusa, so beautiful, legend said, before her metamorphosis by Athena's decree. What deprived her of her beauty was the the loss of her virginity – whether by rape or consent – to Poseidon. After her defilement, a mere glance at her face would petrify the beholder.

Medusa's blood had the power either to kill or to raise the dead; if she could annihilate, she could also give life, and it was this same deadly blood that had given birth to Pegasus, winged horse, author of the Muses' fountain. This ambivalence, the lifegiving and the deadly from the same source, seems to have been attributed to snakes from very early times: the Romans saw guardian-spirit or Genius in snake form, (the gliding serpent at Anchises' tomb is a good example from Virgil), and Coleridge was following classical tradition when he made his Mariner look out upon the 'slimy things' moving on the 'rotting sea' that burns 'like a witch's oils' and see that they are water-snakes of flashing beauty, 'O happy living things!' At that moment the dead Albatross falls from the Mariner's neck and his deliverance from the world of death begins.

Coleridge set 'The Rime of the Ancient Mariner' in a timeless region which had some fairy-tale, almost mock-medieval qualities, where Christian language could be used but classical mythology could not. None the less, it is easy to trace both Medusa and Persephone in the figure of Death-in-Life, the Woman whose mate is Death, whose 'locks were yellow as gold', skin 'white as leprosy', who 'thicks man's blood with cold'. When she wins the game of dice whose prize is the Mariner, he is carried into the death-world where at last his spiritual life begins. The *katabasis* pattern here remains very clear in spite of the unusual imagery of open sea replacing the dark underworld. The solitary traveller returns from his shamanistic journey with 'strange power of speech' and a recurrent burning agony which compels him to tell his revelatory story to chosen listeners.

Most *katabasis*-narratives, whether classical or later, use the 'underworld' as a visual image, as well as figuratively to denote the 'underside' of human experience, the unconscious or the unknown areas of life. The journeys of Odysseus and Aeneas, like many others, begin with a trench dug in the ground, a cave hollowed out of rock. The traveller descends into the earth, as Mephistopheles tells Faust he must descend 'below earth's deepest floors'.

In this dialogue from Goethe's most obscure and bewildering work, *Faust* Part II, the Tempter prompts Faust to take the 'way to the Unreachable...the void...the deep of deeps' (though, he adds, 'I might as well say, height'). Here the glow from a burning tripod will allow Faust to see the Mothers, around whom float 'all forms of entity', in endless transformation. The Mothers are never further described or defined,[10] but Faust needs to find them because only they can bestow the creative power he needs in order to bring back to life the supreme human beauty of Paris and Helen. (Faust does succeed in calling up Helen, in a scene both visionary and farcical, but loses her because he cannot control his impulse to seize the incomparable 'phantom'.)

Obscure as it is, *Faust* is full of paradigms, and this descent to the creative Mothers calls up older descent-stories and throws piercing light on aspects of their meaning. The descent into the underworld suggests Mother Earth, who brings forth the gifts of Demeter; the Mothers – who bestow the power to create, as well as themselves creating – fulfil the functions of the ancient Muse, who was Mother as well as inspiring maiden for the poet. Pindar, who habitually speaks of himself as servant or spokesman of the Muses, can also call his songs their 'daughters' (*Nem.* IV. 3); and Orpheus' mother was invariably named as a Muse, Calliope. The femaleness of the Muse may be that of either mother or loved maiden; but if a bride, she might well be snatched away at her wedding, since she cannot take the role of wife, living in a settled parity of status with the poet, but must always be elusive, part of himself yet other, always to be sought and rediscovered.

Muses, or Daughters of Beulah, have the peculiar duality that belongs to figures in dreams: they seem to come from outside in an uncontrollable way, and yet are felt to belong to the dreamer's own mind and cannot be disowned, even if the dreamer would prefer to detach himself from them. Two of the Muse's characteristics point clearly to her nature as an image formed in the subconscious. She is associated with running water (almost invariably so, except in Blake, who speaks only rarely of rivers and fountains)[11] and thus shares in the powerful archetypal character of this most universal symbol for the unconscious life. Secondly, she is always female. Almost all artists, poets, and musicians have been men; the man's unconscious life is naturally enough associated with feminine images, the unknown, the opposite of the familiar conscious self.

The Muse as female guide is felt to be needed by the poet, because his search for the reality of experience – his task of rescuing the moment, the 'spot of time', from oblivion – may take him into regions of darkness and danger where he cannot move on without her help. The journey has to be a kind of *katabasis*, a descent like the journey of Orpheus into Hades; his search for Eurydice is a pattern for all poets seeking the dead or dormant female who is the counterpart he needs.

Orpheus, as lover and as poet, finds in Eurydice both inspiration and material for his songs. Wordsworth regarded Lucy in a similar light: when she was 'Rolled round in earth's diurnal course/With rocks, and stones, and trees', Wordsworth could no longer see her as female Muse 'Beside the springs of Dove'. Instead he drew inspiration with much more toil and spiritual self-denial, from the rocks and stones and trees of his daily world.

When Rilke's Eurydice was drawn away from her impatient lover's sight, she too was taken into the underworld of chthonic darkness where veins of silver ore cross between roots and the hidden sources of life-blood for creatures above. In this non-human world Eurydice, like Lucy, neither hears nor sees:

> sie war schon Wurzel.

> she was already root.

> ('Orpheus, Eurydice, Hermes', 1904)

This is why, as Bowra remarked, she does not recognise Orpheus when he turns round to look at her; she no longer has any human attachments, but is simply part of the natural order.[12]

Eight years later, Rilke amplified this perception in *Gegen Strophen*, 'Antistrophes', a poem which called all women 'Eurydice's sisters', comparing women to bread, the universal symbol for the food of mankind, made from fruit of the earth. Again he sees the woman as dying young, but thereby united with the life of the earth and so able to sustain the man who is her lover:

> Abbruch der Kindheit
> war euch nicht Schaden. Auf einmal
> standet ihr da, wie im Gott
> plötzlich zum Wunder ergänzt.

> Wir, wie gebrochen vom Berg,
> oft schon als Knaben scharf
> an den Rändern, vielleicht
> manchmal glücklich behaun;
> wir, wie Stücke Gesteins,
> über Blumen gestürzt.

> Blumen des tieferen Erdreichs,
> von allen Wurzeln geliebte,
> ihr, der Eurydike Schwestern,
> immer voll heiliger Umkehr
> hinter dem steigenden Mann...

> Childhood's breaking off
> did you no harm. All at once
> you stood there, completed
> as in a god, to a miracle.

> We, as though chipped from a mountain,
> often as boys even sharp
> at the edges, at times

perhaps happily hewn;
we, like bits of rock
hurled on to flowers.

Flowers of the deeper earth levels,
loved by all roots,
you, Eurydice's sisters,
always full of holy conversion
behind the ascending man...

(tr. M. Hamburger)

Rilke was always preoccupied with the idea of the woman dying in youth and so becoming part of a chthonic realm of deeper life. Like Wordsworth's Lucy (and his Ruth, and Louisa), Rilke's Eurydice was one of a series of such figures, recurrent all through his poetic life. In his 'Alcestis' (which, like 'Orpheus, Eurydice, Hermes', was included in the *Neue Gedichte* of 1907-8), the dying woman is a bride taken to the world of death by 'the slender god' on her wedding day. Admetus rushes towards her and struggles to grasp her vanishing form:

Aber einmal sah
er noch des Mädchens Antlitz, das sich wandte
mit einem Lacheln, hell wie eine Hoffnung,
die beinah ein Versprechen war: erwachsen
zurückzukommen aus dem tiefen Tode
zu ihm, den Lebenden –

But once more he saw
the girl's face, that turned towards him
with a smile, radiant as a hope,
that almost was a promise: to spring up,
to come back, out of deep death
to him, the living one.

In 'Orpheus, Eurydice, Hermes', the promise to return is expressed in more Wordsworthian terms: because Eurydice is 'already root', she can be 'poured out like fallen rain, shared like a hundredfold supply':

hingegeben wie gefallner Regen
und ausgeteilt wie hundertfacher Vorrat.

The fallen rain is pouring a life-giving moisture upon the world; as individual, Eurydice (or Lucy) has gone, to become a nameless part of the natural order. The women whom Rilke mourned in actual life, Paula Modersohn-Becker and later Wera Ouckama Knoop, assumed the same function through the 'great death', which made them sources of creativity. Like Wordsworth, Rilke has to find his glimpses of reality, when the woman-Muse has died, in the 'minute particulars' which he is impelled to name in the ninth Duino Elegy:

> Bringst doch der Wanderer auch vom Hange des Bergrands
> nicht eine Hand voll Erde ins Tal, die Allen unsagliche, sondern
> ein erworbenes Wort, reines, den gelben und blaun
> Enzian. Sind wir vielleicht hier, um zu sagen: Haus,
> Brücke, Brunnen, Tor, Krug, Obstbaum, Fenster,
> – höchstens: Saule, Turm...aber zu sagen, verstehs,
> ob zu sagen so, wie selber die Dinge niemals
> innig meinten zu sein.

> Doesn't the wanderer bring back
> from the mountain slopes to the valley
> not a handful of earth
> but rather a word
> hardly won, and pure, the yellow and blue gentian?
> Are we here on earth to say: house
> bridge, fountain, jug, gate, fruit-tree, window
> – or even: column, tower –
> but to say these words, you know, with an intensity
> that never seemed expressible to the things themselves.

Rilke has unfolded the 'tranquillity' in which Wordsworth said specific emotions must be recollected, and revealed the composure, the patience, the attentiveness, which allowed the creative metamorphosis of such emotions to take place in him:

> Ah, poems amount to so little when you write them too early in your life. You ought to wait and gather sense and sweetness for a whole lifetime, and a long one if possible, and then, at the very end, you might perhaps be able to write ten good lines. For poems are not, as people think, simply emotions (one has emotions early enough) – they are experiences. For the sake of a single poem, you must see many cities, many people and things, you must understand animals, must feel how birds fly, and know the gesture which small flowers make when they open in the morning. You must be able to think back to streets in unknown neighborhoods, to unexpected encounters, and to partings you had long seen coming; to days of childhood whose mystery is still unexplained, to parents whom you had to hurt when they brought in a joy and you didn't pick it up (it was a joy meant for somebody else); to childhood illnesses that began so

strangely with so many profound and difficult transformations, to days in quiet, restrained rooms and to mornings by the sea, to the sea itself, to seas, to nights of travel that rushed along high overhead and went flying with all the stars, – and it is still not enough to be able to think of all that. You must have memories of many nights of love, each one different from all the others, memories of women in labour, and of light, pale, sleeping girls who have just given birth and are closing again. But you must also have been beside the dying, must have sat beside the dead in the room with the open window and the scattered noises. And it is not yet enough to have memories. You must be able to forget them when they are many, and you must have the immense patience to wait until they return. For the memories themselves are not important. Only when they have changed into our very blood, into glance and gesture, and are nameless, no longer to be distinguished from ourselves – only then can it happen that in some very rare hour the first word of a poem arises in their midst and goes forth from them.

(From *The Notebooks of Malte Laurids Brigge*)

Unlike Wordsworth, Rilke returned, in the last years of his creative life, to the Orpheus myth and the search for the lost woman, who in *Sonette an Orpheus* is both Eurydice and (in some of the sonnets at least) Wera Ouckama Knoop. This search had been a recurrent subject in nineteenth-century literature on the Continent; French and German writers of the Romantic age felt as keenly as Blake and Wordsworth did the loss of inner vitality in the classic myths, and struggled to re-state them in more profoundly personal ways, whether using the traditional names or not.[13] The *Sonette an Orpheus* succeed with astonishing fulness in pursuing the *katabasis* to its personal depths as well as on a mythological level. Eurydice is not restored, but Orpheus discovers a richer creative power in his union with the natural world, made possible by her loss. It is mourning for the loss of Wera/Eurydice that becomes Rilke's source of a new world, the world of praise that was sung as the girl 'made herself a bed' in the poet's ear

> und schlief in mir. Und alles war ihr Schlaf.
> Die Bäume, die ich je bewundert, diese
> fuhlbare Ferne, die gefühlte Wiese
> und jedes Staunen, das mich selbst betraf.
>
> Sie schlief die Welt. Singender Gott, wie hast
> du sie vollendet, dass sie nicht begehrte,
> erst wach zu sein? Sieh, sie erstand und schlief.

Wo ist ihr Tod? O, wirst du dies Motiv
erfinden noch, eh sich dein Lied versehrte? –
Wo sinkt sie hin aus mir?...
Ein Madchen fast...

and slept in me. And her sleep was all things.
The trees, that I ever wondered at, these
distances perceptible, the meadows perceived,
and every astonishment that seized my heart.

She slept the world. Singing god, how have you
so fulfilled her that she had no longing
ever to be awake? See, she stood up, and slept.

Where is her death? Oh will you yet
discover this theme before your song consumes itself?
Where does she fall away from me?...
A girl, almost...

(*Sonette an Orpheus*, I. 2)

The inward process of the Eurydice-figure's 'world-sleep' revealed itself, with extraordinary certainty as well as speed, in the composition of the two series of the *Sonnets*, within the first two months of 1922. This was a revelatory explosion of creative power comparable to the illuminative experience of Blake in the Truchsessian Gallery in 1804, when, after twenty years of darkness: 'O Glory! and O Delight! ...I was again enlightened with the light I enjoyed in my youth... I am really drunk with intellectual vision whenever I take a pencil or graver into my hand.' With similar abruptness and completeness, the 'dictation of an inner impulse' forced Rilke to attend, in 'a single breathless obedience', to the surge of energy which he called 'a hurricane in the spirit', a 'gust within a god'.[14] Rilke, in the *Sonnets*, writes directly from within the experience of inspiration, the experience which he struggles to describe with meticulous fidelity in the *Duino Elegies*, and which he considers and (still reverently) tries to assess in many of his later letters. These three together form (as Erich Heller[15] has remarked) the only personal account by a twentieth-century writer of his own states of inspiration.

In this record from Rilke's last years of major creative work, he is not simply particularising the materials of transformation, and not merely exhorting to attentiveness and patience, as he does in the passage already quoted from *The Notebooks of Malte Laurids Brigge*. These later poems and letters do not represent Rilke's attempts to 'name' things: rather they set out to convey the exprience of creativity in its lived moments. The poet's task of seizing 'minute particulars', of immortalising 'spots of time', is most fully defined in the memorable letter which Rilke wrote to Witold Hulewicz, his Polish translator, about a year before his death:

> It is our task to imprint this transitory, perishable earth so deeply, sorrowfully, and feelingly within ourselves that its being rises up once more, 'invisible', in us. *We are the bees of the invisible. We desperately gather, in the honey of the visible, to store it up in the great golden hive of the invisible...* The earth has no other recourse than to become invisible: *in* us, since we, with one part of our being, participate in the invisible... *We are*, let me emphasise it once more, *in the sense of the Elegies, we are these transformers of the earth...*

The metaphor of the bees brings a specific and glowing life to the idea of the poet's work as 'harvest'. He had used the same terminology about ten years earlier, in 'Es winkt zu Fühlung':

> Wer rechnet unseren Ertrag?...
> Die Vögel fliegen still
> durch uns hindurch. O der ich wachsen will,
> ich seh hinaus, und *in* mir wachst der Baum.

> Who reckons our harvest?...
> The birds fly silently
> through us and away. O, I who want to grow,
> I look outside, and *in* me grows the tree.

'Interiorisation' is the ugly but perhaps unavoidable term used by W. A. Strauss in his valuable scrutiny of Rilke's late poems and letters.[16] As the poet draws into himself all that he perceives in the world around him, the being of each thing – animate or inanimate – enters into a new life-dimension, transcending its natural existence – like the tree at the opening of the first Orpheus sonnet:

> Da stieg ein Baum. O reine Übersteigung!
> O Orpheus singt! O hoher Baum in Ohr!

> There rose a tree. Oh pure transcendence!
> Oh Orpheus sings! Oh tall tree in the ear!

The whole sequence ends with this theme of transcendence, as Wera the young dancer 'fills out' her movements to a constellation while Orpheus sings, and in the final sonnet Rilke addresses the Orpheus-figure in terms that have biblical overtones, so that he once again evokes the Christ who is in all things and makes all things new:

Stiller Freund der vielen Fernen, fühle,
wie dein Atem noch den Raum vermehrt.
Im Gebälk der finstern Glockenstuhle
lass dich lauten. Das, was an dir zehrt,

wird ein Starkes uber dieser Nahrung.
Geh in der Verwandlung aus und ein.
Was ist deine leidendste Erfahrung?
Ist dir Trinken bitter, werde Wein.

Sei in dieser Nacht aus Übermass
Zauberkraft am Kreuzweg deiner Sinne,
ihrer seltsamen Begegnung Sinn.

Und wenn dich das Irdische vergass,
zu der stillen Erde sag: Ich rinne.
Zu dem raschen Wasser sprich: Ich bin.

Silent friend of many distances, feel
how your breath continually enlarges space,
Let yourself ring out into the beams
of the dark belfry. What feeds upon you

becomes a strength beyond this sustenance.
Go into transformation, out and in.
What is the deepest suffering you have known?
If the drink is bitter to you, become wine.

Be in this night from excess a magic force
at the crossroads of your senses,
sense of their strange encounter.

And if the earthly forgets you,
say to the silent earth: I flow,
speak to the surging water: I am.

If this ecstasy of transcendence is demanded by the things of earth, Rilke also speaks of the poet's need to travel into the inner world which he calls 'the vast landscape of Lament' ('Klage'). The tenth Duino Elegy describes the poet's journey beyond death, led by the maiden Klage through the land of her ancestors, to a dark ravine, where he sees – shimmering in the moonlight – the Spring of Joy. Neither Orpheus nor Eurydice is named in this poem, but these presences assert their own identity; Klage is unmistakably the Eurydice who, in the poem of the *Neue Gedichte*, was 'full of her great death', who already belongs (like Persephone) to that other world.[17]

The descent into the world of the dead is re-interpreted in the plays and films of Jean Cocteau, where Orphée becomes a true poet only after following Death's Angel, to meet a timeless reality. This timeless experience is full of fragments or echoes of remembered life, which take on fuller – though confusing – meanings as he struggles back to earth and seeks to find poetic expression for them.

In these modern developments of the *katabasis* theme, Eurydice – or Lucy – has the role of Muse as well as that of lost memory or treasure, to be discovered and (even if lost again) made the material of art. Because this female figure has both functions, she cannot provide the sense of steadfast and benevolent companionship which the ancient poet could find in his Muse; a companionship which included a sense of awe, but much reassurance. For the modern poet, the Muse is likely to seem ever more elusive, as he moves on and downwards to discover what he needs to say. This *katabasis* can only be described by modern critics – and poets themselves – as a descent into the unconscious. They may also, if they look back at the metamorphoses of Orpheus over the centuries, see it as analogous to the discipline of purification imposed in Orphic cults in order to recover lost knowledge of eternal truths.

The poet is one who continually seeks for a creative element which is in his own nature but also 'other'. He has an intermittent relation with this other, but an awareness of loss, or of damage done to this relation, and is impelled always to renewal of active search for what is lost. The search will take him into the realm of the unconscious, where he will meet experiences of anguish and terror. The creative work that can issue from such a journey will be unpredictable, and its forms may be almost infinitely various. Whether popular or esoteric, traditional or innovative, its authenticity must depend on the degree of humility and courage with which he has undertaken the journey, as well as on the nature of his poetic gift.

XI

Roman Choice

AFTER Virgil, the fullest and the most appalling realisation of *katabasis* in Latin literature is found in Seneca's tragedy *Hercules Furens*, probably written during the reign of Nero. In this play Hercules emerges from the world of the dead, only to be overcome by an hallucination which leads him to slaughter his own family. The structure of the drama is that of Euripides' *Heracles*, but Seneca has added choral lyrics describing the world of Hades, and also an extremely long narrative spoken by Theseus, recounting the journey into the underworld. These passages have a Virgilian poignancy as well as much visual detail that is clearly drawn from Virgil's two accounts of *katabasis*, that of Orpheus in *Georgics* IV and that of Aeneas in *Aeneid* VI. Seneca's generation would recognise the dark silences of this underworld, and the countless souls flocking in baffled despair, as the realm visited by Aeneas and by Orpheus in the poems written about a century before. No writer of Rome's Silver Age, or those that followed, could have escaped Virgil's imprint.

Seneca's play, however, has taken more than elements of imagery and diction from Virgil. In Euripides, the hero descends to Hades as his final Labour, commanded by Hera to bring up the three-headed Cerberus; he also rescues Theseus, who in gratitude receives him as an afflicted friend when he recovers from his madness. This structure stands in the Latin play also, but the emphasis is changed, chiefly by making Juno speak the prologue (convention did not allow the Greek Hera to do this). Juno declares that the journey to Hades will lure Hercules into madness. She realises that his successful capture of Cerberus may lead him to attempt the restoration of shades to the world of the living, and the assumption of cosmic power for himself:

> patefacta ab imis manibus retro via est
> et sacra durae mortis in aperto iacent.

Up opened is from lowest ghostes the backward way to skye,
And sacred secrets of dire death in open sight do lye.

(*H.F.* 55-6, tr. Heywood)

This hope of conquering death is a delusion which Juno will use to destroy her enemy.

Hercules does arrive from Hades with Cerberus tamed and Theseus rescued, but these achievements are given little emphasis in the play. Hercules' boast is that he has seen Hades and returned unharmed (606-13).[1] As the Chorus of Thebans await Hercules' return from Hades, they sing of Orpheus' comparable journey and its outcome. The very straightforward account of Orpheus' descent seems at first to be presented as an encouraging example to Hercules:

Immites *potuit* flectere cantibus
umbrarum dominos...

He had the power to sway the ungentle
lords of the shades by his songs...

(569-70)

But although the rulers of the Underworld are moved, their command to the lovers as they start on their homeward way is implacably stern:

tandem mortis ait 'vincimur' arbiter,
'evade ad superos, lege tamen data:
tu post terga tui perge viri comes,
tu non ante tuam respice coniugem,
quam cum clara deos obtulerit dies
Spartanique aderit ianua Taenari'.

Wee conquer'de are, chyefe kyng of death sayd then
To Gods (but under this condition) goe,
Behynde thy husbandes backe keepe thou thy way,
Looke thou not backe thy Wyfe before to see.
Than thee to sight of Gods hath brought the day
And gate of Spartane Taenare present bee.

(582-7, tr. Heywood)

Obedience to this 'law' is impossible for Orpheus and Eurydice; precisely because they are true lovers. The narrative ends starkly. By his backward glance Orpheus 'destroyed' what he hoped to win:

odit verus amor nec patitur moras;
munus dum properat cernere, perdidit.

Love hates delay, nor could abyde so long.
His gift, hee lost, while hee desires the sight.

(588-9, tr. Heywood)

Orpheus' journey to Hades, in Seneca as in Virgil, was undertaken with the single aim of recovering Eurydice. This he fails to do, because he cannot control his impatient love. Hercules goes to Hades as a task which he sees as an opportunity for glory; although he does carry out the task, he also fails to achieve his wider purpose. This is because he is gripped by *furor*, more destructive than the passion of Orpheus but still described by the same term (*H.F.* 991; the word is here used by Amphitryon, of the state predicted by Juno at 98; Eurydice recognises Orpheus' state of *furor* in *Geo.* IV. 495). The heroic endeavour of these journeys to the underworld proves to be futile and deluded. Both Orpheus and Hercules finally destroy what they love, and the lost bride is lost for ever. The path through the underworld does not lead to the Spring of Joy revealed by Rilke's Klage.

· The *katabasis* which Virgil described so much more fully in his later work was undertaken for a different reason and brought to a different end. Aeneas has a female guide on his terrifying journey: an aged woman, not a bride. The Cumaean Sibyl is a venerable prophetess, who seems to be – and perhaps is – more than human. Aeneas needs her guidance, but there is no personal emotion between them. He goes to seek help from his dead father, who will point his way as future conqueror, ruler, and founder of the Roman nation. All this has little to do with a lost bride, poetic inspiration, and the Spring of Joy.

Aeneas' first (and dearly loved) wife Creusa is not encountered in Hades, and cannot be, since she did not die but was 'snatched away' from him in the burning city of Troy. He does, however, meet his second love, Dido, in one of the most memorable passages in Virgil's epic. The shade of the queen who killed herself for his love appears before him, in the grove haunted by the souls of unhappy lovers; when she turns away and will not speak to him, Aeneas begs her to stay, follows her with his gaze, and weeps (*Aen.* VI. 440-76). He is left alone, as he was by the fleeting form of Creusa in Troy (II. 771-94). The Creusa scene echoed very closely Virgil's account of Eurydice's withdrawal from Orpheus' gaze, on the road back to earth, in the *Georgics*; the parallels have been noted by many editors. The lover sheds tears, tries to grasp the vanishing woman, longs to say 'many things'. In the encounter with Dido, Aeneas does say many things, but again he cannot touch her and is left weeping bitterly. In all three cases in Virgil, the lost wife is lost for ever and the hero must return to continue life alone. At this point the structural parallels break down entirely: Orpheus goes on to mourn in a distracted fashion, sings of Eurydice, and is torn to pieces by the Ciconian women; Aeneas weeps, as long as Creusa, or Dido, remains in sight, but then struggles along his appointed path (*datum molitur iter*, VI. 477) – to the slopes of Ida or to the pale scarred throng of those who died in war.

Creusa and Dido were not the only women to be destroyed (and subsequently irrecoverable) in the course of Aeneas' epic struggle for Rome. The enemies of Aeneas include women as well as men: Juturna and Camilla especially, who die in their youth, cut off from hope and protesting at the cruelty of their lot. Roman legend as well as Roman literature included many stories of heroic young brides or virgins (Verginia, Cloelia, and Lucretia are three well-known examples) who died from causes more glorious than snake-bite, leaving husbands, lovers, or fathers to continue a mourning life alone. These Roman heroines are not rescued by any knightly feat or challenge to death, as Andromeda was, or the Eurydice of the Middle Ages: Roman tradition did not admit the recovery of lost females, and (except in Ovid) any encounter between the lost woman and her lover could only deepen their separation. The woman who died was venerated as an embodiment of Roman self-dedication to the community, but the fulfilment of Roman destiny demanded male achievement in the public world. The examples to be followed would be patriarchal, and would not admit any relation at all with the lost maiden or bride.

The clear-sighted resolution of Aeneas, seen so unsympathetically in the nineteenth century, sharpens the contrast with Dido's cherishing warmth. Virgil's portrayal of her painful death is shocking, but even when they felt this ancient readers did not question the rightness of Aeneas' action. For him to deviate from his divinely ordained way – to look back, as Orpheus had done – would have destroyed him, and Rome too.

That Aeneas, who is clearly presented as national hero, should renounce human passion and the search for further revelation, and turn his face instead towards the practical mission laid upon him in this world, was not at all surprising. The meaning of this renunciation is perhaps hinted at when Aeneas emerges from Hades through the Ivory Gate of False Dreams. What he has seen in the chthonic realm was not false in the simple sense of a lie, or a hallucination, but was a visionary experience which (if he chose to remain within it) might for him represent a labyrinth of error and waste. Virgil makes it plain that all this vision, or journey, must be left behind, and nothing Aeneas has seen is ever mentioned again in the epic, after his return to the everyday world. He will go on to marry Lavinia; a political alliance on which Rome's position in Latium will be based. The Roman hero is not required to be celibate or misogynist; but this Latin wife will not, it appears, bind him to any loyalty outside his national duty as lawgiver, priest, and father of his people.[2]

What is more surprising than Aeneas' behaviour, in Virgil, is the behaviour of Orpheus the supreme poet, when his story is told as climax to the *Georgics*. This poem, a most ambitious work, was written in praise of Italy and its peoples; in this work of his thirties, Virgil was already shaping and defining Roman ideals, for personal and national life. The Orpheus story could not be chosen to conclude such a work simply because it offered a touching fanciful contrast.

The fourth of the 'Farming Poems' deals principally with bee-keeping, after the subjects of agriculture, trees, and farm animals in *Georgics* I to III. Mythological references, as well as contemporary affairs, abound in all of the *Georgics*, so that the shift of scene from actual Italian landscape to the world of Hades or to the subaqueous cavern of Cyrene does not jolt the reader. But the length of this mythological Orpheus-narrative, its emotional intensity and richness of poetic detail, command a different response from the pleasure and interest aroused by the diversities of the *Georgics* before this point.

The Orpheus story itself occupies seventy lines 'nested' within the episode of Aristaeus' recovery of his bee-swarm (IV. 281-558).[3] The Greek hero Aristaeus was traditionally the protector of shepherds and of vines and olives, who taught farmers the art of bee-keeping and other skills; his mother was a water-nymph, Cyrene, and his father (in the most prevalent tradition) Apollo. Veneration of Aristaeus, in the Greek world, was ancient but (as far as we know) entirely unconnected with Orpheus. The link between them seems to have been made by Virgil himself, who for the first time in extant literature[4] provides a reason for Eurydice's incautious treading upon the serpent on the river-bank: she was running 'headlong' to escape the pursuit of Aristaeus. To find the Greek culture-hero in the role of sexual predator, destroyer of Eurydice and finally of Orpheus himself, may seem startling.

This aspect of the beneficent demigod becomes less incongruous if he is set with others of the same character such as Heracles and Theseus, or even with gods such as Apollo and Poseidon. The instruction of mankind, the imparting of secrets, or gifts of especial value for civilisation, usually came from male figures of rapacious virility. (Perhaps the only exception to this pattern is Athena, giver of the olive and of many crafts and intellectual pursuits; she is a goddess without feminine attributes, and without mother or child.) The attempted rape of Eurydice is quite in keeping with Aristaeus' nature, as one who discovered and taught practical arts in the post-Saturnian world. His purposeful aggressiveness is demonstrated again when he ambushes and overcomes Proteus, having learnt from Cyrene that the Old Man of the Sea can tell him how to recover his bees.

Most explicitly, Virgil's endearing agricultural Italy is not the world of the Golden Age. In *Georgics* I, he attributes the hardships and frustrations of the farmer's life to Jupiter's deliberate purpose, impelling men to struggle, to learn, and above all to work for survival and for human advancement.[5] The natural obstacles and dangers set in man's way were designed by Jupiter:

> ut varias usus meditando extunderet artis
> paulatim

> so that experience, by attentive thought, might gradually beat out the various arts.

(I. 133-4)

The work is to be both intellectual and practical; the strenuous image of a metal-worker is suggested by *extunderet*, which is Virgil's own addition to the passage in Lucretius used here as source. Lucretius speaks of the struggles of early men to develop practical skills, like eager travellers on an unknown road, where

> usus et impigrae simul experientia mentis
> paulatim docuit pedetemptim progredientes

> experience, and the inventiveness of the lively mind,
> gradually taught them as they moved on, step by step.

(*de Rerum Natura*, V. 1452-3)

Virgil adds to the idea of exploration that of dominating hard material by strength of will and tenacity, to produce a useful work of technical expertise.

As editors of the *Georgics* have observed, the same verb, *extundere*, is applied in *Georgics* IV (315-6, again with *experientia*) to the practice of *bougonia*, the regeneration of a swarm of bees from the body of a slaughtered ox. This technique was supposedly taught to farmers by Aristaeus, whose skilful care had already 'beaten out' the successful practice of farming in general (328), and who now complains to his mother Cyrene because his swarm has unaccountably failed him. To gain a new swarm he will be required to slaughter four bulls and four heifers, and leave them in a thicket to rot. The account of this slaughter is ritualistic, not violent, though when Virgil describes the practice as followed in Egypt he speaks of the farmer struggling to stop up a calf's nostrils and battering its body to pulp in a closed shed (295-304). Ruthlessness as well as exact technique is needed for this. Aristaeus is told to leave 'poppies of oblivion' with the carcasses and a black ewe as a funeral gift to Orpheus, and to sacrifice another calf in honour of 'Eurydice placated' (545-7). Aristaeus asks no questions when he is told to do all this; he acts instantly, *haud mora, continuo...*, 'without delay, at once'

(548). Immediately he finds miraculous clouds of bees, humming about the putrefied bodies, or hanging like grapes in the treetops above.

This image of abundant agricultural life springing from death ends Virgil's whole poem, and it follows immediately after the narrative of Orpheus' disastrous *katabasis* and his own death. Throughout this narrative, Virgil laid emphasis on the contrast at all points between the figures of Orpheus and Aristaeus. The tale is told to Aristaeus by Proteus, the Old Man of the Sea, as an explanation of Aristaeus' loss and also perhaps of the implacable doom that may await inertia. Orpheus, unlike Aristaeus, has not offended divine powers by any aggressive wrongdoing, but by failure of will and of resourcefulness. This is heavily punished, while Aristaeus, who worked unsparingly and humbly in spite of everything, received only a temporary disappointment as reprimand for his aggressiveness, and after that a material reward.

The swarm of bees which is restored so abundantly to Aristaeus is the living treasure that he cared for and worked for until he was (momentarily, it seems) distracted by a sudden impulse of sexual rapacity. Bees have been described in the first half of this final *Georgic* in the most delicate and often anthropomorphic detail. They are shown as inventive, loyal, courageous, devoted to their fellows and to the work of the hive. They never give way to any self-indulgences, and they know no sexual pleasure. The separate functions of drones, queen, and workers are said to correspond to particular social roles in a human community, and there is specific resemblance to an ideal community in the terms of Roman tradition.[6] The upholder of this tradition, who secures its continuity at all costs, is the somewhat unattractive Aristaeus. As Otis and others have observed, it is Orpheus who is presented to the reader with 'empathetic' warmth, and Aristaeus who is seen with objective judgment – and approved, when he bitterly complains to Cyrene, uses violence against the devious Proteus, and finally offers his sacrifices as instructed, without emotion. Both Orpheus and Aristaeus have to undertake journeys to another world, below the earth; in Aristaeus' case, the traveller is amazed by what he sees, but there is no emotional link between him and any person or thing seen in the world beyond or below ordinary consciousness.

Orpheus stirs sympathy and astonishment even in Hades, but he is shown as turning round at the edge of daylight because he has forgotten what he was told to do *(immemor*, 491). He can then only struggle for speech, wander aimlessly, and utter his lament, with pitiful repetition like the nightingale's artless song. The Thracian women tear him to pieces because they feel flouted *(spretae)* by his devotion to Eurydice, and the episode ends with the picture of his severed head floating down the Hebrus, its cold tongue uttering the name of unhappy Eurydice. The mention here of the singing head includes no reference to its oracular powers or to any poetic merit in its song. Indeed, the Orpheus of this poem does not have the role of *vates*, 'prophet', or *poeta*, 'maker', at all; neither master craftsman nor vehicle of divine truth, he is simply a suffering human being, whose voice appeals to all creatures and to the powers of the underworld because it expresses human grief with so much poignancy and truth.

These were qualities of Virgil's own poetry also, but in the *Georgics* – and still more in the *Aeneid* – it is evident that he did not believe such expression to be an adequate aim for any poet. Passages of such emotional quality were made to take a subordinate place in the design of his work, to be received as dramatic rather than authorial utterance. Virgil was writing carefully constructed poetry on themes of the highest public importance, and in most of his work his peculiar imaginative richness only deepens that public significance. Sometimes doors open upon regions beyond the public precinct; Virgil, we realise, is aware of irrationalities and cosmic terror.[7] But the intensity of such moments in his poetry (the farmer in distant future times whose plough will turn up the bones of Roman dead on the battlefields of Greece, for example, or the apocalypse revealed in burning Troy when Venus draws back the veil before Aeneas' mortal vision)[8] is subject to the firmest discipline of total design. The fate of Orpheus in *Georgics* IV is a vivid example of the self-destruction which, in the judgment of the public poet, would be encountered, and deserved, by a singer – however inspired – who simply spun music from undisciplined personal emotion. Virgil's Orpheus, like Seneca's, breaks a divine law because he is a true lover. For this reason he cannot be a Roman hero, and in Roman terms he cannot even be a good poet.

Romans, Virgil plainly says, were not chosen to be poets, or metal-workers either. (In the famous passage which makes this disclaimer, the verb for those who will 'beat out' the 'breathing bronzes' of statuary is *excudere*, not *extundere* – close enough to recall the passages in *Georgics* IV, but suggesting blows that are hammered with slightly less aggressive impact; 'beat' rather than 'batter'.)

> excudent alii spirantia mollius aera,
> credo equidem, vivos ducent de marmore vultus,
> orabunt causas melius, caelique meatus
> describent radio, et surgentia sidera dicent:
> tu regere imperio populos, Romane, memento –
> hae tibi erunt artes – pacisque inponere morem,
> parcere subiectis et debellare superbos.

> Let others fashion from bronze more lifelike, breathing images –
> For so they shall – and evoke living faces from marble;
> Others excel as orators, others track with their instruments
> The planets circling in heaven and predict when stars will appear.
> But, Romans, never forget that government is your medium!

> Be this your art: – to practise men in the habit of peace,
> Generosity to the conquered, and firmness against aggressors.

> (*Aen*. VI. 847-53, tr. Day Lewis)

The true poetic task is the work of craftsmen, needing a life of dedication and divine aid; a lofty and demanding vocation, as were those of all artists, speakers, mathematicians, grouped with them in this prophetic pas- sage spoken by Aeneas' dead father. The Roman, whose whole vocation was the public one of government, could not take such a role. At this point Virgil writes as if he were not a Roman at all, but a quite anonymous mouthpiece, hailing Aeneas the inarticulate, the man of *prudentia*, Aeneas who suppresses his own feeling and forgets his vision of the chthonic realm, as exemplar for Rome and for the new world order. The poetry which this world would need was to be public in theme, noble in moral content, and craftsmanlike in its making. It would not be the music of Orpheus, whose lyre (in E.T.A. Hoffman's striking phrase) 'opened the door of the underworld of feeling'.

This dichotomy between poetry and practical life was not thought to be inevitable by most Greeks. Aristotle had regarded government as the supreme art, but he did not marginalise poetry and music as Virgil does in these words of Anchises. Along with the tradition of poetic inspiration, enhanced by the mythology of Apollo and the Muses, the Greeks had maintained another (not deeply conflicting) tradition of poetry as a craft, and a craft of positive social value. Such a poet as the Spartan Tyrtaeus, whose songs inspired his countrymen to greater ferocity and patriotic fervour, might be seen as exemplifying this public tradition. The Roman Ovid, whose frivolous or otherwise subversive poetry led Augustus to banish him for life, might be seen as betraying it.

Plato did not trust poets to compose within this second, socially valuable tradition; the unaccountable gusts from the Muses might blow too strongly. So, for example – and here Plato is speaking of dramatic poetry, but the force of his argument will apply to many other forms also –

> we shall bow down before a being with such miraculous powers of giving pleasure; but we shall tell him that we are not allowed to have any such person in our commonwealth; we shall crown him with fillets of wool, anoint his head with myrrh, and conduct him to the borders of some other country. For our own benefit, we shall employ the poets and storytellers of the more austere and less attractive type, who will... conform to those rules we laid down when we began the education of our warriors.

> (Plato, *Rep*. 398b, tr. Cornford)

The image of the poet as social cement-layer, or source of a community's motive-power, is seized by Horace as the really significant strand in the Orpheus legend as it reached him. The whole tradition of Orpheus the animal-charmer is said by Horace to derive from his actual achievement in raising men from savagery, as other poets also did, to begin a civilised way of life in communities.

> Silvestres homines sacer interpresque deorum
> caedibus et victu foedo deterruit Orpheus,
> dictus ob hoc lenire tigris rabidosque leones.
> Dictus et Amphion, Thebanae conditor urbis,
> saxa movere sono testudinis et prece blanda
> ducere quo vellet. Fuit haec sapientia quondam,
> publica privatis secernere, sacra profanis,
> concubitu prohibere vago, dare iura maritis,
> oppida moliri, leges incidere ligno;
> sic honor et nomen divinis vatibus atque
> carminibus venit. Post hos insignis Homerus
> Tyrtaeusque mares animos in Martia bella
> versibus exacuit; dictae per carmina sortes;
> et vitae monstrata via est.

> Before men left the jungle, a holy prophet of heaven,
> Orpheus, made them abhor bloodshed and horrible food.
> Hence he is said to have tamed rabid lions and tigers.
> It is also said that Amphion, who built the city of Thebes,
> moved rocks by the sound of his lyre and led them at will
> by his soft appeals. This was the wisdom of olden days:
> to draw a line between sacred and secular, public and private;
> to bar indiscriminate sex, and establish laws of marriage;
> to build towns and inscribe legal codes on wood.
> That is how heavenly bards and their poems came to acquire
> honour and glory; after them Tyrtaeus and Homer
> won renown, for their verses sharpened the courage of men
> · to enter battle. Song was the medium of oracles, song
> showed the way through life.

(Horace, *Ep.* II. 3, *de Arte Poetica*, 391-403, tr. Rudd)

It is in this role that Orpheus appears in Virgil's Elysium in *Aeneid* IV, 'the Thracian priest in his long robe', venerated as teacher by the spirits of great heroes and men of true virtue. The Orpheus of the *Georgics* has no place in the Hades of Aeneas' *katabasis*.

The idea of the poet's function as social teacher – sometimes still combined with the prophetic role (which also had Greek sources) in the Renaissance – was popular in Tudor England, particularly in the works of Spenser,[9]

Chapman, and Bacon. Orpheus' understanding of divine law and moral truth, and his command of the poetic art as a supreme skill, made him the best teacher for early communities as the Renaissance thinker imagined them in their struggle towards civilised life. In developing such an image of Orpheus, and of the poet in general, the writers and thinkers of the Tudor age were accepting the Roman choice which asserted a social value for the arts and a vocation of disciplined craft for the artist, while the door to 'the underworld of feeling' remained locked, with Eurydice dead and unsought behind it.

What is a poet, if he follows the path opened before him by the Roman act of choice? He is one who exercises a craft learnt through purposeful discipleship, and used to influence mankind for good. He is a social teacher, a civiliser who devotes his skill to high ends and so must reject limited personal themes and dangerous emotions. He rejects, therefore, the journey into the unconscious which other artists have often regarded as the source of their own creativity; he turns away from the art and literature of man's 'dark side', the formless, the irrational, and the chthonic. To carry out his task, he will try to work with clarity, proportion, and decorum.

The mainstream of the European tradition since the Renaissance concerning the artist's identity and the value of the artist's work in society has accepted this Roman choice, and consciously so; Roman civilisation provided the exemplar and the channel by which all that was found most valuable in ancient Greece had reached the modern world. Rome provided the principles of taste, as well as of law and morality, for educated men in the seventeenth and eighteenth centuries. For them, the medieval period, with its anonymous craftsmen whose view of themselves was biblical rather than classical, often seemed a kind of aberration, and was not highly regarded. Neither could the *katabasis* of Orpheus be incorporated into the Roman poet-icon, except as a minor adventure (retold as a sad tale or sometimes a mock-tragic ballad, by a number of eighteenth-century poetasters in England). The search for Eurydice began to be reinterpreted only in the nineteenth century, by the French and German Romantics, who insisted on re-opening for artists and poets the dark world of death and of the dream, in order to find new images and new language. Sometimes this has been possible simply through a more attentive approach to 'minute particulars', sometimes through obviously experimental movements such as surrealism. Poets, artists, and musicians of the twentieth century have renewed the search for Eurydice in many ways. By doing so they have often encountered not only the lost bride, but other mythological entities that had been forgotten and denied. In recognising and naming these presences, they have also recognised themselves as heirs of Orpheus.

Notes

Introduction

1. Philostratus, *Heroica*, V. 704; *Life of Apollonius of Tyana*, IV. 4. One of the most recent representations of the Orpheus legend uses the hostility of Apollo as its central theme: Harrison Birtwistle's opera *The Mask of Orpheus* (1986) ends with Apollo (in the form of a huge sun-face) triumphant above the stage while Orpheus lies dead.

Chapter I *The Backward Glance*

1. The poem was printed in the Academy catalogue for 1864. It was reprinted in the *Selections* of Browning's poems which appeared in 1865, and in later editions of *Dramatis Personae*.

2. In their biography *Lord Leighton* (New Haven, 1975), L. and R. Ormond speak of the painting's 'over-upholstered look' (61) and 'theatrical lighting ... chilly tonality' (86). These qualities relate to Leighton's habit of seeing his figures in terms of sculpture, and Hellenistic sculpture at that. His agonised Orpheus resembles nothing so much as the struggling Alcyoneus on the Great Altar of Pergamum, clinging with one foot to Ge while Athene pulls him by the hair. The Ormonds also relate Leighton's Orpheus painting to his *Fisherman and Syren*, painted about seven years earlier, in which a young fisherman, very handsome in Greek style, lies against a rock, outstretched in the pose of crucifixion, while a voluptuous pearl-braided mermaid entwines her tail about his limp figure. The male rejection in the Orpheus picture is more positive and more tormented, but the theme is recognisably the same.

3. In the year before *Orpheus and Eurydice* was shown at the Academy, Leighton had designed the tomb erected for Elizabeth Barrett Browning in the Protestant Cemetery at Florence. It is an imposing structure decorated with medallions and emblems of poetry including the lyre.

4. When Virgil speaks of her following behind Orpheus because Proserpina had imposed this law (*Geo.* IV. 487), he is not necessarily implying that

Eurydice knew of a ban on any backward looking. Eurydice's close association with Proserpina has been differently interpreted by many scholars,
from Jane Harrison onwards; cf. Ch. X.

5. The Lorelei image finds expression in Leighton's *Fisherman and Syren*
(cf. n. 2), but in general he avoided it: his women are usually noble and
innocent even when they bring men to their doom (e.g. *The Last Watch of
Hero*).

6. In a letter of 22 November, 1817, to Benjamin Bailey: 'I am certain of
nothing but the holiness of the Heart's Affections and the truth of the
Imagination.'

7. Charles Dickens, *David Copperfield* (1850), Ch. 64: the last words of the
book.

8. The suggestion that *furor* here refers not to Orpheus' uncontrollable
impulse but to a destructive frenzy in the *crudelia fata* themselves was made
in 1840 by the Rev. F. G. Cooper (*Works of Virgil*, New York) and has recently
been reiterated by James Seaton in his *Reading of Vergil's 'Georgics'* (Amsterdam, 1983), 167. The whole interpretation of *fatum*, and of Jupiter's part
in the world order, takes a different turn (as Seaton sees) if this view is
accepted. Seaton seems to me to be mistaken in supposing that Orpheus in
494 cannot be both object of the verb and vehicle of its subject, *furor*. *Quis
tantus furor te perdidit?* is exactly parallel in thought to *subita dementia cepit
amantem*, six lines earlier.

9. On this aspect of Orpheus' disobedience, cf. G. B. Miles, *Virgil's
'Georgics'* (Berkeley, 1980), 276.

10. On the contrasting figures of Aristaeus and Orpheus in *Geo.* IV., v.
Ch. XI.

11. Cf. Ch. II, n. 4.

12. M. Owen Lee, 406-7.

13. *Alc.* 357-62. The scholiast on this passage states that Orpheus succeeded in bringing his wife back.

14. Hermesianax, *Leontion* III (= Kern, *Orph. Fragm.*, test. 61), ap.
Athen. XIII. 597b.

15. Isocrates, *Busiris*, II. 8; Diod. Sic. *Bibl.* IV. 25. 4. The author known as
pseudo-Heraclitus also speaks of Orpheus bringing up Eurydice from
Hades, just as Heracles brought up Cerberus (*de Incred.* 21).

16. *Symp.* 179d.

17. Jane Harrison remarked that in Greek mythology 'passionate lovers
are always late' (*Prolegomena to the Study of Greek Religion*, Cambridge,
1908, 603). The *Orphic Argonautica*, with its journey to Hades, cannot be
earlier than the second century AD.

18. Peri's *Euridice* has been revived in recent years, notably in performance by Music Theatre Wales. This version, with 'new and free'
accompaniment by Stephen Oliver, revealed great beauty in the melodic line,

and also keen intelligence and warmth in Rinuccini's libretto. However, the work remained an exciting philosophic demonstration rather than a drama.

19. This was in 1616, when Monteverdi rejected a proposal for a setting of *Le nozze di Tetide* because he thought it impossible to write music for winds: 'Ariadne moved us because she was a woman, and similarly Orpheus because he was a man, not a wind.'

20. This translation of Alfred's Old English is largely that of W. J. Sedgefield (Oxford, 1900, 116-8).

21. Expansion of Boethius' Latin (Book III, Metrum 12), either to explain classical references or to draw out Christian implications, has been ascribed largely to commentaries such as that of Remigius of Auxerre; some additions may come from Alfred himself.

22. Bersuire was a Benedictine of Avignon, who wrote the allegorical commentary on the *Metamorphoses* which seems to have attached the biblical moral to Ovid's story for the first time. He was writing in the fourteenth century, at least a century before the illustrated version of the *Ovide Moralisé* was printed in Paris.

23. 'calm of mind, all passion spent': v. *Samson Agonistes*, 1755-8.

24. The 'empathetic' Orpheus narrative is closely analysed by Otis in *Virgil: A Study in Civilised Poetry* (Oxford, 1963), 197-209.

25. 'Can you bear this?' is from a letter of Charles James Fox commenting on Aeneas' 'complacent' *sum pius Aeneas* in *Aen*. I. 378; *sunt lacrimae rerum*, I. 462; in context the phrase clearly means 'men weep for (human) disasters', but the long accepted sense 'there is grief at the heart of life' may not be wholly unjustified as undertone.

26. Brooks Otis, *Ovid as an Epic Poet* (Cambridge, 1970), 184.

27. Some critics do not regard this catena of stories as a miscellany. Otis (183) discovers an ingenious pattern, and some other commentators have been even more schematic.

Chapter II *The Magic Flute*

1. Graf, 80.

2. 'The Story of Orpheus and Eurydice', in *Poems of the Earthly Paradise Time* (c. 1865-70). Morris wrote many verse tales on the theme *Love Is Enough* (title of a drama of medieval colouring, 1875).

3. H.D., *Collected Poems* (New York, 1925).

4. 'Orpheus and Eurydice', *CQ* n.s. II (1952), 113-26.

5. Guthrie (1935), 187-91, Appendix to Ch. V. These vases show Orpheus performing his music in Hades, but they do not show the rescue of Eurydice.

In two of them (one said to be in Naples, the other in the Fenicia collection) there is a woman whom some have identified as Eurydice, but she is not named and other identifications are possible.

6. Paus. I. 37. iv.

7. Eusebius, *In Praise of Constantine*, 14.

8. In Jean Anouilh's play *Eurydice* (1941).

9. E.g. Plato, *Protagoras*, 326a-b. Alexander Polyhistor (as reported by Plutarch, *De Mus*. 5) said that Orpheus' compositions bore no resemblance to auletic music, and that he imitated no one; his style was followed by Terpander of Lesbos, who lived in the seventh century BC and was said to have received the lyre of Orpheus from some fishermen.

10. The earliest known representation of the lyre, on the famous sarcophagus from Hagia Triada in Crete, shows an instrument with seven strings. The *Orphic Argonautica* (381-4) speaks of the *cithara* as Apollo's instrument, and associates the *phorminx* (an older and smaller version of the lyre) with Hermes. Both are played by the centaur Chiron.

11. Nicomachus of Gerasa (c. 100 AD) relates that Hermes, not Apollo, was the teacher of Orpheus; but no earlier writer by-passes Apollo in this way.

12. Soph. *Ichn.* 307, 337, 366. Only about four hundred lines of this play are known, from papyrus discovered in 1907, and about half of these lines are incomplete. Much, therefore, remains obscure. The compilation known as the *Library*, handed down under the name of Apollodorus, also makes the theft of the cattle precede the lyre, and distinctly states that these cattle furnished the gut for the lyre's strings (III. 10. ii).

13. Paus. VIII. 54, vii. Aversion to the tortoise seems to have become stronger in Roman times, together with admiration for tortoiseshell as a luxury material for decoration. For the early Christians, the tortoise became a symbol of evil, and the word *tartarucus* ('dweller in Tartarus') often replaced *testudo* as its Latin name. (OED, however, derives 'tortoise' from the Latin *tortus*, 'twisted'). Cf. J.M.C. Toynbee, *Animals in Roman Life and Art*, (New York, 1972), 221-3.

14. Tony Harrison, *The Trackers of Oxyrhynchus* (London, 1990), 44-5. The mysterious sounds which bear a disturbing resemblance to a cow's mooing are like the lowing sound which comes from the meat on the spits when Helios' cattle are roasted in *Od*. XII. Cf. Linforth, 135-6, on the Grimm folk-tale 'The Singing Bone'.

15. Paus. IX. 30. i.

16. On the *Ichneutae*, and the satyr-play in general, v. the admirable survey by D.F. Sutton, *The Greek Satyr-Play* (Meisenheim am Glan., 1980). On Marsyas, cf. Ov. *Met*. VI. 382-400. The hideous fate met by Marsyas is paralleled by many other mythical characters who struggled to practise some form of art, free from divine dictation; this structure is well discussed by

Eleanor Winsor Leach, 'Ekphrasis in Ovid's *Metamorphoses*', *Ramus* 3 (1974), 102-42. For the somewhat surprising appearance of a Marsyas-statue in the Roman Forum, and his demotion along with the exaltation of Apollo by Augustus, v. J.P. Small, *Cacus and Marsyas in Etrusco-Roman Legend* (Princeton, 1982).

17. E.g. Asclepiades of Tragilos, cited by Schol. Eur. *Rhes.* 895; and probably Pindar. *Pyth.* IV. 176. Cf. Linforth, 4, 22-3.

18. *Busiris,* XI. 7.

. 19. Linforth, 21. Agriope or Argiope as late as the third century BC, in Hermesianax (ap. Athenaeus, XIII, 597B); Eurydice is not mentioned in literature before Moschus' *Lament for Bion* (second century BC, Moschus, III. 124); however, the name Eurydice is written on one of the Apulian vases mentioned on page 30.

20. For shamanism in general v. M. Eliade, *Shamanism: Archaic Techniques of Ecstasy* (Paris, 1951, tr. London. 1964); and for shamanism in the Greek world, v. Dodds, 142, 164, n. 47, and W. Burkert, 'Γοης, zum griechischen *Schamanismus*', *Rh. Mus*. CV (1962).

21. Isocrates, *Busiris*, XI. 38.

22. Genesis, 19:26.

23. Hoban, ed. Picador. The killing of the tortoise by Orpheus has no classical model, as far as I know. Hoban also telescopes the myth in other ways, and in some important details departs from its tradition entirely; for instance, he makes Hermes the father of Orpheus.

24. On Masonic elements in *The Magic Flute*, v. H.C. Robbins Landon, *Mozart's Last Year* (London, 1988), 127-31.

25. Macrobius, *Saturn*. I. 18, 22; Eur. ap. Macrob. id.: 'O Lord Bacchus, lover of the laurel, Healer Apollo skilled with the lyre.' Macrobius also quotes Aeschylus: 'Apollo crowned with ivy, the Bacchic one, the prophet.'

Chapter III *The Healer of the Soul*

1. E.g. the Dorian expresses self-control and moderation, the Mixolydian sadness and gravity, the Phrygian fire and inspiration (*Pol*. VIII. 5, 1340b). The whole passage on music in education (VIII. 5-7) naturally assumes familiarity with Greek musical language and styles, and also with a considerable literature on musical subjects, much of it now lost.

2. v. especially *Rep.* III. 398-401, 410-12; cf. *Protagoras*, 326b, and *Laws,* II. 656a.

3. This is not to suggest that the illuminators of Hebrew manuscripts were familiar with Greek vase-painting, or any other ancient source. What did exist

was a continuous tradition representing Orpheus, or an Orpheus-figure, as bringer of spiritual health and also tamer of animals through music. David could not fulfil his biblical role without following this Mediterranean pattern.

4. The Jerusalem mosaic was discovered near the Damascus Gate, in 1901, and would appear to be part of the floor of a tomb. For a detailed account, v. F. Cabrol and H. Leclercq, *Dictionnaire d'archéologie chrétienne* (Paris, 1936), XII, 2740-6. Another remarkable example in mosaic was discovered in 1965 near Gaza, a synagogue floor showing David, in the dress of a Byzantine emperor, playing to wild beasts who listen with heads bowed. This mosaic is dated by an inscription, 508-9 AD.

The inattentive dog whose master plays the flute to him on the monastery floor at Beth Shean in Israel forms part of a large and attractive design using many Greek themes; the Orphean tradition here is weakened but still evident.

Illustrations of David composing the Psalms, or tending his sheep as a boy, follow the Orpheus iconography in both Jewish and Christian manuscripts of the medieval period.

Orpheus and David are side by side as healers of strife in an endearing passage of Spenser:

> Wicked Discord, whose small sparkes once blowen
> None but a God or godlike man can slake;
> Such as was Orpheus, that when strife was growen
> Amongst those famous ympes of Greece, did take
> His silver Harpe in hand, and shortly friends them make.
> Or such as that celestiall Psalmist was,
> That when the wicked feend his Lord tormented,
> With heavenly notes, that did all other pas,
> The outrage of his furious fit relented.
> Such Musicke is wise words with time concented,
> To moderate stiffe minds, disposed to strive...

> > > (*Faerie Queene*, IV.2.i-ii)

5. Ps. 89:15.

6. In 'Poetry and Drama' (1951), printed in *On Poetry and Poets* (1956).

7. The story of Heracles' apotheosis goes back at least to Homer's time (*Od.* XI. 600); the Aeneas tradition was much older than Virgil, and had its living witness in the worship of the hero, well attested in Latium. The interpretation of the *Aeneid* as record of a spiritual pilgrimage leading to a heavenly realm goes back at least as early as Fulgentius' *Vergiliana Continentia* in the sixth century. Bernardus Silvestris, in the twelfth century, developed this analysis in terms of Chartrian Platonism, and draws a comparison between Aeneas and Orpheus at the moment of entry into the underworld (*Commentum super sex libros Eneidos Virgilii*). For Orpheus as teacher in Virgil's Elysium, v. *Aen.* VI. 645-7.

8. Summarised by Winthrop Wetherbee in *Platonism and Poetry in the Twelfth Century* (Princeton, 1972), 96-7. For Guillaume and the 'School of Chartres' to which he belonged, the supreme texts from the ancient world were Plato's *Timaeus* and Boethius.

9. Robert Henryson, *Orpheus and Eurydice*, 414, 561-4. The details of Henryson's allegory appear to derive from the Commentary on Boethius written in the late thirteenth century by Nicholas Trevet.

10. Bersuire begins his Commentary with a clear statement of these alternatives: *dic allegorice quod Orpheus, filius (s)olis, est Christus, filius Dei patris, qui a principio Eurydicem... animam humanam per caritatem et amorem duxit ipsamque per specialem prerogativam a principio sibi coniunxit. Verumtamen serpens...* ('Say in allegorical terms that Orpheus, son of the Sun, is Christ, the son of God the Father, who from the beginning has led Eurydice...the human soul, through (his) charity and love, and by special prerogative, has joined her to himself from the beginning. Yet the serpent...'). Orpheus leads Eurydice out of hell, singing *Surge, propera, amica mea, et veni* ('Arise, hasten, my love, and come'). Bersuire goes on: *Vel dic quod Orpheus est peccator... qui amat animam suam perdet eam* ('Or say that Orpheus is a sinner...(he) who loves his own soul shall lose it').

11. The author of this hymn is unknown. It is discussed in Peter Dronke's important article 'The Return of Eurydice' (*C&M* 23, 1962, 198-215). Dronke suggests that this Orpheus-Christus *figura* goes back to Prudentius and probably earlier. Moses' brazen serpent is compared with the crucified Christ in the words attributed in John 3:14 to Jesus himself. In the Easter sequence, Orpheus' lyre is implicitly set in analogy both with the brazen serpent and with the Cross.

12. A third icon of the Good Shepherd, found especially in medieval manuscript illumination, shows him attended by various animals as he walks along, cradling a lamb in his arms (the lamb often haloed as Lamb of God). This *figura* has no pagan forerunner, as far as I know.

13. R. Eisler, *Orpheus* (Leipzig and Berlin, 1925), 97. Cf. Guthrie (1935), Ch. III, n. 14.

14. O. Kern, *Die Religion der Griechen*, II (1935), 199, n. 1.

15. For the Domitilla *arcosolium*, v. P. du Bourguet *Early Christian Art (Le Peinture paleo-chrétienne*, Amsterdam and Paris, 1965), 53.

16. The discussion of this amulet in Guthrie (1935), 265-6, considers Eisler's theory that it represents purely pagan traditions that Dionysus and Orpheus both suffered crucifixion. Another 'syncretist' object of great interest is a gold signet ring, thought to date from the fifth century, which shows Orpheus playing his lyre, beside a tree entwined by a serpent; a Greek inscription evidently refers to the Revelation. The ring is in the British Museum; v. J. Godwin, *Mystery Religions in the Ancient World* (London, 1981), 145.

17. B. Walters, 'The Orpheus Mosaic in Littlecote Park, England', in *Atti del III Colloquio internazionale sul Mosaico Antico* (Bologna, 1984), 433-42.

18. These details depend on descriptive evidence from early antiquarian witnesses, and the series of engravings by Samuel Sysons, dated 1796. The pavement itself suffered serious damage in the eighteenth and nineteenth centuries and it has now been re-buried. A replica of the mosaic as it would have appeared originally was made in 1973 by Bob and John Woodward.

19. A much smaller and simpler Orpheus-floor at Withington, in Gloucestershire, was laid at approximately the same date as the Woodchester one; it had a rectangular panel added later, with fish and a bearded head with tendrils springing from it. This is certainly intended as Neptune, since there is also a hand holding a trident. This design is very inferior to the Woodchester one (and came from a different workshop) but may have used ideas from the Corinium artists' work.

20. The scholiast is quoted by Kern (*Test.* 82): 'The philosopher Heraclides says that some tablets of Orpheus actually exist. He writes that a claim is made in the same way for (the cult of) Dionysus in Thrace, on the (mountain) called Haemus, where they say certain records exist on tablets.' (The name of Orpheus was added to the text by Wilamowitz.)

21. Athan. *cod. Reg.* 1993 f. 317 (= Kern, *Test.* 154).

22. The text is known to us from Eusebius (*Praep. Evang.* XIII. 12) and, in a shorter version, from ps-Justin (*de Mon.* 2, *Coh. ad Gent.* 15). These texts, and other citations, are collected in Kern, 255-66. For a very useful discussion of the poem, v. Friedman, 13-28. This includes appraisal of the use of Greek myth and Greek literary conventions in Alexandrian Jewish apologetic.

23. To say that the Testament is addressed to Greek readers, in the attempt to prove to them that monotheism is compatible with familiar mythic and philosophic ideas, need not exclude a different set of readers – the Jews and/or Christians – who might be imagined as realising through Orpheus' message that the pagan heritage was not wholly senseless and intolerable.

Chapter IV *Eternal Life*

1. The phrase is Bowra's: *Pindar* (Oxford, 1964), 369. Pindar also gives us the earliest extant account of a heavenly region to be attained by those who have 'kept their souls pure from all wrongdoing' (*Ol.* II. 61-77). The scene is again one of radiant light, golden flowers, garlands, fresh water; but the gods and kings who live there in the *Odyssey* version (IV. 561-5) are joined by '*all those* who ...' R. G. Austin's note on the Elysium passage in *Aen.* VI points out that this ode of Pindar was composed for Theron of Acragas, a city where

Pythagorean ideas and Orphic cult were likely to be very familiar.

2. On this 'priamel' pattern, v. E. Fraenkel, *Horace* (Oxford, 1957), 230-2. Milton used it for the activities of the fallen angels, *P.L.* II. 528-76.

3. Vat. lat. 3225, fol. 52, recto; Angelo Mai, *Virgilii picturae antiquae ex codicibus Vaticanis* (Rome, 1835), pl. 49; T. B. Stevenson, *Miniature Decoration in the Vatican Virgil* (Tübingen, 1983), 72.

4. Nothing could be more unlike the Elysium of Tibullus (I. 3. 57-66), who is introduced there by Venus, not the Sibyl, and sees Amor rather than Orpheus as presiding over the activities of the blessed.

5. As do the 'bright Spirits' of C. S. Lewis's *Great Divorce*, who on attaining to heaven find the 'kernel' of all that they ever desired in their earthly life.

6. *Crat.* 400 c4. On Plato's use of the prison metaphor, cf. Burnet's note on *Phd.* 62b.

7. *Symp.* 179d, *Rep.* 364-5.

8. Plato, *Rep.* X. 618b, 620a.

9. v. W. Burkert, *Greek Religion* (Oxford, 1985), 300.

10. E.g. Eleusis, Soph. fr. 753, 805; Aristoph. *Frogs*, 426-31; Orphic disciplines, Eur. *Hippol.* 952-5; philosophic ideas, Eur. *Phrixus*, fr. 833, *Chrysipp.* fr. 839.

The Athenians who fell at Potidaea in 432 were officially commemorated in an inscription asserting different bourns for spirit and body: 'The heaven received the souls of these men, the earth their bodies' (CIA I. 442). Rohde (437) cites this epigram as implying a view of the soul's survival already commonly accepted. In contrast with this inscription, it is noteworthy that Pericles' oration in praise of the dead in the first year of the Peloponnesian War (Thuc. II. 35-46) contains no reference to their souls' survival; and Socrates in Plato's *Apology* is hesitant.

11. Diog. Laert. VIII. 8, Clem. Alex. *Strom.* I. 131, both citing Ion of Chios as their source.

12. For Dionysus, cf. Ch. IX: Persephone, Ch. X. Rhea, *Orphic Hymn* XIV, cf. Ov. *Met.* XI. 92, Justinus, *Hist. Phil. epit.* XI. 7, 14; Megale, Hippolytus, *Refutatio*, V. 20.

13. Linforth, 291.

14. Guthrie, 238.

15. Hdt, II. 79. Herodotus attributes the same prohibition to the Egyptians and associates it also with Bacchic and Pythagorean custom. The Orphic rules of diet were also Pythagorean.

Theseus' derisive reference to those who 'take Orpheus as King' in Euripides' *Hippolytus* (952-4) implies that pride in sexual abstinence might characterise a devout Orphic, but the dramatic context makes this speech a wild flailing at the supposed seducer; Hippolytus the huntsman could hardly have been an Orphic, as Barrett points out.

16. Theophrastus, *Charact.* XVI. 11.

17. Plato. *Protag.* 316d, *Rep.* 364e; Dem. *In Aristogeitona* I. 11; *Rhes.* 943-4; Hor. *A.P.* 391-2.

18. Pausanius, describing rites conducted at Phlya in Attica, refers to them as 'performances' (IX. 30. xii).

19. Clem. *Protrept.* II. 17-18; Arnob. *Adv. Nationes* V. 19. These passages seem to be confirmed in their reference to representation, not merely verbal commemoration, when one of the writers of the *Mythographi Vaticani* tells the story of Bacchus' dismemberment and adds: *hanc etiam fabulam in sacris eius (Sc. Orphei?) repraesentasse leguntur* (III. 12. v.). Cf. Macrobius, in *Somn. Scip.* I. 12. xi, Diodorus III. 62. viii. For discussion of the 'representations', v. Guthrie (1952), 132, 203-4, 207-13.

20. Mallius Theodorus, *de metris* IV. 1, p. 589, cites the Athenian Critias for this claim (which makes the tradition nine centuries old at the time of our surviving text). Other authors are not so categorical about Orpheus' metrical inventions: Musaeus, Linus, and Homer are named as rival claimants, also Phemonoe, the first Pythian priestess.

Alcidamas, *Odysseus* 24, ascribes the invention of the alphabet to Orpheus, but this was not a common belief; cf. Linforth, 37. Music is never said to be an invention of Orpheus: what he discovered was the right use of language and musical sounds to bridge the gulf between human and divine.

21. Pap. Berol. 44 = Kern *Fr.* 49, restored by Diels.

22. Eur. *Alc.* 966-9; cf. p. 59. For details of these representations, v. Guthrie (1952), 36-9.

23. For discussion of this and related questions about the *Hymns*, v. Linforth, 179-89; Guthrie (1952), 257-61.

24. The presence in the theogonic literature of philosophic ideas related to those of Heraclitus and Empedocles was pointed out as long ago as 1926 by Otto Gruppe. He believed that the Orphic cosmology originated in the sixth century BC, and that the *Rhapsodic Theogony* was an attempt – made perhaps many generations later – to assemble the various ideas and tales that had proliferated from those beginnings. But v. West, 227-9, on the date and currency of this work.

25. 'Guard all these things in your mind, dear child, in your heart, knowing indeed that all of them were spoken long ago, and from Phanes' (Rhaps. Theog. 4, ap. Aristocrit. Manich. *Theosophia*, 116 = Kern, fr. 61).

26. The most detailed and impressive study of the gold plates is that of Zuntz (277-393). He considers the texts Pythagorean and in no way Orphic. The distinction between these two sets of ideas is not easy to maintain, and probably was not always clearly maintained in practice. But Zuntz's caution against 'vast and vague' 'Orphic' interpretations is most salutary. v. also Burkert, *Greek Religion* (Oxford, 1985), 293, on the further discovery in 1969 at Vibo Valentia in Bruttium.

27. Cf. the detailed account of these tablets, in West, 17-18.

28. *Hipp.* 952-4.West thinks that the links with Pythagorean doctrine which the bone plates seem to suggest were not likely to be derived from Pythagoras' own disciples: he suggests a common origin for both Orphic and Pythagorean strands in Ionia.

29. Now in the possession of the Liverpool Museum. For details on this marble, v. B. Ashmole, *Catalogue of the Ancient Marbles at Ince Blundell Hall* (Oxford, 1929); A.T.F. Michaelis, *Ancient Marbles in Great Britain* (Cambridge, 1882). The relief is discussed by Kerenyi in his *Pythagoras und Orpheus* (Zurich, 1950). Kerenyi wished to emphasise links between Orpheus and the untamed world of the forest; he assumed the existence of a wolf-cult connected with the Lycomedai at Phlya (cf. p. 71) and with Apollo Lycaeus.

30. *AP* 391-3. *Fauni enim silvicolae... quos poeta Lucanus secundum opinionem Graecorum ad Orphei lyram cum innumerosis ferarum generibus cantu deductos cecinit*, 'The Fauns, dwellers in the woodlands,... whom the poet Lucan described as drawn by song – according to the belief of the Greeks – with countless kinds of wild beasts, to the lyre of Orpheus' (*Liber monstrorum*, I. 6, ap. Haupt, *Opuscula*, II, p. 224). Michaelis cites another example of a satyr listening to Orpheus, in a Greek vase-painting (*Arch. Zeit.* 1868, pl. 3).

31. Rev. of Schreiber's *Griechische Satyrspiel-reliefs*, in *Berliner Philol. Wochenschrift* (1910), 785 ff.

32. *Phaedo*, 107d; references to this idea in other writers are cited by Burnet *ad loc.*

33. Plutarch, *de facie in orbe lunae*. The belief that souls would go to the moon after death is discussed with many references in Norden's edition of Virgil, *Aen.* VI.

34. *De vita Pythagorica*, 18. ii.

35. The tradition of the Orphean Christ lingers in the popular song *Lord of the Dance*, and its spirit animates Stevie Smith's short poem *The Airy Christ*, where he sings ceaselessly and only wishes that men would hear him. It is not always apocryphal: Gregory Nazianzen (*Orat.* II. 1. ix) speaks of Jesus guiding his flock 'with the sweet sound of the syrinx'. Music, and the dance, as divinely given means to praise and to approach God, are of course part of Hebrew tradition: 'they that sing, as well as they that dance, shall say, "All my fountains are in Thee" ' (Ps. 87:7).

36. Manilius, V. 326-8:

> Oeagrius Orpheus
> et sensus scopulis et silvis addidit aures
> et Diti lacrimas et morti denique finem

Orpheus, son of Oeagrus, gave consciousness to rocks, ears to the woods, tears to Hell, and finally an end to Death.

The emphatic *denique* in this line makes the conquest of death Orpheus' final and characteristic achievement, surely referring to his role as saviour for initiates rather than to the one occasion of his quest for Eurydice. Bowra (118) thought that Manilius was simply choosing the earlier version of the Eurydice-story, in which she was successfully brought to life; this does not seem an adequate understanding of *morti denique finem*, or of *domuit infernas carmine leges* in I. 927.

Chapter V *The Music of the Spheres*

1. Like the water endlessly poured into leaking jars by the Danaids, who are regularly introduced into accounts of Hades, and depicted on the Apulian vases.

2. On memory in the *Aeneid*, v. E. Henry, *The Vigour of Prophecy* (Bristol, 1989), 132-7.

3. Paus. IX. 39. On the two fountains, v. also Rohde, 575, n. 151.

4. Hdt. IV. 95.

5. This practice is described in detail by Iamblichus, *VP* 164-5, and attributed by him to the witness of Aristoxenus. Little critical attention has been given to Iamblichus, but Burkert is sceptical about this account of Pythagorean discipline (*Weisheit und Wissenschaft zu Pythagoras, Philolaos und Plato*, Nuremberg, 1962). Most critics have been ready to accept it, however; v. Simondon, 158-60.

6. The first kind of knowledge is probably more influential in later European thought, through the theory of innately known *notiones* or abstract ideas, put forward in the treatises of Cicero and other writers on Roman Stoicism.

7. v. *Meno*, ed. R.S. Bluck (Cambridge, 1961), 275-6, on the relative importance here of Orphic, poetic, and Pythagorean traditions. Bluck was inclined to disbelieve in a Pythagorean origin for the Platonic doctrine of recollection; but other scholars (e.g. A. Cameron, *The Pythagorean Background of the Theory of Recollection*, Wisconsin, 1938; J. Burnet, *Introduction to Plato's 'Phaedo'*, 1911) take the opposite view. Burnet considered that *anamnesis* was part of the original teaching of Pythagoras, discarded by some of the 'scientific Pythagoreans' of the fifth century, but then re-examined in a mathematical context by Socrates (*Phaedo*, ed. Burnet, 72c).

8. In his 1964 lecture on *The Law of Nature and the Structure of Material*: 'The mathematical structures are actually deeper than the existence of mind or matter.' This return to the Pythagorean tradition has been inspiring to scientists in many fields: so Michael Polanyi in *Personal Knowledge* (1957)

acclaimed 'the beauty and power inherent in the rationality of contemporary physics', returning to a true source after the Descartian centuries.

9. *The Ascent of Man* (1973), 156.

10. *Comm. in Metaph.* 83.

11. The essay on astrology attributed to Lucian identifies the seven strings of Orpheus' lyre with the seven planets, and these are presumably the seven stars shown round the head of Orpheus, or Christ, on the Berlin seal and on several other objects of a syncretist character (and dubious date).

Specific details on the theme of the cosmos as cithara, in ancient times, is given by West, 30-1. An alternative version of this 'correspondence' was that of Boethius, who spoke of a four-stringed lyre which imitated 'the cosmic music that consists of the four elements'.

Both of these theories are discussed in a brief and lucid chapter in Burkert's *Lore and Science in Ancient Pythagoreanism* (Cambridge, Mass., 1972).

On the planetary diagrams, v. A. K. Heninger, Jr., *Touches of Sweet Harmony* (California, 1974); he discusses in detail, for example, that shown in Franchino Gafori's *Practica Musicae* (Milan, 1496).

12. Aristotle, *Metaph.* 986 a 3.

13. Similarly, in his notes to his unfinished epic *Davideis* (published 1656) Abraham Cowley insisted that the whole tradition of the heavenly music must be taken metaphorically. The music, Cowley says, stands for the mathematical order of the universe, and also for the order in the good man's soul. In the poem, God creates the universe of the four elements, which correspond to the different voices in a choir: earth is the bass, fire the treble, and water and air combined the tenor. Thus (Cowley adds):

> *David's Lyre* did *Saul's* wild rage control,
> And tun'd the harsh disorders of his *Soul.*

> (*Davideis*, I. 479-80)

14. v. Cornford's 1930 essay, 'The Harmony of the Spheres' (*The Unwritten Philosophy*, Cambridge, 1950, 14-27). George Steiner has pointed out the significance of the word *patine*, or *paten*, here: in addition to its meaning 'metal disc', it is the term applied to the flat dishes used for the Host at the Eucharist; the heavenly bodies seen by Lorenzo and Jessica are sacred (Steiner, 'Silence and the Poet', in *Language and Silence*, London, 1966, 61-2).

15. Cf. pp. 150, 158.

16. G.K. Chesterton, *Autobiography.*

17. E.g. in Edouard Schuré's *Les Grand Initiés* (Paris, 1889).

18. They included Léger, Delaunay, and Picabia; v. Virginia Spate, *Orphism* (Oxford, 1979). Marc Chagall, Delaunay's friend, was on the fringe of

this group, and was much influenced at the time by Orphic ideas. His painting *Hommage à Apollinaire* (1911-12; now at Eindhoven) represents a hermaphroditic figure with two singing heads, at the centre of a planetary disc.

Chapter VI *The Daughters of Memory*

1. E.g. the sonnet 'The world is too much with us' (published 1807).

2. Wordsworth dates his experience of joy as 'universal sentiment of Being' from his seventeenth year, when he felt himself communing with 'every form of creature':

> One song they sang, and it was audible...
>
> (*The Prelude*, II. 352-418, 1850 version)

3. The process is exemplified in some of Wordsworth's best-known poems, such as 'Tintern Abbey' and 'The Daffodils'. The memorable phrase comes from the Preface to *Lyrical Ballads*, where poetry is – in spite of this impetus of personal emotion – defined as a philosophic form of expression, in which 'no words which fancy or imagination can suggest will be to be compared with those which are the emanations of reality and truth'.

4.　　Brook! Whose society the Poet seeks,
Intent his wasted spirits to renew...
If wish were mine some type of thee to view,
Thee, and not thee thyself, I would not do
Like Grecian Artists, give thee human cheeks,
Channels for tears; No Naiad should'st thou be...

> (Sonnet, 1806)

5. On this question, v. M. Moorman, *William Wordsworth*, Vol. I (London, 1968), 423-6.

The identity of 'Lucy Gray' is another matter, though 'Oft I had heard...' seems to be speaking of a girl who has a supernatural being akin to that of 'Lucy' in the five poems discussed; she comes and goes inexplicably, and

> sings a *solitary* song,
> That whistles in the *wind*.

6. 'All Religions are One', c.1788. Blake's references to 'the forms of all things' have a Platonic ring; evidently, his thinking about perception and the nature of reality continued to be deeply Neoplatonic even after he

denounced Plato (together with Homer, Ovid, and Cicero) as the author of 'stolen and perverted Writings...which all men ought to contemn' (Preface to *Milton*). Blake's attitude to the classical tradition changed radically after his experience of 'restoration to the light of Art', which enabled him to identify the 'spectrous Fiend' that frustrated his work for twenty years as 'the Jupiter of the Greeks' (Letter to William Hayley, 23 October, 1804). Even so, the Platonic Theory of Forms, which he had studied in the voluminous works of Thomas Taylor, was never discarded.

Taylor had translated the *Hymns of Orpheus* as well as much of Plato, Plotinus, and Proclus: Blake's debt to him is admirably discussed in G.M. Harper's *The Neoplatonism of William Blake* (North Carolina, 1961).

7. Hesiod, *Theogony*, ed. M.L. West (Oxford, 1966),75: 'Hesiod's enthusiasm for the Muses...leads him to speak of them at some length, but he has not a great variety of things to say about them.'

The translation quoted here is by Richmond Lattimore (Michigan, 1959).

8. E.g. on the superb red-figured hydria at Palermo (Banco di Sicilia, Fondazione Ignazio Mormino 385); the musician in Phrygian dress has been identified with Orpheus; he holds a lyre but is looking at the Muse, who (as often) is shown holding an open roll from which she is apparently reading to him.

9. The earliest traditions seem to have spoken of three Muses. Pausanias (IX. 29) gives them names: Melete (Practice), Mneme (Remembrance), Aoide (Song). Cicero mentions one version which spoke of four (*N.D.* III. 21). However, nine became the accepted number at an early date.

10. Hor. *Od.* II. 1. xxxvii; III. 3. 1.1xx; Prop. II. 13A. iii; Pope, *Du Fresnoy's Art of Painting*, 2.

11. *Od.* VIII. 488-91. It is because the Muses know what really happened that the singer tells the tale 'very correctly'; so Dante calls on 'those Ladies' to inspire him, '*si che dal fatto il dir non sia diverso*', 'so that the word may not be at variance with the fact' (Inf. XXXII. 12).

12. *Theog.* 22-34; Callim. fr. 2; Ennius, *Pers.* Prol. 1-3). On these experiences, cf. West's commentary on *Theog.*, 158-61; he cites valuable parallels both within and outside the Greco-Roman tradition.

13. *A.P.* 385; Cic. *de Off.* I. 31.

14. Solon I. 51-2; cf. Theognis 876. D.A. Campbell prefers to take 'wisdom' in Solon's lines as meaning 'technical skill'. The language will certainly bear this sense, but the position of the Muses' pupil between the series of practical workers and craftsmen (43-50) and the prophets inspired by Apollo (53-6) seems to suggest 'wisdom' in a more general sense.

15. There is nothing comparable in the atmosphere or the attitude expressed in Propertius' dream of Apollo's rebuke and Calliope's blessing on Helicon (Prop. III. 3). Other examples of this poetic theme are collected in O. Falter, *Der Dichter und sein Gott bei den Griechers und Romern* (Würzburg, 1934).

16. Cf. C.M. Bowra, *Pindar* (Oxford, 1964), 33-41. The whole of Ch. I, and also Ch. VI, is closely relevant to the poet's relation with the Muses.

17. For more detailed consideration of the 'damsel', v. K.M. Wheeler, *The Creative Mind in Coleridge's Poetry* (London, 1981), 25-7.

18. The mingling of honey, milk, and dew in the 'drink of song' which Pindar sends to Aristoclides in *Nem.* III may not have been a source for Coleridge's poetic food, but the coincidence – if it is one – is notable.

Keats' Belle Dame also gave her pale knights 'honey wild and manna dew' to drink; his first version had 'honeydew'.

19. Preface to 'Kubla Khan' (1798).

20. Preludium to *The First Book of Urizen*, 1794; cf. *Europe*, 'My Fairy sat upon the table and dictated...' and the introductory lyric to *Songs of Innocence* (1789), where the command to 'pipe' comes from a child seen on a cloud.

The visitant 'dictating' to the poet had appeared in *Paradise Lost*; in Book VII Milton gives her the name Urania, and later calls her

> my Celestial Patroness, who deignes
> Her nightly visitation unimplor'd,
> And dictates to me slumbring, or inspires
> Easy my unpremeditated Verse.

> > (*P.L.* IX. 21-4.)

Dante also had called his Muse 'Urania' (*Purg.* XXIX. 41), but it is with the identity of Love that inspiration 'dictates' to him:

> I'mi son un che, quando
> Amor mi spira, noto, e a quel modo
> ch'è ditta dentro vo significando.

> I am one who, when Love breathes upon me, takes heed, and in this way I go on, revealing what has been spoken inwardly.

Chapter VII *The Naming of Creatures*

1. 'Les grands poètes et les grands artistes ont pour fonction sociale de renouveler sans cesse l'apparence que revêt la nature aux yeux des hommes' (*Les Peintres Cubistes*, 1913).

2. Apollinaire did, of course, find the Orpheus myth a congenial subject. His poem 'Le Bestiaire' had the subtitle 'Le Cortège d'Orphée'. It was set to

music by Poulenc. However, it was always the image of Orpheus and the natural world that interested Apollinaire, not the story of Eurydice.

3. v. C.M. Bowra, *The Creative Experiment* (London, 1949) for a brief and lucid account of Hopkins' understanding of the communication possible between nature and man. This Hopkins called 'instress', by which the identity of particular living beings or objects (their 'inscape') passed into the individual consciousness of another. These moments Bowra describes as 'truly supernatural experience', and 'Dionysiac', as against the 'Apollonian' experiences of Hopkins' friend Bridges.

4. Cf. D.F. Bauer, 'The Function of Pygmalion in Ovid's *Metamorphoses*', *TAPA* XCIII (1962), 1-21. This article comments in a perceptive way on the prominence of Pygmalion in this part of the poem, and also on Ovid's use of the image of stone throughout the work. The inanimate part of creation, used for protective walls and for tombs – and a kind of death at the sight of Medusa – can come to life in the story of Deucalion and, at this central point in the narrative, in response to the passion of the artist. This certainly is a climactic point in the structure of the *Metamorphoses*, but I would not like to follow Bauer's excursion into numerology and his meticulous tracing of the Golden Section.

Bauer cites a dissertation which I have not been able to see: W.C. Stephens, *The Function of Religious and Philosophical Ideas in Ovid's 'Metamorphoses'* (Princeton, 1957).

5. The only mention of the Orpheus myth which has any significance in Keats occurs at *Endymion* I. 793- 4, where Keats develops the idea of holy utterance or music imparting a sanctity which lingers in particular places:

> from the turf, a lullaby doth pass
> In every place where infant Orpheus slept.

It is a detail which suggests how congenial the Orphean theme might have been to Keats, if he had chosen it.

6. On this original and divine language, cf. Stephen R.L. Clark, *The Mysteries of Religion* (Oxford, 1986), 56-7. 'The yearning for a Really Appropriate Language' (Clark rather drily comments) 'is one explanation for the reverence often felt for "Science".'

Ben Jonson found this notion a rewarding theme for a satirical knockabout:

> Mammon: I'll shew you...a treatise penn'd by Adam –
> Surly: How!
> Mammon: Of the philosopher's stone, and in High Dutch.
> Surly: Did Adam write, sir, in High Dutch?
> Mammon: He did: Which proves it was the primitive tongue.

> (*The Alchemist*, II. i)

7. Simonides, fr. 62.

8. The acorn sufficed as food for men in their primitive state of goodness, according to Rousseau in his *Discours de l'Inegalité* (1754). Rousseau's immediate source for this detail was Dicaearchus; he might also have found it in several of the ancient poets, e.g. Tibullus II. 3. 73.

9. Kern, *Orpheus* (Berlin, 1920), 63. pl. 1. Cf. also Strzygowski, *Armenia*, on a frieze of the same subject.

10. C. S. Lewis uses the word 'enactment' for the speaking of names by his Venusian Adam, in the scene of almost rococo efflorescence which forms the climax to his science-fiction *Perelandra* (1943). He had used the same themes in the chapter called 'The Founding of Narnia', in *The Magician's Nephew* (1955): Aslan the divine lion paces about an empty land, singing, and the world around him is filled with growing trees, flowers, and animals of every kind, forming a circle around him. (This story also includes a Deplorable Word which can blight a world and destroy all living things.) Aslan had roared in *Prince Caspian*, to summon Bacchus and Silenus to join a throng of dancing trees. The nature of Lewis's Narnia is essentially Orphean.

11. Apollod. I. 9; Herod. II. 49.

12. An enjoyable account of Renaissance examples, with numerous illustrations, is by G. Scavizzi in *Orpheus: The Metamorphosis of a Myth*, ed. J. Warden (Toronto, 1985). Orpheus is seen in many versions, charming assorted animals, often including the three-headed Cerberus: the *ianitor inferorum* hangs his head at this new kind of sop, and stops barking.

13. In the event the lady was so embarrassed by Orpheus' nudity that she refused to wear the tiara in London society. A detachable loincloth was therefore made for Orpheus. The tiara is now owned by the Worshipful Company of Goldsmiths.

14. Godo Lieberg has carefully analysed the artist-figure in ancient literature; v. especially Lieberg, 159-73, for examples of the 'craftsman-poet'. The true creator, in the Jewish-Christian sense, is not found in the artist-figure until the Renaissance, Lieberg suggests: he quotes Leonardo de Vinci, *'il pittore è Signore d'ogni sorte di gente e di tutte le cose'*, 'the painter is lord of every kind of people, and of all things'.

15. This passage is discussed by Sewell, 72-4, noting its parallels with Sidney's *Apologie*, and the wedge of separation eventually driven between imagination and reason by Baconian thinking. Sidney, as Sewell observes, regretted and even resented this separation, but failed to resist it. He failed 'by presenting the poet as exceptional, aloof from the general endeavour of knowledge and justified on other grounds. He thus plays straight into Sprat's hands'.

16. Sewell, 179. The virtual omission of Blake from this very rich and discerning study is surprising.

17. The phrase was first used by T.S. Eliot in his essay 'The Metaphysical Poets', published in 1921. The particular exemplification of this psychic schism in the writing of Bacon was discussed in an important essay by L.C. Knights, 'Bacon and the Seventeenth-Century Dissociation of Sensibility' (1943), first published in *Scrutiny*, and reprinted in *Explorations* (1946). This essay is concerned with Bacon's own sensibility rather than his ideas; it makes Blake's hostility towards him more deeply comprehensible.

Chapter VIII *Furor Poeticus*

1. Ps. 40 is a good example of this shared experience in Hebrew poetry.

2. *Apol.* 22b-c; cf. the comparison of a poet with a fountain, *Laws* IV. 719c.

3. Quoted and discussed in relation to Thomas's poem 'After the Funeral' in C. Day Lewis's study of creativity *The Poetic Image* (London, 1947), 122.

4. *Conversations of Goethe with Eckermann*, tr. Oxenford (Everyman's Library, 1935), 205.

5. A remark cited by John Press in *The Fire and the Fountain* (Oxford, 1955), 5.

6. In her important article 'Poetic Inspiration in early Greece', *JHS* CI (1981), 87-100.

7. Stephen Spender, 'The Making of a Poem' (London, 1955), 52. This essay describes in close detail the experience of inspiration as Spender has known it, the kind of verbal craft-work that he found had to follow it, and the place of memory in the poetic vocation.

8. *An Anatomy of Inspiration* (London, 1940).

9. D.H. Lawrence, *Letters*.

10. No translator has found a wholly satisfactory equivalent for the Greek: 'mournful dirge' (Thomson) misses entirely, and 'tuneless tune' (Fraenkel), 'tuneless song' (Vellacott), and 'song unmusical' (Lloyd Jones) keep the oxymoron but have no appropriateness; if Cassandra's song recalls the nightingale's, it cannot be merely unmusical. The nearest to Aeschylus is perhaps Headlam's version, 'Lamenting in *lawless measures*, like the brown sad nightingale...'. This keeps the more general sense of 'without law' rather than 'without melody', and brings out Cassandra's disregard for – or ignorance of – musical expertise; her song lacks the detached craftsmanship of the Muses' disciple.

11. The phrase is Rilke's, from a short poem of 1923, describing the terror of the creative moment with great immediacy.

Wir sind nur Mund. Wer singt das ferne Herz,
das heil inmitten aller Dinge weilt?
Sein grosser Schlag ist in uns eingeteilt
in kleine Schlage. Und sein grosser Schmerz
ist, wie sein grosser Jubel, uns Zu gross.
So reissen wir uns immer wieder los
und sind nur Mund.

Aber aufeinmal bricht
der grosse Herzschlag heimlich in uns ein,
so dass wir schrein...
Und sind dann Wesen, Wandlung und Gesicht.

We are mouth, no more. Who sings the distant heart,
that dwells, whole, within all things?
Its powerful beating is shared among us,
in little beats. And its great sorrow
is – like its great jubilation – too great for us.
So we tear ourselves away once more
and are only mouth.

But all at once breaks out
the great heartbeat, at home within us,
so that we cry out...
and then we are Being, Transformation and Sight.

12. Elegy I. 1-7, tr. Mitchell. The moment when Rilke 'knew that the god had spoken', crying to him out of a (literal) storm so that he began to write this poem, is described by Princess Marie von Thurn und Taxis-Hohenlohe, in *Erinnerungen von Rainer Maria Rilke*, 40-1.

13. 'All Religions are One', c. 1788.

14. Preface to *Milton*, 1804-8.

15. *Approach to Painting* (1927), 19.

16. Letter to Hayley, 18 December, 1804. This letter, and the one written a year later (11 December, 1805, again to Hayley), express with great immediacy Blake's sense of blinding illumination when he felt the divine energy touching him, and the deprivation of the years when he did not.

17. Murray's article (n. 6) shows clearly how comparatively late was the idea of ecstatic possession in the Greek tradition of poetic inspiration.

Chapter IX *Poets' Sinews*

1. A more commonplace, if perhaps more sophisticated, variant on this motive of sexual jealousy, is suggested by Hyginus, who relates that each of the Thracian women was stirred by Venus to desire Orpheus for herself. This the goddess did in anger against Orpheus' mother Calliope, who had been chosen by Jupiter as judge between Venus and Proserpina for possession of Adonis.

2. E.g. Aesch. *Bassarids*.

3. Cf. Ch. IV, n. 19; West, 15-26; Herodotus (II. 81) speaks of 'Orphic and Bacchic rites', as if they were popularly conflated.

4. Cf. the account of these in E.R. Dodds' edition of *Bacchae* (Oxford, 1944), Introduction, II. iii. The whole of this Introduction remains indispensable for any consideration of Dionysian religion; cf. also Rohde, Ch. VIII.

5. Plut. *Them*. 13, ii. Even if we think this story incredible, it is evident that Plutarch did not expect his Greek and Roman readers to find it so.

6. 'Come, heroic Dionysus, to the pure temple of Elis...spotless bull' (Plut. *Quaest. Gr.* 36, 299b); cf. *de Is. et Osir.* 35 on statues of Dionysus Tauromorphos.

7. Paus. VIII. 37; cf. Soph. *Fr.* 874,

8. v. Rohde, 340-1, with Notes; Guthrie (1935), App. 1 to Ch. IV.

9. Guthrie (1950), 156.

10. On the conviction of immortality among the Thracians, cf. Hdt. IV. 93-4, and Plato, *Charm*, 156d.

11. Linus and flax, v. Robert Graves, *The Greek Myths* (Harmondsworth, 1955), 147, with considerable range of reference.

12. Proclus, Commentary on Plato's *Politicus*, 398.

13. *Catast.* XXIV. 140.

14. Not at all securely; v. R.S. Conway, *From Orpheus to Cicero* (Bull. J. Rylands Lib., 1933), 71.

15. Pico's insight was highly unusual in the fifteenth century, by which time Dionysus had assumed the persona of Bacchus, giver of sensual enjoyment.

16. This story also appears in an epigram which survives in a rhetorical declamation of uncertain date:

> Orpheus, servant of the Muses, the Thracians buried here. Zeus who rules on high struck him with a smoking dart, dear son of Oeagrus, who taught Heracles, and discovered letters, and wisdom, for mankind.

> (Quoted by Linforth, 15)

17. E.g. Ov. *Met*. XI. 50-5. Ovid's account goes on to describe an attack on the head by a snake; Apollo intervenes and turns the snake to stone. Virgil (*Geo*. IV. 523-7) leaves the head before it even reaches Lesbos.

18. *Heroica*, V. 704. For a particularly fine example of the head-oracle in a vase-painting, v. E. Vermeule, *Aspects of Death in Early Greek Art and Poetry* (Berkeley, Calif., 1979), 179 and fig. 21.

19. Boccaccio, *Genealogia Deorum Gentilicium*, II. 2. v.

20. *Life of Apollonius of Tyana*, IV. 14.

21. *The Ignorant Book-Collector*, 11-12.

22. The running Orpheus animates Schubert's song 'Der Musensohn', with its shifting of key and endless rhythmic movement, as all things in all seasons respond to him. The song is a setting of the early lyric by Goethe:

> Durch Feld und Wald zu schweifen
> Mein Liedchen wegzupfeifen,
> So geht's von Ort zu Ort...

> To roam through field and forest,
> To pipe my song on its way,
> So it goes on, from place to place...

23. First performed in 1986. Birtwistle's preoccupation with this theme appeared even before he began his ten years' work on this opera, in the *Nenia on the Death of Orpheus* (1970). Birtwistle was not, of course, the first operatic composer to make the *sparagmos* an important theme in an Orpheus opera: Haydn did so, and so had Poliziano's *favola di Orfeo*. Poliziano's version followed Euripides closely at many points.

24. Anouilh, *Eurydice* (1941).

25. *Two Gentlemen of Verona*, III. 2.

26. Hölderlin lived to be seventy-three; but his mental illness came upon him when he was about thirty, and he never recovered.

Chapter X *The Lost Bride*

1. Carcanet Press, 1982.

2. The same aspects of Hades are the strongest elements in Seneca's memorable account in *Hercules Furens*, where Orpheus is introduced as parallel to Hercules in his victorious journey to the world of the dead. The choral narrative about Orpheus (569-99) is less striking than the descriptive passage preceding it (547-57), especially in the image of motionless dark water (550-1, 554). Cf. pp. 183-5.

3. Cf. pp. 19-20

4. The most notable example of a tamed dragon is found perhaps in the legend of St Martha, who was said to lead her dragon on a chain, after subduing it. A chained dragon is also depicted with the elegant Princess of Uccello's well known *St George* (in the National Gallery, London). It is not clear why the dragon who is so nonchalantly controlled in this picture must also be killed by St George.

5. On Minerva's relation with the Muses, v. esp. Ov. *Met.* V. 254-71, and cf. Ch. VI (pp. 108-14).

6. This tradition disregards the text of Revelation, which speaks of the Woman 'travailing in birth, in pain to be delivered'.

7. Disregarding the command of God, in the state of unashamed nakedness before the Fall, that man and wife should 'be one flesh' (Gen. 2:24-5). The moral questions raised by this passage are complex, for both Jewish and Christian theologians, and the present discussion touches only on aspects that concern the Orphean theme.

8. Cf. pp. 69-72.

9. The identification of Eurydice as a goddess of the underworld was first discussed at length by Maass (*Orpheus*, München, 1895).

Eisler also examined links between Eurydice and Hecate (e.g. the dedication to Hecate of the first hymn in the Orphic collection; cf. Paus. II. 30. ii).

10. Goethe said that he had read of these goddesses in Plutarch. A temple of the Mothers, in Sicily, is mentioned in *Marcellus*, 20, but the reference does not in itself illuminate the *Faust* passage. However, a wider context is considered in the interpretation by Harold Jantz (*The Mothers in 'Faust': The Myth of Time and Creativity*, Johns Hopkins, 1969).

11. Blake evidently did not experience water as life-giving so much as life-destroying; images of deluge and destruction are frequent, and he uses the sea as image for the material world threatening to swallow up the spiritual. His Platonist source, Thomas Taylor, cited Heraclitus' enigmatic saying, 'Moisture is the death of the soul'.

12. v. C.M. Bowra's essay on the *Neue Gedichte*, in *R.M. Rilke: Aspects of his Mind and Poetry*, ed. W. Rose and G. Craig Houston (London, 1938).

13. E.g. Novalis, Goethe, de Nerval; all three are discussed in W:A. Strauss, *Descent and Return* (Cambridge, Mass., 1971).

14. William Blake, letter to William Hayley, 23 October, 1804; R.M. Rilke, letters to Countess Margot Sizzo-Noris-Crouy, 12 April, 1923; to Xaver van Moos, 20 April, 1923; to Princess Marie von Thurn und Taxis-Hohenlohe, 11 February, 1922; *Sonnets to Orpheus*, I. 3.

15. Erich Heller, *The Disinherited Mind* (London, 1952). Heller found the only comparable personal account (in the nineteenth century) in Nietszche.

16. *Descent and Return*, Ch. V: v. esp. 150-2, and 165-6.

17. The idea of the 'great death' which every individual is called to achieve through full and free assent (*Bejahung*) was with Rilke as early as *The Book of Hours*, published in 1905:

> der grosse Tod, den jeder in sich hat,
> das ist die Frucht, um die sich alles dreht.
>
> the great death, which everyone has in himself
> that is the fruit, on which all depends.

He insisted many times in his correspondence that the awareness of life and of creative power could come only from the acceptance of death and the 'eating of the poppy'.

In more objective terms, the critic Cleanth Brooks suggested something of this profound paradox when he spoke of the poet as one who 'triumphs over the apparently contradictory and conflicting elements of experience by unifying them into a new pattern' (*The Well-Wrought Urn*, London, 1949, 174).

Chapter XI *Roman Choice*

1. The story of Alcestis' successful restoration to life by another encounter of Heracles with Death is not mentioned in this play.

2. Lavinia is young, beautiful, and docile; otherwise, she is hardly characterised at all. It is notable, however, that she is first mentioned as the passive bearer of a supernatural sign (fire burning on her head, VII. 71-7) similar to that borne by Aeneas' son in Troy (II. 680-4). She is standing beside her father at the altar when this happens, and she does not act as interpreter of the omen or initiate any action.

3. The 'nested' structure has been analysed by Adam Parry ('The Idea of Art in Virgil's *Georgics*', *Arethusa* 5, 1972, 35-52).

4. It is, of course, possible that this circumstance was drawn from the lost Hellenistic epyllion which Bowra and others (following Wilamowitz *der Glaube der Hellenen*, 244, n. 2) have posited as source for the whole episode in the *Georgics*. No such poem is mentioned in ancient times. L.P. Wilkinson, *The Georgics of Virgil* (Cambridge, 1969), 117, points out that Virgil's 'allusive manner', sometimes taken as evidence of Alexandrian and similar sources, may well be a literary artifice offering no proof that there was anything to allude to. Wilkinson also rejects modern analyses of the Aristaeus-Orpheus antithesis in Virgil as inappropriately moralistic.

5. The theme is at least as old as Hesiod (*WD* 90-105; in this version Zeus'

infliction of troubles upon men is precipitated by the curiosity of Pandora).

6. On the 'Roman' virtues of Virgil's bees, v. the valuable chapter on the *Georgics* in Jasper Griffin, *Latin Poets and Roman Life* (London, 1985). Griffin also makes a telling comparision between Aristaeus' inadvertent destruction of Eurydice and the casual killing of Silvia's stag and of the Cretan deer in the *Aeneid* (VII. 483-502, IV. 69-73). In each case the killer is not vicious, but relentless, and he is the intended builder of a new community. Cf. also E.M. Stehle, 'Virgil's *Georgics*: The Threat of Sloth' (*TAPA* 104, 1974, 347-69) on the contrast between Aristaeus' productive *labor* and the erotic inertia that characterises Orpheus in this poem).

7. On this dimension of Virgil's poetry, two remarkable studies in recent years have enlarged critical understanding with an unusual widening of vision: they are W.R. Johnson's *Darkness Visible* (Berkeley, Los Angeles, and London, 1976) and P.R. Hardie's *Cosmos and Imperium* (Oxford, 1986).

8. *Geo*. I. 493-7; *Aen*. II. 604-18.

9. Spenser unites this idea of the poet's function with that of the 'healer of the soul' – David, for example, as considered in Ch. III. He writes, for instance, of the poet as true and decisive peacemaker who can end 'wicked Discord':

> Such as was Orpheus, that, when strife was growen
> Amongst those famous ympes of Greece, did take
> His silver harpe in hand and shortly friends them make;
> Or such as that celestiall Psalmist was,
> That, when the wicked feend his lord tormented,
> With heavenly notes, that did all other pas,
> The outrage of his furious fit relented.
> Such musicke is wise words with time concented,
> To moderate stiffe minds dispos'd to strive...
>
> (*The Faerie Queene*, IV. 2. i-ii)

Select Bibliography

This short and probably idiosyncratic list is intended as a pointer to the most important reference-material on Orpheus and Orphic themes. Interpretative literature which has been valuable in this study is referred to in the Notes.

ALDERLINK, L.J., *Creation and Salvation in Ancient Orphism* (Chico, Calif., 1981).

CAMERON, A., *The Pythagorean Background of the Theory of Recollection* (Menash, Wis., 1938).

DODDS, E.R., *The Greeks and the Irrational* (Berkeley, Calif., 1951).

FRIEDMAN, J.B., *Orpheus in the Middle Ages* (Cambridge, Mass., 1970).

GRAF, F., 'Orpheus, A Poet Among Men' in *Interpretations of Greek Mythology*, ed. J. Bremmer (London, 1987).

GUTHRIE, W.C.K., *Orpheus and Greek Religion* (London, 1935).

───── *The Greeks and their Gods* (London, 1950).

KATZ, R., *Divining the Powers of Music* (New York, 1986).

KERN, O., *Orphicorum Fragmenta* (Berlin, 1922).

OWEN LEE, M., 'Orpheus and Eurydice: Myth, Legend, Folklore', *C. & M.* 26, 402-12.

LIEBERG, G., *Poeta Creator* (Amsterdam, 1982).

LINFORTH, I.M., *The Arts of Orpheus* (Berkeley, Calif., 1941).

ONORATO, R.J., *The Character of the Poet: Wordsworth in 'The Prelude'* (Princeton, 1971).

ROHDE, E., *Psyche* (Heidelberg, 1893; tr. Hillis, London, 1925).

ROSENBERG, A., *Die Zauberflöte: Geschichte und Deutung von Mozart's Opera* (München, 1972).

SEWELL, E., *The Orphic Voice* (London, 1960).

SEZNEC, J., *The Survival of the Pagan Gods* (New York, 1953).

SIMONDON, M., *La Mémoire et l'Oubli dans la Pensée Grecque* (Paris, 1982).

SPERDUTI, A., 'The Divine Nature of Poetry in Antiquity', *TAPA* 81 (1950), 209-40.

STRAUSS, W.A., *Descent and Return: The Orphic Theme in Modern Literature* (Cambridge, Mass., 1971).

WARDEN, J., (ed.) *Orpheus: The Metamorphoses of a Myth* (Toronto, 1982).

WEST, M.L., *The Orphic Poems* (Oxford, 1984).

WIND, E., *Pagan Mysteries in the Renaissance* (London, 1968).

ZUNTZ, G., *Persephone* (Oxford, 1971).

Index

DATE DUE